THE FIRE

⤳ -IN- ⤳

FICTION

passion, purpose, and techniques
TO MAKE YOUR NOVEL GREAT

Donald Maass

WRITER'S DIGEST BOOKS
Cincinnati, Ohio
www.writersdigest.com

For more resources for writers, visit www.writersdigest.com/books.

To receive a free weekly e-mail newsletter delivering tips and updates about writing and about Writer's Digest products, register directly at http://news letters.fwpublications.com.

13 12 11 10 09   5 4 3 2

Distributed in Canada by Fraser Direct
100 Armstrong Avenue
Georgetown, Ontario, Canada L7G 5S4
Tel: (905) 877-4411
Distributed in the U.K. and Europe by David & Charles
Brunel House, Newton Abbot, Devon, TQ12 4PU, England
Tel: (+44) 1626-323200, Fax: (+44) 1626-323319
E-mail: postmaster@davidandcharles.co.uk
Distributed in Australia by Capricorn Link
P.O. Box 704, Windsor, NSW 2756 Australia
Tel: (02) 4577-3555

Library of Congress Cataloging-in-Publication Data

Maass, Donald.
   The fire in fiction : passion, purpose & techniques to make your novel great / Donald Maass.
      p. cm.
   Includes index.
   ISBN 978-1-58297-506-1 (pbk. : alk. paper)
   1. Fiction–Authorship. 2. Fiction–Technique. I. Title.
   PN3365.M243 2009
   808'.3–dc22   2008045800

Edited by Kelly Nickell
Designed by Terri Woesner
Production coordinated by Mark Griffin

DEDICATION

For Lisa

ACKNOWLEDGMENTS

Writer's Digest: Grateful thanks to Jane Friedman for getting it immediately, for listening, and for her long-term support. Thanks, too, to my editor Kelly Nickell, who is simply the best. Thanks, as well, to marketing guru Greg Hatfield and the rest of the team at F+W.

Donald Maass Literary Agency: Thanks to my stalwart crew who kept the ship moving at full steam while I completed this book: Jennifer Jackson, Cameron McClure, Stephen Barbara, J.L. Stermer, Charlie Noyes, plus interns Kat Sherbo and Amy Boggs.

Free Expressions: Thanks to my colleagues in the *Writing the Breakout Novel* workshops, excellent sounding boards all: Lorin Oberweger, Brenda Windberg, Jason Sitzes, Roman White, and Lisa Rector-Maass.

TABLE
⟿ OF ⟿
CONTENTS

INTRODUCTION

We've all read them: the sixth novel in a mystery series that disappoints, the splashy-looking hardcover that proves to be empty inside, the latest novel by a favorite author that is just plain *off*. We wonder what went wrong. Was the author rushed, or not edited, or maybe just not trying?

Lackluster stories turn up every day, too, in the submissions sent to my literary agency in New York. The manuscripts of published and unpublished authors alike too often lie flat on the page. They fail to engage, to excite my imagination. Feeling little for the characters and unenthusiastic about where the story may go, I scribble notes for my rejection letters.

Then there are those manuscripts that effortlessly lift off. From the first sentence, I am immediately drawn into the world of the story. The protagonist is someone about whom I immediately care. Secondary characters come alive, and even the antagonist surprises me. I cannot help but read every page as the author unfolds his purpose, whether it is to scare me, to satirize, to uplift me, or just to amaze me.

No doubt you have felt that way about one published novel or another. You may also have noted with envy that the publisher got behind that lucky book. You can tell that from the gorgeous cover and the book's front-of-store placement. Reviewers also gush, declaring that *it's her best ever*.

What is it that puts authors at the top of their game? Is it the result of accumulated craft, experience reaped, confidence built over twenty or more books? Is it a sage suggestion from a veteran agent or editor? *Why not tackle thus-and-such subject?*

Masterpiece novels look like singular events. We imagine that this novel is the story that the author has been burning to write. He's been saving it up, planning it for years, worked on it for a decade between delivering lesser works. In our more envious moments we may imagine that this corker was born from a one-time lightning flash of inspiration.

I don't buy that. A lightning flash bright enough to light four hundred pages? A suggestion so brilliant that forty or more elegantly shaped scenes flow easily onto the page? A decade-long project that did not ever once grow stale?

A masterpiece novel may be singularly inspired, and it certainly can be a once-in-a-career event. But even so, it is not magic. It may feel that way to the author. He may hype its close-to-my-heart genesis and confess in *The Writer* or on NPR that the manuscript wrote itself.

It disappoints me when authors perpetuate the myth that writing is magic. Some allow it to be so. It's a shame that those writers fail to understand their own process. What's wrong with that? What's wrong is simply that magic is unpredictable. A method that's mysterious cannot be repeated.

I believe that passion is available to every author, every time she sits down to write. Every novel can be inspired. Every scene can have a white-hot center. It is not a matter of conjuring demons, being obsessed, or just plain luck. The passion that inspires great fiction can be a writing technique as handy and easy to use as those with which all fiction writers are familiar. Passion can be a practical tool.

What do I mean by passion? Simply put, it is the underlying conviction that makes the words matter. It is the burning drive to urgently get down something specific, something that the reader has to see. It could be as big as a universal truth about human nature or as small as the quality of the light on an autumn afternoon on the Nebraska prairie.

Whatever it is, the words flow, or seem to, and as readers we are blown away by the author's precision and emotional force. A passionate author has us in her grip. Passionate fiction is not bogged down, wandering, low in tension, or beset by the many bugbears of by-the-numbers novel writing, like stereotypical characters, predictable plots, cliché-ridden prose, churning exposition, buried dialogue, and so on.

Passionate writing makes every word a shaft of light, every sentence a crack of thunder, every scene a tectonic shift. When the purpose of every word is urgent, the story crackles, connects, weaves, and falls together in wondrous ways. No wonder such novels feel as if they are writing themselves. Actually, it is the author who has found a groove. Wouldn't it be nice if every manuscript flowed so easily?

STATUS SEEKERS AND STORYTELLERS

Why do some novels by published writers go wrong? To start to answer that question, I think we must first go back to the beginning and examine the two primary reasons why people write fiction.

For thirty years I have observed fiction careers. I've seen them succeed and fail. The more I see, the more I feel that novelists fall into two broad categories: those whose desire is to be published, and those whose passion is to spin stories. I think of these as *status seekers* and *storytellers*.

It can be tough to tell the difference, at least at first. Before their first contract, most fiction writers will urgently tell me what they believe I want to hear: *I am totally committed to making it, to being the best writer I can be, no matter what it takes. I want to achieve excellence.*

I believe such sentiments are sincere but I have learned to take them with a grain of salt. It is over time that I discover an author's true motivation for writing. Authors themselves may not know, and all have a mixture of motives. Still, their primary reasons for writing will ultimately emerge.

You can begin to see the difference as fiction writers try to break in. The majority of writers seek representation or publication years too soon. Rejection slips quickly set them straight. How do they respond?

Some cleave to the timeless advice *get it in the mail, keep it in the mail.* The more thoughtful pull their manuscripts and go back to work.

Here's another clue: once in a while an unready but promising manuscript will cross my desk. Wanting to be encouraging, I send a detailed e-mail or letter explaining my reasons for rejecting it. What do you suppose is the most common response? It's the immediate offer of a trunk manuscript; a shame, since what is needed is not something else but something better.

Serious fiction writers sooner or later reach a point where their command of craft seems good enough for them finally to break in. Their supporters agree. Critique groups proclaim the latest manuscript the best ever. Mentors say *this should be published* and introduce the no-longer-newcomer to New York agents at the next regional writers conference. Interest is expressed. The big break seems imminent.

Still, rejections arrive, often glib brush-offs like *I didn't love this enough* or *this would be difficult to place in the current market.* In response, status seekers grow frustrated. They decide that landing an agent is a matter of timing or luck. Storytellers may be understandably bewildered at this stage but recognize that something is missing from their writing. They resolve to do something about it.

At my *Writing the Breakout Novel* workshops I again notice the difference between these two types of writer. Some want to know how to make their manuscripts acceptable. *If I do this and I do that, will I be okay?* When I hear that question my heart sinks a little. That is a status seeker talking.

A storyteller, by contrast, is more concerned with making his story the best story that it can be, with discovering the levels and elements that are missing, and with understanding the techniques needed to make it all happen. Status seekers rush me fifty pages and an outline a few months after the workshop. Storytellers won't show me their novels again for a year or more, probably after several new drafts.

You would think that at long last finding an agent who says *yes, it's time to show your novel to publishers* would relax the status seeker's anxiety for validation, but that isn't true. Generally speaking, authors are never more work than during the submission process. It is normal to want updates on how submissions are going, but with status seekers the process can get nutty. If declines keep coming, I hear unhelpful suggestions. *What about Viking? Didn't they launch Stephen King? Should we submit my comic vampire novel there?* There also are impossible questions: *What does it mean when an editor doesn't respond after six weeks?*

As you can see, questions like that don't really need an answer. What the status seeker wants is a contract. He wants to know that his years of effort will pay off.

The first contract is a watershed that finally divides the status seekers from the storytellers. Once in the hands of an editor, a status seeker will focus on what he is getting (or not) by way of cover, copy, blurbs, and "support" like advertising and promotion. It certainly is okay to want the best for one's novel. It is also normal for publishers to put only modest effort into launching debut fiction.

Why? Because two-thirds of fiction sales are *branded*—fans buying new titles by authors whose work they already love. For unknown authors, ad and promo dollars produce few unit sales. That drives status seekers crazy. *Why throw money at authors who are already bestsellers? How am I supposed to grow if my publisher doesn't spend some bucks pushing me?*

Storytellers have a more realistic grasp of retail realities. They may promote, but locally and not for long. They'll put up a website, maybe, then it's back to work on the next book. That's smart. The truth, for newer authors anyway, is that the best promotion is between the covers of the last book.

What about later stages of career? Do status seekers correct course and grasp the fundamentals of success? I wish. Typically, in mid-career, status seekers go full time too soon. They grow to rely on advances for their living. Revisions become perfunctory. Frustration grows. A friend gets a film deal and panic sets in. In-store placement, posters, and *shelf talkers* become the keys to salvation. After six or seven books, advance size becomes critical. *I am working too hard to keep getting paid fifteen thousand per book!*

Storytellers ignore the ephemera. Their mid-career focus is hitting deadlines and delivering powerful stories for their readers. The issues that come up are about developing their series or what to write as their next stand-alone.

In advanced stages of their career, status seekers will grumble about publishers, spend on self-promotion (or spend nothing at all), and expound as experts on getting ahead. They change agents, obsess over trunk projects, write screenplays. They wind up at small presses. A typical request from a status seeker at this terminal stage is, *I whipped off a graphic novel last weekend; can you find me a publisher for it?*

Storytellers are different. Storytellers look not to publishers to make them successful, but to themselves. They wonder how to top themselves with each new novel. Their grumbles are not about getting toured but about getting more time to deliver. Storytellers take calculated risks with their fiction. Mostly they try to make their stories bigger.

Therein lies the essence of why storytellers succeed where status seekers fail: Storytellers may seem anointed, but they are anointed by readers. Give readers stories that blow them away every time and they will become the loyal generators of the sales that make career success appear effortless.

Storytellers are oriented the right way; consequently, their stories almost never go wrong. Which type of fiction writer are you? Really? I believe you, but the proof is in your passion and whether or not it gets on the page.

PLAYING WITH FIRE

Readers know when a novel is drifting off course. We may not be able to articulate where the problem lies, but clearly some novels are poorly focused, lacking force, self-indulgent, or just plain ill-conceived.

What went wrong? Was it a stubborn refusal to abandon a difficult idea? Was there something in the story that the author was afraid to tackle? Or was it some flaw in the premise itself, a subject that simply didn't have enough juice?

It is essential, I believe, to realize that the power of a novel doesn't lie in some independent inner life. A timely topic by itself will not make a novel great. Nor can a novelist count on characters to take over the story. The strength of a novel arises, rather, from the author's day-to-day story development. A sound idea and dynamic characters are merely starting points. Greatness comes in the shaping.

If you have read my previous book, *Writing the Breakout Novel*, or used my *Writing the Breakout Novel Workbook*, you know that I believe in learning from others. Everything we need in order to understand the techniques of passion lies within the covers of novels that you will find currently on the shelves. In picking illustrative examples I have selected from many genres, subjects, styles, and intents. There is some bias toward recent novels of long-published writers and toward bestsellers, but those are not the only criteria.

Plot descriptions put my examples in context. Be aware that there are plot spoilers ahead. If you like, read the novels cited herein first for enjoyment and later for technique. I don't care. All that matters to me is that you stop waiting for magic and embrace passion as a daily practice.

At the end of each chapter you will find exercises. These are the practical techniques, the application of the theory. Try them. There is a tendency among writers to read writing advice and think *right, got it*. Then at the next keyboard session, the words flow in the same old way. It's what feels safe, I know, but to grow you must try new things.

Master novelists do. In fact, I believe they are uncomfortable when they are playing it safe. So what about you? Are you ready for a leap into mastery? Are you ready to control your own success? Do you want to blow away your readers every time? If so, put the methods herein to use right away.

If you do that, I think you will feel an immediate difference in your writing. In a little while you should find every sentence, every scene, and every writing session growing productive in exciting ways. I suspect that since you will be stoking the fire in your stories as a matter of routine, you will soon stop believing in luck. You may ultimately see that mastery is not a mystery, nor a state to be achieved sometime later on. Greatness is within your grasp now.

Showing you the practical methods that, when used by others, we call mastery is the purpose of *The Fire in Fiction*. Applying those methods is your challenge. When you have these techniques working for you, go ahead and tell your fans that it's all magic, if you like. You and I will know that passion is your craft and that you use it every day.

CHAPTER ONE

PROTAGONISTS VS. HEROES

Is there a difference between a protagonist and a hero? A protagonist is the subject of a story. A hero is a human being with extraordinary qualities. A protagonist can be a hero, certainly, but isn't always. Quite often in manuscripts the protagonists are ordinary people. They may face extraordinary circumstances in the course of the story but when we first meet them they, in effect, could be you or me.

That early introductory moment is where many authors begin to lose me. Why? Meeting a protagonist who is a proxy for me, with whom I can readily identify, should be ideal, shouldn't it? Isn't that how sympathy arises? I see myself in the novel's focal character and, therefore, her experience becomes mine? Actually, it doesn't work quite like that. A reader's heart does not automatically open just because some average schlemiel stumbles across the page.

What draws you to people in life? An even better question is, to what *degree* are you drawn to people in life? It varies, doesn't it? Most people leave you indifferent, I'll bet. When you are pushing your loaded shopping cart across the supermarket parking lot, are you filled with love for your fellow shoppers? (You are? Are you tripping on ecstasy?) How about your fellow workers? Probably you find reasons to like them. Your friends? No doubt your shared experiences, values, and interests keep them in your circle.

Now think about the people whom you deeply admire. Who are the individuals for whom you would cancel other plans? Who stirs in you awe, respect, humility, and high esteem? Are these regular people, no different than anyone else? They may not be famous but they are in some way exceptional, right?

Whether they are public figures or just ordinary in profile, our heroes and heroines are people whose actions inspire us. We would not mind spending ten straight hours or even ten days with them. That is important because ten hours is about how long it takes to read a novel and ten days is not an uncommon period of time for readers to commit to a single book. When it is your book, what sort of protagonist do you want your readers to meet? One whom they will regard more or less as they do a fellow grocery shopper?

To create an immediate bond between reader and protagonist, it is necessary to show your reader a reason to care. Pushing a shopping cart is not a reason to care. Demonstrating a character quality that is inspiring does cause readers to open their hearts.

There are many ways to signal to your readers that your protagonist is worth their time. Let's explore a few of them.

AVERAGE JOES, JANE DOES, AND DARK PROTAGONISTS

What if your protagonist is a genuine Everyman, a regular Joe or Jane who is going to be tested, later, by irregular events? Or, what if your protagonist is dark: wounded, hiding, haunted, self-loathing, an outsider, or simply unpleasant?

Can we care about such protagonists? Why should we? We don't spend much time with such people in life, why would we do so with our valuable reading time? Despite that, contemporary literature is packed with dark protagonists about whom consumers are avid to read. Why? What makes them different? What is working when we, by all rights, shouldn't much care? Let's have a look at some successful dark protagonists. We can learn from them what is necessary to make all protagonists people about whom we eagerly want to read.

Thomas H. Cook's nineteenth literary crime novel *Red Leaves* (2005) was a nominee for the Mystery Writers of America Edgar Award for Best Novel; it was also a nominee for the Anthony, Barry, and Golden Dagger awards. It's the story of a small-town photo-store owner named Eric Moore. Eric's life is one of middle-class placidity. His wife is a college teacher. His sulky son Keith hides in his room doing God knows what. Everything's normal. Eric's life is turned upside down one morning when he learns that the little girl that Keith was babysitting the night before has gone missing. As the police repeatedly question Keith, Eric finds that nothing on which he relies is as secure as he believed.

Cook's plan is to introduce unsettling problems into the apparently ordinary life of an ordinary man. Cook knows there is no particular reason we should care about Eric Moore, so his opening must meet that challenge:

> When you remember those times, they return to you in a series of photographs. You see Meredith on the day you married her. You are standing outside the courthouse on a bright spring day. She is wearing a white dress and she stands beside you with her hand in your arm. A white corsage is pinned to her dress. You gaze at each other rather than the camera. Your eyes sparkle and the air around you is dancing.
>
> Then there are brief vacations before Keith was born. You are in a raft on the Colorado River, sprayed with white water. There you are, nearly blinded by the autumn foliage of New Hampshire. On the observation deck of the Empire State Building, you mug for the camera, feet spread, fists pressed to waists, like masters of the universe. You are twenty-four and she is twenty-one, and there is something gloriously confident in the way you stand together, sure and almost cocky. More than anything, without fear. Love, you have decided by then, is a form of armor.

Alert readers will note that those paragraphs break some major rules of openings. They are inactive. They are backstory. How does Cook get away with that? As so often when rules are broken, the secret ingredient is tension. Look at the opening line: *When you remember those times, they return to you in a series of photographs.* The narrator is speaking of happy times; by implication, the present is unhappy. What went wrong? Before we even can formulate the question we are reading ahead to find out, and Cook tells us.

What about Eric Moore, Cook's clueless protagonist? He is a man with his head buried in the sand, but here, looking back, we learn that he is a man capable of great happiness. His wife once adored him. They were young and confident, even fearless. Eric Moore knew the power of love. To put it simply, he was strong. Although Cook will soon enough wreck Eric's life, there is an implied promise that by the novel's end Eric will be strong again. Call it his goal, or his redemption; whatever you call it, it's a strength that attracts us and causes us to open our hearts to Eric Moore.

What if your protagonist is burdened by the past? Authors must be harboring a lot of secrets and regrets because this type of hero turns up constantly in my slush pile. Past secrets and calamities generally are much more dramatic than present action, too, making it difficult to construct a compelling narrative. Many try to maintain story tension by delaying revelation. That's a durable strategy, but over the long haul of a manuscript it's tricky to pull off.

There is also the problem of turning a burdened protagonist into someone about whom we will immediately care. Did you ever know someone who wouldn't let go? Annoying, weren't they? You see my point. Why put up with a whiner?

Sue Miller made an immediate splash with her first novel, *The Good Mother* (1986), and continues to impress today (*The Senator's Wife*, 2008). In *While I Was Gone* (1999), an Oprah's Book Club selection, she spins the story of veterinarian Jo Becker. Jo's life is all but perfect; naturally, the past returns to disrupt it. As a young woman, Jo lived on a commune, where matters ended badly with a murder.

Like Thomas H. Cook, Sue Miller opens her novel looking backward from a moment of serenity, her heroine rowing on a lake with her husband. The challenge of this scene is to introduce a sense of disquiet into Jo's happy life, the long shadow of the past, while at the same time giving Jo an inner strength that gives Miller's readers the signal that it's okay to care:

> I had felt something like this every now and then in the last year or so, sometimes at work as I tightened a stitch or gave an injection: the awareness of having done this a thousand times before, of surely having a thousand times left to do it again. Of doing it well and thoroughly and neatly, as I liked to do things, and simultaneously of being at a great distance from my own actions.
>
> ...
>
> As we rowed back, as we drove home, I found myself wanting to tell my husband about my feeling, but then not knowing what to call it. The shadow of it lingered with me, but I didn't say anything to Daniel. He would hear it as a want, a need. He would feel called upon to offer comfort. Daniel is a minister, a preacher, a pastor. His business is the care of his flock, his medium is words—thrilling words, admonishing or consoling words. I knew he could console me, but consolation wasn't what I felt I wanted. And so we drove along in silence, too, and I looked out the window at the back roads that sometimes seemed utterly rural, part of the nineteenth century, and sometimes seemed abruptly the worst of contemporary suburban life: the sere, beautiful old fields carved up to accommodate the two-wide circular asphalt driveways, the too-grand fake-garrison-colonial houses.

How does Miller meet her challenge here? Jo is unsettled, "at a great distance from [her] own actions." Nothing admirable in that. She wants to talk with her husband but rejects the idea. Nothing noble in that, either. Then Jo explains that her husband's comfort "was not what I felt I wanted."

Ah. What *does* Jo want? Miller doesn't say, but clearly it is more than just talking things over. By implication, Jo feels an urge to do something. She wants to take positive action. Without stating so explicitly, Miller hints that Jo wants to bring her past to light and find a way to move beyond it.

The longing for positive change is a strength that we all can understand. In this opening of *While I Was Gone*, that longing is understated, a fleeting impulse. But that is all it takes. It is a shaft of light in the darkness. It's the hint that opens our hearts, and the one that many novelists leave out.

What if your protagonist is imperfect, even a person others do not like? Outsiders, outcasts and pariahs are plentiful in contemporary fiction and in submissions to my agency. *I want my protagonist to be flawed* is one of the most common remarks I hear when manuscripts are pitched to me at writers conferences. That's nice, but too often when the manuscripts turn up later I find that the flaws are fatal. Quickly turned off, I find little reason to continue reading.

Joseph Finder is a top (maybe our only) author of business thrillers. He hit his stride with *Paranoia* (2004) and followed strongly with *Killer Instinct* (2006) and the *New York Times* bestseller *Power Play* (2007). *Company Man* (2005) boxes corporate CEO Nick Conover into a bad decision, after which his situation gets progressively worse.

To accomplish this, Finder has to make Nick Conover a man with enemies. As the CEO of an office furniture company charged with laying off thousands of Michigan workers and moving manufacturing operations overseas, that isn't hard to do. The trick is to make Nick nevertheless highly likable.

Finder tackles this difficult task by giving Nick a host of instantly redeeming qualities. He struggles to keep his family together and his kids happy a year after the death of his wife, whose memory he honors by trying (not entirely successfully) to complete the home renovations she planned. Nick is a local boy made good. He was captain of the high school football team and rose through the company ranks. He has friends. He tries to minimize the damage to the workforce, but after five thousand layoffs this is not possible.

One morning a disaffected worker named Louis Goss storms the executive offices to threaten a sickout and let Nick know that he, Goss, literally knows where Nick lives. After hearing insults about his Mercedes (Nick actually drives a Chevy Suburban) and personal threats, Nick faces Goss square on:

> "Let me ask *you* something, Louis. Do you remember the 'town meeting' at the chair plant two years ago? When I told you guys the company was in a shitload of trouble and layoffs seemed likely but I wanted to avoid them if possible? You weren't sick that day, were you?"
>
> "I was there," Goss muttered.
>
> "Remember I asked if you'd all be willing to cut your hours back so everyone could stay on the job? Remember what everyone said?"
>
> Goss was silent, looking off to one side, avoiding Nick's direct stare.
>
> "You all said no, you couldn't do that. A pay cut was out of the question."
>
> "Easy for you to—"
>
> "And I asked whether you'd all be willing to cut back on your health plan, with your daycare and your health-club memberships. Now, how many people raised their hands to say, yeah, okay, we'll cut back? Any recollection?"
>
> Goss shook his head slowly, resentfully.
>
> "Zero. Not a single goddamned hand went up. Nobody wanted to lose a goddamned hour of work; nobody wanted to lose a single perk." He could hear the blood rushing through his ears, felt a flush of indignation. "You think I slashed five thousand jobs, buddy? Well, the reality is, I *saved* five thousand jobs."

Later, Goss invades Nick's home, and in self-defense, Nick shoots him. Because feelings against Nick are running so hot, and because his company would be torn apart if it became known that he has not only fired thousands but has actually shot one of them dead, Nick is persuaded by his security chief to dump the body. This fatal mistake leads to legal jeopardy, but it is the least of Nick's problems. A management cabal turns deadly, too, and so Nick must save simultaneously his own hide and the company to which he is, he finds, deeply devoted.

Nick Conover proves to be a good guy, but Joseph Finder does not ask his readers to wait to find that out. He establishes quickly that Nick is both human and caring—or, at least, caring for a CEO. Finder also reinforces Nick's essential goodness through the remainder of his novel.

As the author of novels like *Fight Club* (1996), Chuck Palahniuk has some experience with unpleasant protagonists. In *Choke* (2001), Palahniuk cooked up a loathsome hero of the class of Humbert Humbert from Vladimir Nabokov's *Lolita* (1955). Victor Mancini is a failed med student who supports himself (and pays his mother's elder care bills) by scamming restaurant patrons: He pretends to choke on food and, after being rescued, plays on their sympathy. That is not his only bad habit. He trolls for dates at sex addiction recovery meetings and more. There's not a lot to like about Victor.

Why should we read about someone so despicable? Palahniuk knows we have little reason to do so. He must therefore capture us quickly and make us care about a hero who deserves scorn. But how? Palahniuk takes a bold approach:

> If you're going to read this, don't bother.
>
> After a couple of pages, you won't want to be here. So forget it. Go away. Get out while you're still in one piece.
>
> Save yourself.
>
> There has to be something better on television. Or since you have so much time on your hands, maybe you could take a night course. Become a doctor. You could make something of yourself. Treat yourself to a dinner out. Color your hair.
>
> You're not getting any younger.

> What happens here is first going to piss you off. After that it just gets worse and worse.
>
> What you're getting here is a stupid story about a stupid little boy. A stupid true life story about nobody you'd ever want to meet. Picture this little spaz being about waist high with a handful of blond hair, combed and parted on one side. Picture the icky little shit smiling in old school photos with some of his baby teeth missing and his first adult teeth coming in crooked. Picture him wearing a stupid sweater striped blue and yellow, a birthday sweater that used to be his favorite. Even that young, picture him biting his dickhead fingernails. His favorite shoes are Keds. His favorite food, fucking corn dogs.
>
> Imagine some dweeby little boy wearing no seat belt and riding in a stolen school bus with his mommy after dinner. Only there's a police car parked at their motel so the Mommy just blows on past at sixty or seventy miles an hour.
>
> This is about a stupid little weasel who, for sure, used to be about the stupidest little rat fink crybaby twerp that ever lived.
>
> The little cooz.

What keeps us reading that passage? Is it the funny side of the narrator's self-deprecation? Is it the pathos of the little boy's childhood in the hands of an obvious Monster-Mommy? Is it the reverse psychology challenge of the opening line?

Victor Mancini continues to excoriate himself for the next several pages. Clearly he hates himself; or at least the passive boy that he was. That, I believe, is why we care. Victor is berating himself for putting up with an intolerable childhood. (I mean, really, corn dogs?) Palahniuk's narrator has found strength in adulthood: strength enough to see that he was neglected and to be angry about that. Who wouldn't be sympathetic? Who hasn't kicked themselves?

To put it differently, Victor Mancini has achieved self-awareness. He judges himself harshly, but even so he is open-eyed. He knows he is not perfect and we have to respect that. He is brutally funny about himself. How many of us can say the same? His voice rings clear and strong.

What about protagonists who are simply lost, wandering, down-and-out, or without hope? Judging by their frequency in submissions, such protagonists must be easy to imagine; however, they are hard to like. I rarely do. Not in submissions, anyway. I not only want to turn away from their unhappy situations, there's often little reason to feel they are worth my pity. Anxious to delve into their suffering, their authors forget to give me a reason to wish them free of it.

Could there be a hero with less hope than the nameless father in Cormac McCarthy's *The Road* (2006)? Alone with his young son in a gray, post-apocalyptic landscape, the man has no goal other than to push their shopping cart of meager supplies further down the road in front of them and survive. *The Road* is grim. Hope is nowhere. These are the end times. Nothing is going to get better. The few other survivors are desperate cannibals. The man and his son have a gun with two bullets, saved in case suicide is necessary.

Depressed yet? Hey, wait until the movie. Still, *The Road* won the Pulitzer Prize for Fiction, plus the James Tait Black Memorial Prize for Fiction. It was a finalist for the National Book Critics Circle Award. It was widely praised by reviewers. *Entertainment Weekly* named it the best book of the last twenty-five years. It was an Oprah's Book Club pick, and the best-selling trade paperback novel in the year of its reprint. What gives? Was everyone in the mood for a downer?

I doubt that. So many readers can't be wrong, and indeed *The Road* is compelling and heartbreaking. How does McCarthy make us care? There is only one way: We must feel compassion, and quickly, for his hero, referred to in the text only as *the man*. After speedily setting the scene, McCarthy shows us in the man's dismal morning routine what matters to him:

> When he got back the boy was still asleep. He pulled the
> blue plastic tarp off him and folded it and carried it out
> to the grocery cart and packed it and came back with

their plates and some cornmeal cakes in a plastic bag and a plastic bottle of syrup. He spread the small tarp they used for a table on the ground and laid everything out and he took the pistol from his belt and laid it on the cloth and then he just sat watching the boy sleep. He'd pulled away his mask in the night and it was buried somewhere in the blankets. He watched the boy and he looked out through the trees toward the road. This was not a safe place. They could be seen from the road now it was day. The boy turned in the blankets. Then he opened his eyes. Hi, Papa, he said.

I'm right here.

I know.

Hemingway-esque minimalism is an unforgiving style. Stripping a text of its emotion means that emotion can only be evoked through the action of the story—not as easy as it sounds. McCarthy, though, has mastered minimalism. The man's spare gestures (preparing breakfast such as it is, worrying that "this was not a safe place," assuring his son "I'm right here") quickly convey that in this hopeless world there is, after all, one thing that matters to the man: his son. He loves his son. In most stories that would not be remarkable. In the world of *The Road*, to feel anything so strongly is a miracle.

In other words, even the hopeless man has something to hope for, a cause to chase, a reason to push on, someone to save. In the gray wasteland, his human spirit lives. The man in McCarthy's novel is dying. What will happen to his son when he goes? The story's tension derives in part from whether the author's vision of mankind will in the end prove bleak or hopeful. What keeps us reading, I believe, is that for one man, at least, love is a big enough reason to keep going.

Here, then, is some good news: The techniques of putting over dark protagonists are applicable to all protagonists. Find the secret strength in your main character, and it won't matter whether you are working with a hero or an anti-hero. Your readers will bond with both.

CUTTING HEROES DOWN TO SIZE

We have been looking at how to quickly show what is heroic in pro-tagonists who aren't. What about protagonists who *are* heroic? If your protagonist is strong, do-right, active, principled, and upstanding, then you don't have an issue, right?

Wrong. Genuine heroes present as big a challenge, in their way, as downers. Heroes or heroines who are noble and true can easily become cardboard. Think of feisty romance heroines, hard-boiled detectives, save-the-world suspense heroes, fantasy orphan-princes, sassy vampire slayers … these familiar lead characters cannot hold our interest over the long haul of a novel if they are one-dimensional. Indeed, if they are to keep us reading for more than a chapter or two, they must quickly become human.

Suspense novelist Tami Hoag is good at tough-as-nails protago-nists. In *The Alibi Man* (2007), she reintroduces former undercover cop Elena Estes (previously featured in *Dark Horse*, 2002). Injured in a prior case, burdened with guilt over the death of a friend and co-worker in a bust gone wrong, Elena now lives in the guest house of a wealthy Palm Beach friend who owns a stable where Elena has found a happier life, sort of:

> I am not a cop. I am not a private investigator, de-spite all rumors to the contrary. I ride horses for a living but don't make a nickel doing it. I am an outcast from my chosen profession and I don't want another.

Get the idea? Elena is the kind of kick-ass heroine who domi-nates contemporary women's suspense. Outspoken, opinionated, take no you-know-what, Elena's got a big chip on her shoulder. So, how do you feel about her? Is her strength attractive or off-putting? A bit of both, perhaps, but it is the off-putting quality that matters at the moment. Hoag knows that we need to see another side of Elena, and quickly, so she delivers it to us just a page later:

> All my life I have preferred the company of horses to people. Horses are honest, straightforward creatures

without guile or ulterior motive. You always know where you stand with a horse. In my experience, I can't say the same for human beings.

...

That morning I didn't settle in with my usual first cup of coffee to listen to the soft sounds of the horses eating. I hadn't slept well—not that I ever did. Worse than usual, I should say. Twenty minutes here, ten minutes there. The argument had played over and over in my mind, banging off the wall of my skull and leaving me with a dull, throbbing headache.

I was selfish. I was a coward. I was a bitch.

Some of it was true. Maybe all of it. ...

Here's the other side of this kick-ass heroine: She's not perfect; she knows it, admits it, and (at least a little) regrets it. At this point we don't need to know what the argument was about, or with whom, we just need to know that Elena Estes is human. She is not the embodiment of an impossible ideal. She has personal problems, just like everyone. By quickly cutting her heroine down to size, Hoag makes her not only real but a character who has room for change; that, in turn, signals to us that there also is story to come.

It's a strong story, too. Elena finds in a canal the body of a beautiful young woman with whom she worked in the stables. Drawn into the investigation, she runs afoul of a group of Palm Beach bad boys who provide alibis for each other when needed. One of them is a hated ex-fiancé. Who really did it, though, is a question unanswered until the final pages.

Lisa Gardner is another top suspense writer with a handy knack for tough detectives. In *The Survivors Club* (2002), she introduces Providence, Rhode Island, police detective Roan Griffin and immediately lets us know that he's not a superhero:

At 8:31 A.M. Monday morning, Rhode Island State Police Detective Sergeant Roan Griffin was already late for his 8:30 briefing. This was not a good thing. It was his first day back on the job in eighteen months. He should probably be on time. Hell, he should probably be early. Show up at headquarters at 8:15 A.M., pumped up, sharply pressed, crisply saluting. *Here I am, I am ready.*

And then ... ?

"Welcome back," they would greet him. (Hopefully.)

"Thanks," he would say. (Probably.)

"How are you feeling?" they'd ask. (Suspiciously.)

"Good," he'd reply. (Too easily.)

Ah, shit. Good *was* a stupid answer. Too often said to be often believed. He'd say good, and they'd stare at him harder, trying to read between the lines. Good like you're ready to crack open a case file, or good like we can trust you with a loaded firearm? It was an interesting question.

He drummed his fingers on the steering wheel and tried again.

"Welcome back," they'd say.

"It's good to be back," he'd say.

"How are you doing?" they'd ask.

"My anxiety is operating within normal parameters," he'd reply.

No. Absolutely not. That kind of psychobabble made even him want to whoop his ass. Forget it. He should've gone with his father's recommendation and walked in wearing a T-shirt that read "You're only Jealous Because the Voices are Talking to *Me.*"

At least they all could've had a good laugh.

Measure your feelings about Roan Griffin after this introduction. He's your prototypical wounded detective. (Why has he been off the job for eighteen months? His wife died of cancer.) What makes him appealing despite his all-too-typical psychological flaw? I believe it is the self-deprecating humor that Gardner gives him. At least the guy can laugh at himself.

In the next few paragraphs we find out that before his compassion leave, Roan Griffin was the lead investigator on many high-profile cases. Had Gardner begun with that information, we'd already be pulling away from her protagonist. He'd be too perfect, cardboard, an example none of us could live up to. By first making him human, Gardner makes it possible for us to like him before he even makes a move.

Roan Griffin will have to make some big moves, too. He's immediately plunged into a twisty case in which a brutal rapist is assassinated on the opening morning of his trial. Minutes later, the assassin's car blows sky high. The trail of culpability is thus neatly covered. The chief suspects are the three victims who escaped the rapist alive, the Survivors Club of the title. Roan's story is layered with other problems, as well, making for a high-impact read.

Wounded heroes and heroines are easy to overdo. Too much baggage and angst isn't exactly a party invitation for one's readers. What's the best balance? And which comes first, the strength or the humility? It doesn't matter. What's important is that one is quickly followed by the other.

Michael Connelly is one of our most popular crime fiction writers, thanks largely to his passionate and all-too-human LAPD detective Harry Bosch. In *The Brass Verdict* (2008), Connelly brings together Bosch and his half-brother (introduced in *The Lincoln Lawyer*, 2005), defense attorney Mickey Haller.

Connelly opens *The Brass Verdict* with a sequence that establishes Mickey's creds as a tough defense attorney. In the trial of a drug dealer accused of killing two college students, Mickey seizes upon a fatal lie told by the chief witness for the prosecution, a jailhouse snitch. He rips open the prosecution's case. Assistant district attorney Jerry Vincent offers a more lenient sentence, but Mickey's loathsome client wants to roll the dice. Mickey gets him acquitted.

Jerry Vincent is ruined. Zip up to the present day. Connelly knows that although Mickey showed strength in doing his job, morally he was wrong. He set a vicious killer free. If we are to cheer for Mickey now, the moral balance must be leveled. So, we learn that in subsequent years, Jerry Vincent prospered as a celebrity defender in private practice. Jerry even thanked Mickey for showing him the light.

That, though, is not enough to put Mickey Haller on the right side of the ethical line. Mickey must pay a price for his too-dogged defense of a killer, and so Connelly punishes him. Mickey goes out of action for a year for reasons he explains to administrative judge Mary Townes Holder when she summons him to announce that he has inherited the law practice and lucrative open cases of the recently murdered Jerry Vincent:

> "Judge, I had a case a couple years ago. The client's name was Louis Roulet. He was—"
>
> "I remember the case, Mr. Haller. You got shot. But, as you say, that was a couple years ago. I seem to remember you practicing law for some time after that. I remember the news stories about you coming back to the job."
>
> "Well," I said, "what happened is that I came back too soon. I had been gut shot, Judge, and I should've taken my time. Instead, I hurried back and the next thing I knew I started having pain and the doctors said I had a hernia. So I had an operation for that and there were complications. They did it wrong. There was even more pain and another operation and, well, to make a long story short, it knocked me down for a while. I decided the second time not to come back until I was sure I was ready."
>
> The judge nodded sympathetically. I guessed I had been right to leave out the part about my addiction to pain pills and the stint in rehab.
>
> "Money wasn't an issue," I said. "I had some savings and I also got a settlement from the insurance company. So I took my time coming back. But I'm ready. I was just about to take the back cover of the Yellow Pages."
>
> "Then, I guess inheriting an entire practice is quite convenient, isn't it?" she said.

> I didn't know what to say to her question or the smarmy tone in which she said it.
>
> "All I can tell you, Judge, is that I would take good care of Jerry Vincent's clients."

Notice several things about this exchange. The once-arrogant Mickey is now humbled. His tone with Judge Holder is level and respectful. The judge has the power to deny Mickey the cases Jerry Vincent left behind, but it is more than that. Mickey is on shaky ground. He knows it. He is not in a position to demand, but neither does he beg. He just presents the facts. Mickey is a wounded protagonist, quite literally, but Connelly does not overplay it. He instead moves Mickey beyond his angst to a place of dignity. No wallowing for Mickey Haller. As a result, he becomes a hero whose strength comes from his experience and from lessons learned.

Even greater restraint can be observed in the return of Anne Perry's popular Victorian detective Thomas Pitt in *Buckingham Palace Gardens* (2008). In his first outing in several years, Pitt, now working in Special Branch on cases of political importance or special sensitivity, is summoned with his supervisor Victor Narraway to Buckingham Palace. There, a gutted prostitute has been found in a linen closet. The Prince of Wales is in residence, along with several guests with whom he has been discussing an African railway venture. Needless to say, if it becomes known that a whore was in the palace, never mind murdered, the scandal would be explosive. Pitt must uncover the killer, and quickly, as Queen Victoria is due to return to the palace in less than a week.

As Perry's fans know, Pitt is an unusually competent detective; sensitive, passionate, and principled. But that does not mean everyone respects him. The Prince of Wales has squeamishly turned over the ugly matter to one of his guests, the adventurous, charming, and seamy businessman Cahoon Dunkeld. From the outset it is clear that Dunkeld expects the murder to be hushed up, cleared up, and disposed of speedily:

[Pitt] must have made a slight sound, because Dunkeld looked at him, then back at Narraway. "What about your man here?" he asked abruptly. "How far can you trust his discretion? And his ability to handle such a vital matter? And it *is* vital. If it became public, it would be ruinous, even affect the safety of the realm. Our business here concerns a profoundly important part of the Empire. Not only fortunes but nations could be changed by what we do." He was staring at Narraway as if by sheer will he could force some understanding into him, even a fear of failure.

Narraway gave a very slight shrug. It was a minimal, elegant gesture of his shoulders. He was far leaner than Dunkeld, and more at ease in his beautifully tailored jacket. "He is my best," he answered.

Dunkeld looked unimpressed. "And discreet?" he persisted.

"Special Branch deals with secrets," Narraway told him.

Dunkeld's eyes turned to Pitt and surveyed him coolly.

How does Pitt react to being treated like a servant? Not at all. That is the point. It is only when he views the slashed body in the linen closet that his feelings come forward:

Pitt stared at her less with revulsion than with an overwhelming pity for the gross indignity of it. Had it been an animal the callousness of it would have offended him. For a human being to die like that filled him with a towering anger and a desire to lash out physically and strike something. His breath heaved in his chest and his throat convulsed.

Yet he knew he must keep calm. Intelligence was needed, not passion, however justified.

Is Pitt's "overwhelming pity for the gross indignity of it" affected by the condescending treatment he's just been handed by Dunkeld?

Obviously, but Perry is too subtle a novelist to say so. She lets the twin indignities, shown just a page apart, make her point. As the investigation progresses, Pitt suffers much more humiliation at the hands of Dunkeld, but he turns it around. A gamekeeper's son, Pitt is used to his inferior social status. He bears his burden stoically.

Is Pitt wounded? Yes. Anne Perry does not play on that, though, but rather lets it live under the surface. She turns Pitt's afflictions into integrity and makes him human in the highest way.

Is your protagonist a tower of strength? Does he stand up for what is right? Does she kick ass? Do you endow your main character with a cutting wit, a shrewd mind, soaring intellect, mental toughness, keen focus, unstoppable determination?

If so, you may have created a protagonist whom readers will hate. Although it may seem counterintuitive and contrary to the dictum of *heroes for whom we can cheer*, what these paragons of perfection need is humanity. Add it quickly, reinforce it throughout your novel, and we'll know that your tough, do-right, honest-to-a-fault, and formerly flawless protagonist is someone we can believe in because he is real

Just like you and me.

GREATNESS

What makes a protagonist not only a hero or heroine, but great? Indeed, what is greatness? Defining the term is difficult, because it is many different things to many different people.

Perhaps, though, we might agree on one effect of greatness: impact. Great people do not leave the world unchanged. Great characters similarly stir readers and stay with them. Is it possible to construct this effect? How?

It's tricky. Fiction has little impact when it is timid, cliché ridden, uneventful, and formulaic. The same is true of characters. Stereotypes have little impact. They fail to engage us because we don't believe in them. Great characters are especially prone to this problem. If you create someone who is made of goodness, lives by high principles, performs actions of high valor, and is pretty much perfect, then your readers' reaction is likely to be a sneering *yeah, right!*

Fortunately, you don't have to create a paragon in order to conjure greatness. An aura of greatness comes foremost not from who a given character may be, but from the profound impact that character has on others. It is not strictly necessary for a character to have done anything at all for their effect on others to be apparent.

Ethan Canin's novel *America America* (2008) is about a 1970s working-class young man, Corey Sifter, who gets a job as a lawn boy for the rich Metarey family in his upstate New York town. Corey becomes a de facto (though not wholly equal) member of the family. Family patriarch Liam Metarey pays for Corey's education and obtains for him a position as aide to Senator Henry Bonwiller, who is running for the Democratic presidential nomination.

Canin opens his novel many years later at Bonwiller's funeral. From the first lines it is clear that Bonwiller has had an enormous impact on Corey's life:

> When you've been involved in something like this, no matter how long ago it happened, no matter how long it's been absent from the news, you're fated, nonetheless, to always search it out. To be on alert for it, somehow, every day of your life. For the small item at the back of the newspaper. For the stranger at the cocktail party or the unfamiliar letter in the mailbox. For the reckoning pause on the other end of the phone line. For the dreadful reappearance of something that, in all likelihood, is never going to return.

At this point in the novel we know nothing about Bonwiller, Corey or what will happen. All we know is that it was "something like this," which is to say something big, newsworthy and possibly even historic. The after-effects have followed Corey through his life, leaving him alert for echoes.

Bonwiller's funeral is attended by crowds of bigwigs, reinforcing his importance. Corey by this point publishes a respected independent newspaper but chooses not to cover the event himself because, "I was at the funeral for my own reasons." Later in the day, when the crowds are gone, Corey returns to the freshly mounded grave. Regarding it, he reflects:

> That was it. The quiet end of it all.
> There was no one else alive now who knew.

Knew what? There are secrets, obviously; powerful ones worth keeping. It is many pages before we learn what they are. Was the Senator a leader or a rogue or both? Canin hasn't shown us: All he needs at this point is to reveal the impact Bonwiller has had. Greatness already is in the air.

Thirteen Moons (2006) is Charles Frazier's second novel, following *Cold Mountain* (1997). It's the story of a great man, Will Cooper, whose life spans almost the entire nineteenth century. As in Canin's novel, Frazier frames his subject's story. At the turn of the twentieth century, elderly Will Cooper is waiting to die. Notice how Frazier weaves strength into his narrator's final days:

> There is no scatheless rapture. Love and time put me in this condition. I am leaving soon for the Nightland, where all the ghosts of men and animals yearn to travel. We're called to it. I feel it pulling at me, same as everyone else. It is the last unmapped country, and a dark way getting there. A sorrowful path. And maybe not exactly Paradise at the end. The belief I've acquired over a generous and nevertheless inadequate time on earth is that we arrive in the afterlife as broken as when we departed from the world. But, on the other hand, I've always enjoyed a journey.

Will Cooper is clearly a man of wisdom. His days have been long. He has experienced much. More than that, he has lived a unique life that was remarkable in its breadth and reach. In his final days, Cooper pays a visit to the Warm Springs Hotel:

A prominent family from down in the smothering part of the state had come up to the mountains to enjoy our cool climate. The father was a slight acquaintance of mine, and the son was a recently elected member of the state house. The father was young enough to be my child. They found me sitting on the gallery, reading the most recent number of a periodical—*The North American Review* to be specific, for I have been a subscriber over a span of time encompassing parts of eight decades.

The father shook my hand and turned to his boy. He said, Son, I want you to meet someone. I'm sure you will find him interesting. He was a senator and a colonel in the War. And, most romantically, white chief of the Indians. He made and lost and made again several fortunes in business and land and railroad speculation. When I was a boy, he was a hero. I dreamed of being half the man he was.

Something about the edge to his tone when he said the words *chief*, *colonel*, and *senator* rubbed me the wrong way. It suggested something ironic in those honorifics, which, beyond the general irony of everything, there is not. I nearly said, Hell, I'm twice the man you are now, despite our difference in age, so things didn't work out so bright for your condescending hopes. And, by the way, what other than our disparity of age confers upon you the right to talk about me as if I'm not present? But I held my tongue. I don't care. People can say whatever they want to about me when I've passed. And they can inflect whatever tone they care to use in the telling.

The son said, He's not Cooper, is he?

The passage above accomplishes several things at once. It quickly sketches in for us the broad outline of Cooper's life: it's backstory, yes, but in service of the friction between Cooper and the condescending man speaking about him as if he isn't there. Cooper's irritability over how he's spoken of shows a spark of dignity, which right away is tempered by restraint. Step by step, Frazier is building this dying man's strength.

Most telling of all, though, is the son's awed surprise at finding himself in the presence of the legendary Will Cooper. That is impact. It's key is not the great man himself but the people around him. They, in a sense, make him great.

Have you ever been in the presence of someone who awed you? My eyes boggled upon meeting the American poet Robert Lowell in a London pub. Shaking the hand of Ray Bradbury at a publishing party in New York, I found myself unable to speak. I once delivered a contract to Isaac Asimov at his West Side apartment and blathered like a fan boy. (Asimov was amused.) I remember each occasion with vivid clarity. Each time I felt small yet lifted and inspired by the great writers before me.

Is your protagonist great? In establishing her at the outset, it is important to look not toward what she will do later in the story but the impact she has on others now. Her actions will speak, I have no doubt; but who in your hero's circle already has respect, feels awe, so that we can feel it too?

PROTAGONISTS VS. HEROES

Who is at the center of your novel, a protagonist or a hero? Is he merely the subject of the story, or a real human being with extraordinary qualities? I hope it is the latter. Every protagonist can be a hero, even from the opening pages. Indeed, that quality is essential if readers are to tag along with your main character for hundreds of pages more.

It does not matter whether your intent is to portray someone real or someone heroic. To make either type matter to your readers, you need only find in your real human being what is strong, and in your strong human being what is real. Even greatness can be signaled from the outset.

How do you find the strong or human qualities in your protagonist? What will be most effective to portray? The answer to those questions lies in you, the author. What is forgivably human to you? What stirs your respect? That is where to start.

Next, when will you show the readers those qualities in your hero? Later on? That is too late. Too many manuscripts begin at a distance from their protagonists, as if opening with a long shot like in a movie. That's a shame. Why keep readers at arm's length?

Novels are unique among art forms in their intimacy. They can take us inside a character's heart and mind right away. And that is where your readers want to be. Go there immediately. And when you do, show us what your hero is made of. If you accomplish that, then the job of winning us over is done.

Now comes the fun part: spinning a story that won't let us go.

PRACTICAL TOOLS

Finding a Protagonist's Strength

Step 1: Is your protagonist an ordinary person? Find in him any kind of strength.

Step 2: Work out a way for that strength to be demonstrated within your protagonist's first five pages.

Step 3: Revise your character's introduction to your readers.

Discussion: Without a quality of strength on display, your readers will not bond with your protagonist. Why should they? No one wants to spend four minutes, let alone four hundred pages, with a miserable excuse for a human being or even a plain old average Joe. So, what is strength? It can be as simple as caring about someone, self-awareness, a longing for change, or hope. Any small positive quality will signal to your readers that your ordinary protagonist is worth their time.

Finding a Hero's Flaws

Step 1: Is your protagonist a hero—that is, someone who is already strong? Find in him something conflicted, fallible, humbling, or human.

Step 2: Work out a way for that flaw to be demonstrated within your protagonist's first five pages.

Step 3: Revise your character's introduction to your readers. *Be sure to soften the flaw with self-awareness or self-deprecating humor.*

Discussion: Heroes who are nothing but good, noble, unswerving, honest, courageous, and kind to their mothers will make your readers want to gag. To make heroes real enough to be likable, it's necessary to make them a little bit flawed. What is a flaw that will not also prove fatal? A personal problem, a bad habit, a hot button, a blind spot, or anything that makes your hero a real human being will work. However, this flaw cannot be overwhelming. That is the reason for adding wise self-awareness or a rueful sense of humor.

The Impact of Greatness

Step 1: Does your story have a character who is supposed to be great? Choose a character (your protagonist or another) who is, has been, or will be affected by that great character.

Step 2: Note the impact on your point-of-view character. In what ways is she changed by the great character? How specifically is her self-regard or actual life different? Is destiny involved? Detail the effect.

Step 3: Write out that impact in a paragraph. It can be backward looking (a *flashback frame*) or a present moment of exposition.

Step 4: Add that paragraph to your manuscript.

Discussion: Greatness is not always about esteem. Those affected by great people may be ambivalent. Whatever the case in your story, see if you can shade the effect of your great character to make it specific and capture nuances. The effect of one character upon another is as particular as the characters themselves.

CHAPTER TWO

CHARACTERS WHO MATTER

The heroes of popular series are memorable, but quick: Who's the most unforgettable sidekick in contemporary fiction? Takes some thought, doesn't it? Dr. Watson comes easily to mind; perhaps also Sancho Panza or Paul Drake? After that it's easier to think of sidekicks from movies or comic books.

Same question for femmes fatales. Not so easy, is it? Conjuring up the names of Brigid O'Shaughnessy in Dashiell Hammett's *The Maltese Falcon* (1930) or Carmen Sternwood in Raymond Chandler's *The Big Sleep* (1939) tests the depth of your trivia knowledge. Maybe you thought of Justine in Lawrence Durrell's Alexandria Quartet (1957–1960)? Points to you—but what about contemporary fiction? Do you recall the name of Lyra Belacqua's mother in Philip Pullman's *The Golden Compass* (1995)? (It's Mrs. Coulter.) Other femmes fatales?

We could issue the same challenge with respect to the great villains of contemporary literature. After Hannibal Lecter, who is there?

Come to that, how many secondary characters of any type stick in your mind from the fiction you've read in the last year? Do you read chic lit? Have you ever felt that the gaggle of sassy girlfriends in one is pretty much the same as in the rest? How about killers and assassins? Do many of them seem to you stamped from the same mold? How about children? Do precocious kids in novels make you want to gag?

If so, you see my point. Secondary characters in published fiction often are weak.

Supporting players in manuscripts submitted to my agency are too often forgettable, as well. They walk on and walk off, making no particular impression. What wasted opportunities, in my opinion, especially when you consider that secondary characters aren't born, they're built. So, how can you construct a secondary character whom readers will never forget?

SPECIAL

Suppose you want a character to be special. You want this character to have stature, allure, or a significant history with your protagonist. How is that effect achieved? A look at examples of some contemporary femmes fatales may help us out.

James Ellroy's *The Black Dahlia* (1987) probably is the finest noir novel of our time. It's the rich, dark, complex, and highly layered story of a 1940s Los Angeles police detective, Bucky Bleichert, who becomes obsessed with a murder victim, Elizabeth Short, nicknamed the Black Dahlia by the press. Her murder was grisly, the torture beforehand gruesome, and the cast of suspects a roster of corruption. Central to the story, however, is Bucky's fixation on the Black Dahlia. She was beautiful in life, and highly promiscuous, but why is Bucky haunted by this victim over any other?

That, in a way, is the eternal problem of making a character singular. Is there any description of beauty so effective that it would make anyone swoon? Is there a sexual allure that can seduce everyone who opens a book? Do you believe that a crusty cop would really care about a bad news babe?

Making a character uniquely compelling for all readers is pretty much impossible. As readers, we are all too different. What is beautiful, seductive, and dangerous for me may well be laughable to you. What *is* possible is to make momentous the *effect* of one character upon another. As with greatness, creating a feeling that a character is special is a matter of measuring her impact. *The Black Dahlia* opens with Bucky Bleichert looking back after the case has closed:

I never knew her in life. She exists for me through others, in evidence the ways of her death drove them. Working backward, seeing only facts, I reconstructed her as a sad little girl and a whore, at best a could-have-been—a tag that might equally apply to me. I wish I could have granted her an anonymous end, relegated her to a few terse words on a homicide dick's summary report, carbon to the coroner's office, more paperwork to take her to potter's field. The only thing wrong with the wish is that she wouldn't have wanted it that way. As brutal as the facts were, she would have wanted all of them known. And since I owe her a great deal and am the only one who does know her entire story, I have undertaken the writing of this memoir.

What in that paragraph conveys the impact the Black Dahlia has had on Bucky? Is it the elevated tone of his prose? His regret? The Dahlia's refusal to stay small, a "could-have-been"? I believe that it's the simple words "I owe her a great deal." Bucky is in debt to a dead girl. That debt is intriguing by itself but also makes the Dahlia special to Bucky.

Russell Banks's *The Reserve* (2008) is set in a private community for the rich, the "Reserve" of the title, in the Adirondack Mountains in the 1930s. Jordan Groves, a local artist with leftist leanings, falls under the spell of Vanessa Cole, the twice-divorced daughter of a respected brain surgeon and his society wife. Vanessa has secrets and a dangerous side, but at first Jordan is dazzled. As he lands his seaplane at her family's lakeside compound and sees her for the second time, his fascination with her is apparent:

He shut off the motor and sat there for a few seconds and watched Vanessa. She was in a group of perhaps ten people, but he saw no one else. She wore a calf-length black skirt and a dark gray silk blouse with billowing sleeves and over her broad shoulders a black crocheted shawl, and she looked even more beautiful to

Jordan today than when he'd seen her yesterday in the fading, late-afternoon sunlight standing alone by the shore of the Second Lake. She had on bright red, almost scarlet lipstick, and mascara, and though she was pale and her face full of sorrow, she was luminous to him, enveloped by a light that seemed to emanate from inside her. He did not think that he had ever seen a woman with a visible field of light surrounding her like that, a gleaming halo wrapped around her entire body.

What is it that makes Vanessa beautiful? Her black skirt, dark gray silk blouse, and red lipstick? Her black crocheted shawl? Crochet? Um, that doesn't scream siren to me. No, rather it is the aura of light that Jordan sees surrounding her. Would you or I see it? Maybe, maybe not. But Jordan sees it, and his perception is what counts.

Jodi Picoult is a best-selling author and a spinner of morality tales for our time. Her knack for provocative premises is enviable. *The Pact* (1998) revolves around a suicide pact between a teenage boyfriend and girlfriend—Chris Harte and Emily Gold, lifelong next-door neighbors—that goes wrong. Emily's suicide (via gunshot) succeeds. Chris does not go through with it and lives.

For many authors that would be enough tragedy to occasion an aftermath novel, the survivors taking us on yet one more journey of healing and self-discovery. Picoult is a more masterful plotter, though. Doubt about what really happened grows. Eventually Chris is arrested for Emily's murder. Picoult teases out the evidence, swinging our suspicions this way and that, until finally Chris takes the stand and reveals his true feelings about Emily:

> "Do you know," Chris said softly, "what it's like to love someone so much, that you can't see yourself without picturing her? Or what it's like to touch someone, and feel like you've come home?" He made a fist, and rested it in the palm of his other hand. "What we had wasn't about sex, or about being with someone just to show off what you've got, the way it was for other kids our

age. We were, well, meant to be together. Some people spend their whole lives looking for that one person," he said. "I was lucky enough to have her all along."

Picoult has a tough job in *The Pact*. For plot reasons she must withhold from us for most of the novel the truth of what really happened. Finally it comes out: Chris procured the suicide gun and helped Emily hold it to her head. He did this because he cared profoundly about her. She wanted suicide, he hoped to talk her out of it, but in the end he helped her because it was the only thing that would relieve her pain.

That, anyway, is what Picoult wants both the jury and her readers to swallow. We have to, for the jury is going to find Chris not guilty. That's quite a trick. For it to work, Chris has to sway us with a heartfelt declaration of love. Picoult's passage above does the job; at any rate, it did for many readers. To my eye it's clear that for Chris, Emily was special.

Who have been the special people in your life, the ones whose presence looms larger, whose friendships are fundamental, who are indelibly part of your personal story? You have such people in your life, I'm sure. Me too. How is it, then, that protagonists in many manuscripts seem to live in blissful isolation, self-sufficient, wholly self-made, and dependent on no one? Who are these people? They are not real. Consequently they are also unreal for readers. If they are to keep us deeply involved for several hundred pages, protagonists need a personal history.

Who in your story has special stature? Is there an influential teacher, a spouse, a past love, a friend of long standing, a wizard at math, an egotistical-but-gifted auto mechanic? Is there a character in your story who could be given such elevated importance? It isn't that difficult to do. Explore the effect that this paragon has on your protagonist, then find a meaningful moment for that effect to be expressed.

Singular human beings may be rare in life, but this is fiction. You can build them as needed. Who knows? You might even construct for yourself a whole new incarnation of the femme fatale.

ORDINARY

Who are the people in your life whom you take for granted, the ones who are always there, reliable, rock steady? Your family? Your co-workers? Your Starbucks barista? When was the last time you really spent time thinking about them, deep down contemplating who they are and what makes them go?

If it's been a while, you can be forgiven. We've all got a lot to deal with. Part of the gift of steady people in your life is precisely that they *are* steady. You don't have to worry about them. That's fine in life, but in fiction, characters who remain unexamined will be forgettable, even bland.

To see what I mean, let's look at some outstanding sidekicks in recent novels.

Dean Koontz is our indisputable ruler of supernatural and paranoid thrillers. In recent successes like *Life Expectancy* (2004), *The Husband* (2006), and *The Good Guy* (2007), Koontz's paranoid plotting has equaled that of masters like Cornell Woolrich (1903–1968) and Philip K. Dick (1928–1982). It isn't only ordinary men whom Koontz torments, either. In his series of novels featuring southern California short-order cook Odd Thomas, the supernatural plays a big part.

Odd Thomas is perfectly ordinary, except that the dead talk to him. Unfortunately, they usually want something too; frequently revenge. In *Odd Thomas* (2003), a stranger comes to Thomas's town of Pico Mundo. Thomas dubs him "Fungus Man" and suspects something's amiss. It is. In Fungus Man's house, Thomas detects the presence of hundreds of *bodachs*, pain-eating spirits whose presence signals a coming catastrophe.

Many writers would make Odd Thomas a loner. Koontz, though, has a knack for countering our expectations. Thus, Thomas has friends, albeit strange ones like Little Ozzie, a 400-pound man with six fingers on his left hand. Thomas also has a girlfriend. Now, what kind of girlfriend would you give a guy who chats with the recently deceased? Koontz wants to keep the tone of the novel light, so he goes for kooky.

Kooky?

Thomas's girlfriend, Stormy Llewellyn, is introduced buying her and Thomas ice cream cones (coconut cherry chocolate chunk flavor) from the ice cream parlor where she works:

> Her uniform included pink shoes, white socks, a hot-pink skirt, a matching pink-and-white blouse, and a perky pink cap. With her Mediterranean complexion, jet-black hair, and mysterious dark eyes, she looked like a sultry espionage agent who had gone undercover as a hospital candy striper.
>
> Sensing my thoughts, as usual, she sat beside me on the bench and said, "When I have my own shop, the employees won't have to wear stupid uniforms."
>
> "I think you look adorable."
>
> "I look like a goth Gidget."
>
> Stormy gave one of the cones to me, and for a minute or two we sat in silence, watching shoppers stroll past, enjoying our ice cream.
>
> "Under the hamburger and bacon grease," she said, "I can still smell the peach shampoo."
>
> "I'm an olfactory delight."
>
> "Maybe one day when I have my own shop, we can work together and smell the same."
>
> "The ice-cream business doesn't move me. I love to fry."
>
> "I guess it's true," she said.
>
> "What?"
>
> "Opposites attract."

Contrast is the operating principle in creating sidekicks. What distinguishes Koontz, in my mind, is that he doesn't go for the obvious. The obvious contrast to Thomas would be his philosophical opposite: a skeptic or scientific type, say, or perhaps someone who deals with the dead in a practical way, like a funeral parlor director. Thomas's opposite would be serious and goal-driven, unlike lackadaisical Thomas. Their relationship would not be easy but instead knotty.

Instead, Stormy works at an ice cream parlor. An orphan, she has been Thomas's girlfriend since the age of sixteen. Now twenty, her ambition is to own her own ice cream place by twenty-four. She believes she and Thomas are soul mates. (They have a gypsy's fortune telling card that says so.) She teases him and won't have sex with him. She believes in delayed gratification and wants their first time to be pure.

The classic series pattern would be to establish conflicts in their relationship and play them out book after book. In *Odd Thomas*, the first in the series, Stormy dies. (Since Thomas talks to the dead, though, that is not the end of their relationship.)

The point here is that Koontz plays against what we expect. A diametrically opposite Stormy would have been sufficient for his story. The kooky, sweet, innocent-yet-self-aware Stormy that we get is both more endearing and more interesting. Why? Because this Stormy keeps us off balance.

Another principle of effective sidekicks is making them human. That means giving them conflicts. But what kinds of conflicts? Ah. Authors' answers to that question are telling indicators that divide run-of-the-mill writers from true storytellers.

Tess Gerritsen's tense thrillers are noted for their gruesome killers. On that score, *The Mephisto Club* (2006) doesn't disappoint. At Christmastime, Boston is hit with a series of dismemberments—body parts cunningly switched between crime scenes and mystery messages (such as PECCAVI, Latin for "I have sinned") written on the walls in blood. Assigned to this case, their sixth, are medical examiner Maura Isles and homicide detective Jane Rizzoli, who are in a sense each other's sidekicks. Like any good M.E., Maura is detached. Like any good homicide detective, Jane is fiery in her dedication and wounded (literally) by her past.

Gerritsen could easily have left Maura and Jane that way: central casting thriller leads, nicely contrasted and all-too-predictable. But she knows better. Both need other, human, sides. Maura's is shown on this Christmas Eve when she attends a Roman Catholic mass. Afterward, it is clear that she and the priest, Father Daniel Brophy, have a history:

"Hello, Maura."

She looked up and met Daniel's gaze. The church was not yet empty. The organist was still packing up her sheet music, and several choir members were still pulling on their coats, yet at that moment Daniel's attention was so centered on Maura, she might have been the only other person in the room.

"It's been a long time since you visited," he said.

"I suppose it has been."

"Not since August, wasn't it?"

So you've been keeping track, too.

Need a road map, here? Maura's cool and scientific side is softened up in this excruciating flirtation with a priest, which continues over a number of books. Meanwhile, on Christmas day, Jane goes home for dinner with her tension-fraught family. Present this year is someone new: Jane's four-month-old daughter, Regina:

"Let me hold her." Jane opened her arms and hugged a squirming Regina against her chest. *Only four months old*, she thought, *and already my baby is trying to wriggle away from me.* Ferocious little Regina had come into the world with fists swinging, her face purple from screaming. *Are you so impatient to grow up?* Jane wondered as she rocked her daughter. *Won't you stay a baby for a while and let me hold you, enjoy you, before the passing years send you walking out our door?*

Jane's maternal tenderness is not quite what we expect from a woman who, at the crime scene, says to Maura coolly, "I see you found the left hand." Maura's search for a connection and Jane's struggle with her family not only provide extra plot layers, they make human two professionals who could be too easily stereotyped.

Sidekicks can be regular folk (although different than expected and three-dimensional, we hope) or they can be eccentrics. It's a matter of choice and what serves the story, but if you're using misfits or originals, there are issues for you to consider.

David Baldacci regularly climbs to the top of best-seller lists with his political thrillers, many involving the Secret Service. *The Camel Club* (2005) introduces a group of oddball Washington, D.C., conspiracy theorists, the club of the title, who meet once a month to share information and keep tabs on threats to American freedom. A less high-powered group of individuals would be hard to imagine.

Their leader and the series protagonist is a mystery man who has taken the name of his favorite film director, Oliver Stone. He lives in a cemetery caretaker's cottage and in a tent across from the White House in a designated protest area. On the tent is a sign that reads simply, "I want the truth."

Oliver clearly has manifold skills, keen smarts, and some sort of intelligence background. We learn little except that his past is a forgotten life, which is now replaced by his unusual lifestyle and the Camel Club. The club members, on the other hand, have detailed histories and distinct personalities.

The first is Caleb Shaw, a fussy academic type with twin doctorates in political science and eighteenth-century literature. A lifelong protester, his antiestablishment views have exiled him from academia. He works instead in the Rare Books and Special Collections Division at the Library of Congress. What one notices about him first is his manner of dress: suits straight from the nineteenth century, complete with bowler hats, vest pocket watches, and long sideburns and mustache.

The second member of the Camel Club is Reuben Rhodes, a six-foot-four West Point graduate, multi-medal-winning veteran, and former Defense Intelligence Agency operative. Lacking purpose after Vietnam, his life slid into drug use until he ran into Oliver Stone, who helped him turn his life around. When not helping the Camel Club, he works on a loading dock.

The third member is Milton Farb who is able to add long strings of numbers, is possessed of a photographic memory, and once had a promising career at the National Institutes of Health that was unfortunately destroyed by his worsening obsessive-compulsive disorder, a condition born in his childhood in the sideshow of a traveling carnival. His paranoid personality had him close to destitution until he was persuaded by Oliver to become a contestant on the TV show *Jeopardy!* on which he earned a small fortune. Now he runs a successful business designing corporate websites, even though he is prone to ritualistic foot shuffling and adding aloud long strings of numbers meaningful only to him.

A ragtag bunch to be sure; not a collection of people one would expect to be battlers against conspiracy and effective early warning watchdogs for America. But that's the point. Who are the most eccentric people of your acquaintance? Anyone who dresses in antique suits? Any dockworkers who are multiply decorated war heroes? Maybe an obsessive-compulsive math genius sideshow freak or two?

No? Then you see my point. For oddballs and misfits to come across in a sea of secondary characters, they must be genuinely eccentric. But that comes with a problem: Such characters are hard to swallow. We won't buy them unless they are carefully and convincingly constructed, and remain true to their weirdo selves. That's not easy to do. David Baldacci does it.

What about you? How much development have you done of your sidekicks and other secondary characters? Do they provide contrast, yet also counter our expectations? Are they real and human, beset by conflicts with which we can identify? If eccentric, are they genuinely and deeply strange? In what ways? And are those ways justified and detailed?

Whether using sidekicks or secondary characters of other sorts, time spent developing them will considerably raise the interest quotient of your story.

ANTAGONISTS

Villains are some of the worst characters I meet in manuscripts, and not in a good way. What I mean is that they frequently are cardboard. Most are presented as purely evil: *Mwoo-ha-ha villains*, as we call them around the office.

Cardboard villains never work. Far from frightening us, they generally have us rolling our eyes. It's not that I don't enjoy a good baddie, understand; it's just that too many writers get lazy when it comes to these antagonists. Unchallenged by doubt, free of obstacles, never set back, blessed with infinite time and resources, able to work their nefarious schemes on a part-time basis (or, at least, that's how it seems since they crop up only occasionally), these villains strike us as unrealistic and therefore silly.

Even worse can be stories in which there is no villain as such. Literary fiction, women's fiction, romances, and coming-of-age tales are just a few types of story that do not necessarily call for a classic wrongdoer. In such manuscripts, even so, those who oppose the protagonist are often poorly developed and inactive. Lacking strong resistance, one wonders why the protagonist is having a hard time. It is possible to build conflict out of internal obstacles, of course, but over the long haul it's wearisome and hard to maintain readers' interest that way.

People are the most fascinating source of obstacles: that means antagonists, those who work against your protagonist. They can be active opponents or even friendly allies who cast doubt upon your protagonist's actions or undermine his resolve.

Do you go through your days without experiencing friction from others? I doubt it. Do you have ongoing problem people in your daily routine, possibly even active enemies? If you do, then you know that those who oppose you are not easily deterred, and they may even have the best of intentions. Have you ever noticed how your critics are eager to help you? They willingly share what they see as wrong with you and have valuable suggestions for your improvement. Our enemies do not hide.

Keith Ablow's series of thrillers featuring FBI forensic psychologist Frank Clevenger has been noted for its original and chilling villains. The fifth in the series, *The Architect* (2005), revolves around a killer who leaves his victims with one part of their anatomy (their spine, say) exquisitely and meticulously dissected, as if laid open for a medical school class. It's a different piece of anatomy each time, too. All the victims come from money, so Clevenger's task is to make connections and find who is responsible.

Ablow, meanwhile, clues us in. The sick pervert who dissects people is an architect; not only that, a brilliant architect named West Crosse. Crosse is smart. Crosse is successful. Crosse is handsome. Bored yet? We would be except for the creepy and unusual touches that Ablow adds. For instance, when Crosse was twenty years old, he deliberately ruined his perfect face by cutting a jagged facial scar on himself. Professionally, he is blunt to the point of alienating potential clients. Toward the novel's beginning, Crosse brings preliminary plans for a new home in Montana to a rich Miami couple who are choosing an architect. Crosse is openly contemptuous of their ultra-modern digs:

> Crosse sat down. The chair felt stiff and cold. He placed his rolled drawing on the table, laid a hand on the glass. Then he looked Ken Rawlings directly in the eyes. "You're living—or trying to live—in someone else's house. Because it feels safe. But it isn't."
>
> "I'm not following you," Rawlings said.
>
> "This is Walter Gropius's house," Crosse said. He glanced at Heather Rawlings. "It has nothing to do with you, nothing to do with your wife." He felt his own passion beginning to stir, the passion to liberate people from the tombs of fear that kept them from expressing the truest parts of themselves, kept them from feeling completely, exquisitely alive. …

This from a guy who dissects different body parts on living victims? It is exactly that contradiction that makes Crosse so fascinating: He gives life through design; he takes life by design. What is up with this sicko? Of course we read ahead to find out. More to the point, Ablow has created a villain who helps his victims. If he finds them lacking in some respect, he fixes them. Just being helpful, you see? That's far from your usual *Mwoo-ha-ha villain*, and it works.

National Book Award nominee Charles Baxter devised in *The Soul Thief* (2008) a villain who doesn't kill but rather steals lives.

Baxter's protagonist is Nathaniel Mason, a graduate student in Buffalo, New York, in the 1970s. Nathaniel is infatuated with an artistic beauty, Theresa, who unfortunately is the lover of a romantic poseur named Jerome Coolberg.

Coolberg plays head games with Nathaniel, stealing his shirts and notebooks, claiming that episodes of Nathaniel's life happened to him instead. Events occur that are both tragic and that set Nathaniel's life on a disappointingly conventional track. Years later Nathaniel begins to feel that Coolberg had manipulated his fate in even more sinister ways. He tracks down his nemesis, now a famous interviewer on national radio in California, only to find that Coolberg expects him. They walk on to a pier, where Coolberg explains himself:

> "… Are you looking down? Nathaniel? Good. Do you suffer from vertigo? I do. But you see what's down there? I don't mean the ocean. I don't mean the salt water. Nothing but idiotic marine life in there. Nothing but the whales and the Portuguese and the penguins. No, I mean the mainland. Everywhere down there, someone, believe me, is clothing himself in the robes of another. Someone is adopting someone else's personality, to his own advantage. Right? Absolutely right. Of this one truth I am absolutely certain. Somebody's working out a copycat strategy even now. Identity theft? Please. We're all copycats. Aren't we? Of course we are. How do you learn to do any little task? You copy. You model. So I didn't do anything all that unusual, *if* I did it. But suppose I did, let's suppose I managed a little con. So what? So I could be you for a while? And was that so bad? Aside from the collateral damage? …"

That Nathaniel's life was messed up by Coolberg is bad; that Coolberg can rationalize what he did is even worse. (Worse still is Nathaniel's passive acquiescence, which is made sickeningly clear in the novel's last line.) To put it another way, there's no villain so scary as one who is right.

Not all antagonists are creepy or bad. Some are as human as a novel's protagonist. An example can be found in John Burnham Schwartz's *Reservation Road* (1998), a novel about the aftermath of a hit-and-run. The victim is a ten-year-old boy standing by a roadside near a gas station in a northern Connecticut town. His father, Ethan, sees him killed.

The driver of the car is Dwight, whose point of view is one of the three through which Schwartz tells his story. Dwight is at fault but is intended to be sympathetic. For the author, that is a challenge. How can a hit-and-run driver be sympathetic?

In the opening pages, Schwartz deftly sketches in Dwight's circumstances. He is driving his son Sam home from a Red Sox game. The game went to extra innings, so they are late. That's a problem because Dwight's ex, Sam's mother, is a bitch on wheels. Worse, Dwight screwed up a few years earlier after she told him she was leaving him for another man. Dwight struck both her and Sam; he landed on probation, lost his law practice, and was left with tenuous visitation rights to his son.

Thus, Dwight finds himself driving too fast down a nighttime road, one headlight out, distracted and worried. He hits Ethan's son, killing him. This is a crucial moment for Schwartz. Why doesn't Dwight stop? Schwartz has Dwight's son Sam dozing in the car, his face pressed against the passenger door handle. There is the impact. Schwartz executes the moment this way:

> The impact made the car shudder. My foot came off the gas. And we were coasting, still there, but moving, fleeing. Unless I braked now: *Do it.* My foot started for the brake. But then Sam started to wail in pain and I froze. I looked over and he was holding his face in both hands and screaming in pain. I went cold. "Sam!" I shouted, his name coming from deep down in my gut and sounding louder and more desperate to my ears than any sound I'd ever made. He didn't respond. "Sam!"
>
> In the rearview mirror I saw the dark-haired man sprinting up the road after us. His fury and his fear were

in his half-shadowed face, the frenzied pumping of his arms. He was coming to punish me, and for a moment I wanted him to. My foot was inching toward the brake. But suddenly I felt Sam warm against my side, curling up and holding on and bawling like a baby. I put my foot on the gas.

Dwight makes a tragic mistake, but as *Reservation Road* progresses, it is Ethan who does something wrong, allowing himself to become consumed with a desire for revenge. His reasons are carefully developed—so carefully than when he discovers Dwight's name and goes to his house with a gun, it is unclear what will happen. Motives, in other words, abound on both sides. The two antagonists are perfectly understandable. We feel equally for them both.

That is the power of a three-dimensional antagonist: the power to sway our hearts in directions we would not expect them to be swayed. To get us to see, even accept, the antagonist's point of view. You may not want your story to be neutral. You may embrace right and wrong and write an outcome that makes your values obvious. That is your choice.

At the same time, a wholly black-and-white story cannot engage us very deeply. The deck is too stacked, the players too shallow to stir or scare us in memorable ways. Whatever your intension, it's worth investing time in your antagonist, opening up her unexpected sides, justifying her actions and even making her right. That only adds to the drama.

The term "secondary" for characters is misleading. As you can see, secondary characters have a major role to play in making your novel strong. Special, ordinary, or opposition, they are as important as your protagonist and worth some extra time.

PRACTICAL TOOLS

Creating Special Characters

Step 1: Look at the special character through the eyes of your protagonist. List three ways in which they are exactly alike. Find one way in which they are exactly the opposite.

Step 2: Write down what most fascinates your protagonist about this special character. Also note one thing about the special character that your protagonist will never understand.

Step 3: Create the defining moment in their relationship. Write down specific details of the place, the time, the action, and their dialogue during this event. What single detail does, or will, your protagonist remember best? What detail does she most want to forget?

Step 4: At the end of your story, in what way has this special character most changed your protagonist? At the story's outset, in what way does your protagonist most resist this special character?

Step 5: Incorporate the above into your manuscript.

Discussion: Special-ness comes not from a character but from their impact on the protagonist. What are the details that measure their impact? How specific can you make them? The steps above are just a start. Whether for femmes fatales or any other character, it is those details that will bring their special-ness alive.

Making Ordinary Characters Extraordinary

Step 1: How is your ordinary character identified or defined? A friend? A teacher? A cop? Write down five stereotypes attached to such a type. Find one way in which this character is the opposite of that.

Step 2: Find one way in which this character is inwardly conflicted. How strong can you make this conflict? Make it impossible to reconcile. Create a story event in which we will see this conflict enacted.

Step 3: If this character is meant to be eccentric, push his eccentricity to an extreme. What is one common thing this character does in a completely uncommon way? What is the most outrageous thing this character can do or say? How does he look at things in a way that is peculiar or bizarre? Write a passage in which this character explains his unique habits and outlook. Make it so logical and convincing that anyone would agree.

Discussion: Secondary characters often do not stand out. Giving them the qualities that make them memorable involves violating our expectations, making them deeply human and pushing boundaries. Some authors worry about overshadowing their protagonists or creating cartoon characters. In truth, the problem in most manuscripts is that secondary characters are too tame.

Empowering Antagonists

Step 1: Find five ways and times at which your antagonist will directly engage your protagonist.

Step 2: Write out your antagonist's opinion of your protagonist. What does your antagonist *like* about your protagonist? How does your antagonist want to *help* your protagonist? What advice does your antagonist have?

Step 3: How can your antagonist be summarized or defined? A boss? A senator? A mother-in-law? List five stereotypes associated with such a type. Find one way in which your antagonist is exactly the opposite.

Step 4: Create four actions that will make your antagonist warm and sympathetic.

Step 5: Assume that your antagonist is justified and right. Make her case in writing. Find times in history when things ran her way and were good. Find a passage from theology, philosophy, or folk wisdom that supports your antagonist's outlook. Choose one character whom your antagonist will win over. In what way does your protagonist agree with your antagonist?

Discussion: Cardboard villains don't scare us. Stereotypical antagonists lack teeth. By contrast, an antagonist who is human, understandable, justified, and even right will stir in your readers the maximum unease. In creating antagonists, reject the idea of evil. Make them good. Make them active. Bring them on stage and into your protagonist's face. An antagonist who merely lurks isn't doing much for your story.

CHAPTER THREE

SCENES THAT CAN'T BE CUT

Have you ever skimmed through some scenes in the middle of a novel? Worse, have you ever looked at middle scenes in your own manuscript and wondered if they work?

Middles are tough. Too many middles in manuscripts and published novels are routine, lackluster, just there, nothing special. What goes wrong? Is it poor focus? Is it a blank spot in an outline? Were these ho-hum scenes written on rainy afternoons following disturbing parent-teacher conferences when inspiration was lacking?

I suspect many sagging middle scenes slump the way they do not because of bad planning or bad luck but because their purpose hasn't yet emerged. Authors, as they plow through the middle portion of their manuscripts, tend to write what they think ought to come next; furthermore, they write it in the first way it occurs to them to do so. In successive drafts such scenes tend to stay in place, little altered. Unsure what to do, an author may leave a scene in place because ... well, just because.

The push to rack up pages, to meet self-imposed or actual deadlines, makes it easy to avoid tearing apart a scene to find its weakly beating heart and surgically open it. Taking a fresh approach means throwing away time and redoing a lot of work. Who wants to do that? It's understandable that authors leave the troubled middles alone, but the result is too often scenes that are ineffective.

What can you do to fire up your middles? To answer that question, it's first helpful to realize that every scene set down by an author usually has a reason to be. The author may not grasp the reason yet, but the impulse to portray this particular moment, this particular meeting, this particular action, springs from the deep well of dreams from which stories are drawn.

This scene has a point. The task is to draw that purpose out. How? Changing the words on the page won't work. We authors are wedded to our words. Our instinct is to preserve them. So, it's the whole scene that needs to be explored again. Scene revision is, to me, less a matter of expression and more a way of seeing.

To re-envision a scene, look away from the page and look toward what is really happening. What change takes place? When does that change occur (at what precise second in the scene)? In that moment, how is the point-of-view character changed? The point of those questions is to find the scenes' *turning points* (note the plural).

Having identified the turning points, you will find focusing the scene becomes easier. Everything else on the page either contributes to, or leads readers away from, those changes. All the extra stuff—the nifty scene setting, clever character bits, artful lead-ins and lead-outs—are now expendable, or perhaps they are tools to help selectively enact the scene's main purpose.

Practice re-envisioning scenes in this way; after a while you will find yourself not only dissatisfied with flabby middle scenes as you write them, you'll also have at hand the tools to shape them effectively from the outset—possibly even a few handy tricks and master techniques to use in orchestrating scenes of multiple impact on many characters.

All of this revision does not mean that some scenes shouldn't be cut. Sad to say, some scenes don't deserve to live. The purpose of this chapter, though, is not to set rules for scene triage, but rather to illuminate why middle scenes rock when they do. Once you have that understanding, it's my hope that revision will get easier and, for the majority of your scenes, may prove unnecessary.

Let's look at some of the factors that contribute to scenes that can't be cut.

OUTER AND INNER TURNING POINTS

A moment ago I mentioned a scene's turning *points*. I used the plural because every change (which, after all, is the reason to include a scene in the first place) has two dimensions: 1) The way in which things change that everyone can understand; 2) the way in which the scene's point-of-view character also changes as a result. To put it plainly, scenes work best when they have both *outer* and *inner* turning points.

Marisha Pessl's sparkling debut novel, *Special Topics in Calamity Physics* (2006), was widely noted for a clever stylistic trick. The novel's young narrator, Blue van Meer, is the daughter of a colorful but drifting college professor. During their early wanderings, Blue's father advises her with regard to her writing, "Always have everything you say exquisitely annotated, and, where possible, provide staggering Visual Aids." The text of Pessl's novel thus formally cites hundreds of other works and includes many carefully numbered Visual Aids (illustrations).

Pessl's bold stylistic approach, though, is not enough to carry readers through more than five hundred pages. Story is needed too; this Pessl provides in a mystery surrounding the death of a charismatic film teacher, Hannah Schneider, at the prep school where Blue spends her senior year. From the outset we know that Blue found Hannah hanged by an orange electrical extension cord from a tree. Was it suicide or was she murdered? Pessl flashes back to recount Blue's peripatetic childhood, her involvement at the St. Gallway School with a clique called the Bluebloods, and the tangled webs that, ultimately, will reveal the truth.

There's a lot of ground to cover. Along the way, Pessl faces the chore of bringing Blue to St. Gallway and getting her involved with the Bluebloods. She also needs to imbue this group of friends with the exclusivity and special-ness that makes them alluring, as well as making Hannah Schneider seem a teacher of charisma and openness, not to mention invoking the progressive atmosphere of St. Gallway.

In most manuscripts, tasks like these defeat their authors. Arriving somewhere, introducing people, and creating atmosphere are almost always low-tension traps. Scene after scene of slogging middle are taken up with getting the players and pieces in place so that something neato can happen later on. Pessl knows this. So she constructs these set-up scenes in ways that make them matter.

Consider the chapter titled "Les Liaisons Dangereuses" (a reference to Pierre Choderlos de Laclos's novel of the same name, 1782). After chickening out on several invitations from members of the Bluebloods, Blue decides finally to accept an invitation to meet them at room 208 of Barrow Hall one afternoon … only to find herself in a meeting of a Dungeons & Dragons club. Blue is crestfallen:

> In the aftermath of being brazenly hoodwinked or swindled, it's difficult to accept, particularly if one has always prided oneself on being an intuitive and scorchingly observant person. Standing on the Hanover steps, waiting for Dad, I reread Jade Whitestone's letter fifteen times, convinced I'd missed something—the correct day, time or location to meet, or perhaps *she'd* made a mistake; perhaps she'd written the letter while watching *On the Waterfront* and had been distracted by the pathos of Brando picking up Eva Marie Saint's tiny white glove and slipping it onto his own meaty hand, but soon, of course, I realized her letter was teaming with sarcasm (particularly in the final sentence), which I hadn't originally picked up on.
>
> It had all been a hoax.

This is the scene's turning point: the moment when the protagonist's fortunes take a turn. In this case it's a low moment. Blue is deflated. Set up for new friends, she's been let down by a trick. That realization is the demarcation point, the precise moment when things change. That would be good enough to give the scene shape, but Pessl knows that turning points have both outer and inner components. In the next paragraph she creates the scene's *inner turning point*:

> Never had there been a rebellion more anticlimactic and second rate, except perhaps the "Gran Horizontes Tropicoco Uprising" in Havana in 1980, which, according to Dad, was composed of out-of-work big band musicians

and El Loro Bonito chorus girls and lasted all of three minutes. ("Fourteen-year-old lovers last longer," he'd noted.)
And the longer I sat on the steps, the cruddier I felt. I pre-
tended not to stare enviously at the happy kids slinging
themselves and their giant backpacks into their parents'
cars, or the tall boys with untucked shirts rushing across
the Commons, shouting at each other, cleats slung over
their bony shoulders like tennis shoes over traffic wires.

Strickly speaking, it might not have been necessary to explore
how cruddy Blue feels. But look again. Pessl draws a contrast between Blue's humiliation and the ease of the other students, whose
parents, unlike Blue's father, have arrived to collect them. Blue longs
to be like them but isn't. This sudden ache is the inner change, the
surfacing recognition that she needs friends. What about outward
consequences? Pessl adds that too: Immediately after this, Hannah
Schneider comes along to chat with Blue and summon her to lunch
on the following Sunday. Blue's life takes a fateful turn.

This scene does a lot of work: It humbles precocious Blue, it makes
her aware of her loneliness, and it introduces the agent of change. For
a set-up scene, that's pretty dynamic. In many manuscripts this scene
would be weak, a candidate for cutting. Pessl uses a nicely defined
turning point and a well delineated *inner* turning point to make the
scene necessary.

Khaled Hosseini's debut novel, *The Kite Runner* (2003), had a
long run on best-seller lists; his second novel, *A Thousand Splendid
Suns* (2007), has also gripped readers. It's the story of two Afghan
women, Mariam and Laila, and their friendship and mutual suffering through several decades. The story spans the Soviet occupation
years, the Taliban era, and beyond. In addition to portraying the
condition of Afghan women, Hosseini also wants to convey some of
the magnificence of Afghanistan's history.

Uh-oh. Portraying the *majestic sweep of history* is, for many writers,
a recipe for lengthy self-indulgence and low tension. Hosseini, however, is too skilled for that. In the novel's second section he switches point of view from unhappily married Mariam to young Laila,

daughter of a neighboring couple. Laila has a best friend, Tariq, for whom in adolescence she develops more powerful feelings. Hosseini needs to portray the evolution of this friendship to something deeper. He wants to simultaneously include Afghan history.

In chapter twenty-one of *A Thousand Splendid Suns*, Hosseini sends Laila, Tariq, and Laila's father, Babi, on an excursion to see Shahr-e-Zohak, the Red City, and the enormous twin Buddhas at Bamiyan (later dynamited by the Taliban) carved into a cliffside. On their way from Kabul, Hosseini signals the era by having Tariq shout taunts at passing Soviet tanks. Later, they see remnants of many invasions. Their driver remarks:

> "And that, my young friends, is the story of our country, one invader after another," the driver said, flicking cigarette ash out the window. "Macedonians. Sassanians. Arabs. Mongols. Now the Soviets. But we're like those walls up there. Battered, and nothing pretty to look at, but still standing. Isn't that the truth, *badar*?"
> "Indeed it is," said Babi.

Many writers would let it go at that, but Hosseini knows that travelogue and story are not the same. At Bamiyan, Laila, Tariq, and Babi climb to the top of the statues. The view of the Afghan countryside provokes Babi to reveal to Laila why he married her now-sour mother and how much he misses Laila's two dead brothers. He then shocks her with an admission: "As much as I love this land, some days I think about leaving it." That adds an element of tension to the day and to the novel, and is the scene's turning point for Laila. Her future now could be extremely different, possibly in a different land.

Hosseini also knows that every outer turning point has an inner counterpart. That occurs at the end of the chapter. Babi's revelation triggers a realization in Laila:

> There was something she hadn't told Babi up there atop the Buddha: that, in one important way, she was glad they couldn't go. She would miss Giti and her pinch-faced

earnestness, yes, and Hasina too, with her wicked laugh and reckless clowning around. But, mostly, Laila remembered all too well the inescapable drudgery of those four weeks without Tariq when he had gone to Ghazni. She remembered all too well how time had dragged without him, how she had shuffled about feeling waylaid, out of balance. How could she ever cope with his permanent absence?

Maybe it was senseless to want to be near a person so badly here in a country where bullets had shredded her own brothers to pieces. But all Laila had to do was picture Tariq going at Khadim with his leg and then nothing in the world seemed more sensible to her.

Hosseini thus accomplishes several things at once: He conveys Laila's inner turning point, sets a larger conflict, and connects the violent history of Afghanistan directly to the lives of his characters. Not bad for a scene that began as a sightseeing trip. The scene advances the story but does so not through the mild action of visiting an historic site but by using that site as a springboard for twin turning points.

What about your scenes? Does every scene of travel, arrival, aftermath, investigation, meeting—all the business of getting your characters from beginning to end—capture a sharply defined turning point and reveal its inner meaning? Are you sure? What if you were to do a scene draft of your novel? Suppose that you broke down every discrete unit of the story, pinned down its turning point, and measured in words the change it brings to each scene's point-of-view character? Would your story get stronger?

I suspect so. You might even find that a scene you considered cutting is now vital to the progression of the plot.

DIALOGUE

A common downfall of many scenes is dialogue. The characters talk, talk, talk, but scenes spin in circles and don't travel much of anywhere. Plenty of dialogue in manuscripts also is hard to follow. Choked with incidental action, broken into fragments, and strewn over the length of a page, it can take almost archaeological skill to piece together an exchange.

Dialogue not only needs to do its own work, it also can bring clarity to middle scenes that would otherwise be muddy and inactive. Dialogue is strong (or can be). The process of stripping it down and finding the tension in it can be revealing. It can help define the purpose of a scene.

Brunonia Barry's best-selling debut novel, *The Lace Reader* (2008), spins a story of the present-day denizens of Salem, Massachusetts, in particular the eccentric clan of Whitney women, who have the ability to "read" people by holding pieces of lace in front of their faces. The novel initially is narrated by Towner Whitney, another in the army of unreliable narrators who crowd the pages of contemporary fiction. Towner is called home to Salem when her mother, Eva, an often-arrested rescuer of battered and abused women, goes missing and later is found dead.

Deeper in, *The Lace Reader* switches to other points of view, principally John Rafferty, another in contemporary fiction's army of wounded big city cops who've retreated to small towns. It falls to Rafferty to investigate Eva's death, and thereby dig up Salem's dirt. Salem has a bona fide witch in Ann Chase, a contemporary of Towner's, to whom Rafferty turns for help. When a teenage runaway named Angela also goes missing, Rafferty asks Ann to do a reading on Angela using Angela's toothbrush as a focal object. Ann won't do the reading but offers to guide Rafferty in doing a reading himself.

Now, how would you handle this middle scene? Would you portray Rafferty's first eerie experience of seeing with second sight? Would you work from Ann's knowing point of view? Barry does neither. She portrays the reading and its aftermath in dialogue:

> "When you're ready, open your eyes."
>
> He opened them.
>
> He felt embarrassed, and completely inept. He'd totally failed.
>
> "Describe what you saw," Ann said.
>
> Rafferty didn't speak.

"Go ahead," she said. "You can't make a mistake."

"Well, first of all, I didn't go up, I went down."

"All right, maybe *you* can make a mistake."

"It was a ranch house," he said, trying to explain. He expected her to end the exercise right there. Or tell him to stop wasting her time. Instead she took a breath and continued.

"What did you see when you went down the stairs?"

"I didn't see anything," he said. "Nothing at all."

"What did this nothing at all look like?"

"What kind of question is that?"

"Humor me," she said.

"It was black. No, not black, but blank. Yeah. Dark and blank," Rafferty said.

"What did you hear?"

"What do you mean, what did I hear?"

"Where there any sounds? Or smells?"

"No. ... No sounds. No smells."

He could feel her eyes on him.

"I didn't see anything. I didn't hear anything. I kept trying to go back up the stairs. I failed Psychic 101," Rafferty said.

"Maybe," Ann said. "Maybe not."

"What's that supposed to mean?"

"I went into the room with you," Ann said. "At least I thought I did."

"And what did you see?

"Nothing. It was too dark."

"I told you," Rafferty said.

"I heard something, though ... a word."

"What word?"

"Underground."

"Underground as in hiding? Or underground as in dead?"

Ann didn't answer. She had no idea.

Notice that Barry keeps her dialogue short. The exchange is not rat-a-tat, but even so it's quick. There's tension between Rafferty and Ann, however rudimentary it may be. Consider, too, what this snippet of the novel has to accomplish: It has to show that Ann is a true parasensitive, while Rafferty is not, and reveal a morsel of information about the missing Angela.

Dialogue lets Barry accomplish all that with immediacy and tension. We also do not have to believe in second sight. Barry doesn't force us to accept whether it's real or not. By remaining objective, with dialogue, she leaves the choice to us, which in a way preserves the mystery of it. More to the point, a sloggy and potentially off-putting middle scene has become taut and dramatic. Wouldn't you like all of your middle scenes to have that effect?

We can pretty much count on thriller writer Harlan Coben for crackling dialogue. Coben never wastes words and is particularly good at speeding his middles along with tension-filled talk. In *The Woods* (2007), he spins another of his patented stories in which a past secret haunts his protagonist and someone who was presumed dead returns to stir things up.

Paul "Cope" Copeland is a county prosecutor in New Jersey. His past is clouded by a summer camp tragedy in which he and a girlfriend snuck into the woods along with four others, including Paul's sister. While Paul and his girlfriend were fooling around, the four others were slashed to death. Two bodies were found; the two others (including Paul's sister) were not. Guess what happens? Yup, the dead return. Or do they? And why is suspicion now directed at Paul?

Meanwhile, Paul is prosecuting a college frat house rape case. Thrillers (hopefully all fiction) are built on the axiom *make it worse for the protagonist*. This, Coben does. One obstacle he throws in Cope's way is EJ Jenrette, the father of one of the frat boys. He's rich. His friends support a cancer charity that Cope established in memory of his dead wife. Jenrette convinces these friends to back out of their commitments. There are a number of ways in which Coben could have handled this stakes-building step in his story, but he chooses a late-night phone call from Cope's brother-in-law, Bob, who runs the charity:

"What's the matter?" I asked.

"Your rape case is costing us big-time. Edward Jenrette's father has gotten several of his friends to back out of their commitments."

I closed my eyes. "Classy."

"Worse, he's making noises that we've embezzled funds. EJ Jenrette is a well-connected son of a bitch. I'm already getting calls."

"So we open our books," I said. "They won't find anything."

"Don't be naive, Cope. We compete with other charities for the giving dollar. If there is even a whiff of a scandal, we're finished."

"Not much we can do about it, Bob."

"I know. It's just that … we're doing a lot of good here, Cope."

"I know."

"But funding is always tough."

"So what are you suggesting?"

"Nothing." Bob hesitated and I could tell he had more to say. So I waited. "But come on, Cope, you guys plea-bargain all the time, right?"

"We do."

"You let a lesser injustice slide so you can nail someone for a bigger one."

"When we have to."

"These two boys. I hear they're good kids."

"You hear wrong."

"Look, I'm not saying that they don't deserve to be punished, but sometimes you have to trade. The greater good. JaneCare is making big strides. It might be the greater good. That's all I'm saying."

"Good night, Bob."

"No offense, Cope. I'm just trying to help."

"I know. Good night, Bob."

Dialogue allows Coben to introduce this obstacle with brisk efficiency. In less than a page, and with plenty of tension, he raises Cope's stakes. The passage is easy to read. Bing, bam, boom, it makes its point. No slogging here.

How many of your dragging middle scenes could be tightened and torqued up with dialogue? How tight is your dialogue generally? Is it lean and mean or is it choked up with incidental action and lengthy attributives? Strip it down. Pump it up. Taut dialogue is one of the secrets of making sure that middles scenes are not candidates for cutting.

STRIDING FORWARD, FALLING BACK

Most instruction in writing scenes begins with the sound advice, *send your character into the scene with a goal*. Well, duh. You would be surprised, though, in how many middle scenes in how many manuscripts there seems to be no particular reason for a character to go somewhere, see someone, learn something, or avoid something. What do they *want*?

It can be hard to tell. Now, this is not to say that the immediate goal needs to be flatly stated. *If he didn't sell his boss on his idea for marketing organic toothpaste, and right now, then he was finished!* How clunky. Most authors would like their characters' needs to emerge more artfully, to infuse the action of the scene rather than squat atop it like an elephant on an egg. I'm good with that. But this restraint is too often a convenient excuse for not working out what a character wants or needs at this particular moment.

Working that out is essential to shaping a scene in which everything that happens has meaning. At the end of a scene, we want to feel that something important occurred. A change took place. The fortunes of the character and the path of the story have shifted. We won't get that feeling unless we get, in some way, a prior sense of what we're hoping for—a hope that in the scene is either fulfilled or dashed or delayed.

George R.R. Martin is the best-selling author of a massive fantasy saga A Song of Ice and Fire that began with *A Game of Thrones*

(1996) and *A Clash of Kings* (1999). In the third volume, *A Storm of Swords* (2000), Martin advances the epic struggle for the Iron Throne. Summarizing the plot is impossible. There are so many points of view that each volume contains a character guide with hundreds of listings grouped by family and spheres of influence. Suffice it to say that everyone has an agenda and no one is wholly good or bad.

One of the recurring points of view in *A Storm of Swords* is that of Jon Snow, bastard son of the king of the North. Jon is a Sworn Brother of the Night's Watch, a badly depleted force charged with guarding an immense wall that protects the southern lands from a mysterious race to the north called the Others. Not all humans live south of the wall. North of the wall, deserters and outcasts called wildlings have formed their own quasi-kingdom. Captured, Jon meets the self-appointed King-Beyond-the-Wall, Mance Rayder, who will decide Jon's fate.

What is Jon's goal in this scene? Survival? Sure. But Jon is loyal to the Night's Watch. In fact, he has allowed himself to be captured so that he can spy. His plan is to make the wildlings think he's a Night's Watch deserter, and he has killed one of his own company to prove it:

> "When Mance hears how you did for Halfhand, he'll take you quick enough," [Ygritte] told him.
>
> "Take me for what?"
>
> The girl laughed scornfully. "For one o' us. D'ya think you're the first crow ever flew down off the Wall? In your hearts you all want to fly free."
>
> "And when I'm free," he said slowly, "will I be free to go?"
>
> "Sure you will." She had a warm smile, despite her crooked teeth. "And we'll be free to kill you. It's *dangerous* being free, but most come to like the taste o' it." She put her gloved hand on his leg, just above the knee. "You'll see."
>
> *I will*, thought Jon. *I will see, and hear, and learn, and when I have I will carry the word back to the Wall.*

THE FIRE IN FICTION

Thus, Jon's opening goal is to maintain the illusion that he is a "crow." Everything in the scene works to advance him toward that goal or away from it. His captors are at first undecided about him. Dire threats are made:

> "Might be you fooled these others, crow, but don't think you'll be fooling Mance. He'll take one look a' you and know you're false. And when he does, I'll make a cloak o' your wolf there, and open your soft boy's belly and sew a weasel up inside."

Charming. Observing the wildlings' surprisingly large camp, and noting that they are not entirely warlike, Jon is then brought to the tent of the King-Beyond-the-Wall. Inside, the scene again is not entirely as Jon expected. A gray-haired man plays a lute and sings. A pregnant woman roasts a brace of hens. Jon picks out a large bearded man as the king but he's wrong. It's the lute player.

Mance Rayder recognizes Jon and calls him by name. Jon's peril deepens as Mance describes where they've previously met, at Jon's father's castle, Winterfell, when Mance snuck into a feast to take the measure of his foes. Jon knows his charade is weak:

> "... So tell me truly, Jon Snow. Are you a craven who turned your cloak from fear, or is there another reason that brings you to my tent?"
>
> Guest right or no, Jon Snow knew he walked on rotten ice here. One false step and he might plunge through, into water cold enough to stop his heart. *Weigh every word before you speak it*, he told himself. He took a long draught of mead to buy time for his answer. When he set the horn aside he said, "Tell me why you turned your cloak, and I'll tell you why I turned mine."

Jon is stalling. He doesn't know how to convince Mance Rayder. Mance makes Jon guess his reasons for deserting, but then reveals it was because of the Night's Watch cloak. One day an elk shredded his, and cut Mance up as well. He was tended by a wilding woman, who not only sewed up his wounds but his cloak too, patching it with some scarlet silk that was her greatest treasure. The experience changed him:

> "I left the next morning ... for a place where a kiss was not a crime, and a man could wear any cloak he chose." He closed the clasp and sat back down again. "And you, Jon Snow?"
>
> Jon took another swallow of mead. *There is only one tale that he might believe.* "You say you were at Winterfell, the night my father feasted King Robert."
>
> "I did say it, for I was."
>
> "Then you saw us all. Prince Joffrey and Prince Tommen, Princess Myrcella, my brothers Robb and Bran and Rickon, my sisters Arya and Sansa. You saw them walk the center aisle with every eye upon them and take their seats at the table just below the dais where the king and queen were seated."
>
> "I remember."
>
> "And did you see where I was seated, Mance?" He leaned forward. "Did you see where they put the bastard?"
>
> Mance Rayder looked at Jon's face for a long moment. "I think we had best find you a new cloak," the king said, holding out his hand.

By appealing to his emotions, Jon convinces Mance that he is genuine. He achieves his goal.

George R.R. Martin is a gifted storyteller, but A Song of Ice and Fire is a vast saga composed of uncounted points of view and scenes. To hold our interest over so long a stretch—the fourth volume, *A Feast for Crows* (2006), leapt to the best-seller lists so it's fair to say that it has—it is necessary for each of Martin's scenes to have a strong structure. Each one needs to advance the story a step. How does Martin do that? By identifying goals and making sure that every element in every scene in some way makes the goal more likely or more remote. You could say that Martin knows his characters, but I would say that he knows how to fix them in any given moment, understand what they want, make that clear to his readers, and then keep us in suspense about the immediate outcome.

Step-by-step scene building is the business of advancing toward goals or away from them. Striding forward or falling back or simply playing with our expectations ... it doesn't matter. What's important is that each scene keeps moving. Toward what? Answer that question and you will find a scene's purpose.

FIRST LINES, LAST LINES

Why do you suppose that at the end of auto races they wave checkered flags? It isn't strictly necessary. It's obvious that the cars are crossing the finish line, right? I'm sure there once was a practical reason for it, but whatever the case, the checkered flag does add drama to the final lap.

Does it matter what is the last line of your scene, or the first? Apparently, many authors do not think it does. Most last and first lines in manuscript scenes are quite forgettable. That's a shame. Like a handshake, an opening and closing line can create impressions and expectations. They can set a tone. They can signal where we're going, or what we've done, or serve any number of other useful story purposes.

Or not. So many first and last lines don't do anything at all. I suspect that many authors are afraid of being obvious, or are trying to be artful. Perhaps they imagine that the first thing readers want is some detail about the setting, or something incidental to the action. Or maybe writers just don't know where to begin, or don't know when to quit.

Whatever the case, solid first and last lines can give a scene shape. Creating them deliberately is a discipline worth developing.

Marisa de los Santos's novel *Love Walked In* (2005) is about Cornelia Brown, a café manager in Philadelphia who experiences life (or hopes to) as movie moments. When a Cary Grant lookalike, Martin Grace, walks into her café and engages her in banter that could have been scripted in Hollywood's golden age, she knows her life is about to change.

How and who changes it, though, is a surprise. It isn't debonair Martin but rather his eleven-year-old daughter, Clare, who shows Cornelia the meaning of love. Martin's ex, Clare's mother, is slowly going nuts. Clare knows she needs a better situation but she's not close to her father. When her mother finally vanishes altogether, Clare winds up in Cornelia's care. The scene in which this happens is a crucial turning point for everyone and for the novel.

Assume that the groundwork for this development has been laid. Choose as the point of view Clare. Her mom has just gone AWOL. She's with her father and is frightened and unhappy. Cornelia has come over to talk with Martin; she's full of compassion and completely unprepared to assume the care of an eleven-year-old. But that is what is going to happen. Now, what would be your opening line? Here is what de los Santos chose:

> Clare lay on her side on the guestroom bed in her father's apartment, not sleeping, trying to imagine herself as a piece of driftwood.

Since Clare is adrift in her life, the image makes sense. Notice that the moment is inactive. The author is telling not showing. Or is she? Take another look. Clare is lying on her side, *not sleeping*. Her anxiety is plain. Also, the idea of an eleven-year-old imagining herself as driftwood is arresting. De los Santos needs for us to feel Clare's worry. Behind that is a need to signal Clare's goal: find safety.

With those things neatly accomplished in a tidy, if unsettling, first line, de los Santos is free to maneuver events so that Clare winds up staying over at Cornelia's apartment.

How would you close off this scene? With Clare drifting to sleep in a strange place? That's the obvious choice, almost unavoidable. De los Santos elects it but is skilled enough to know that a falling asleep moment, by itself, is too common to have any impact. Thus, she goes a step further:

> Clare fell onto the bed, kept falling and falling and falling. When she woke up, it was dark and, into the dark, Clare was calling for her mother.

Do you see what de los Santos is doing here? The relationship between Cornelia and Clare is clearly not going to be easy (there wouldn't be any story if it were), so why not signal the underlying issue now, so the chapter ends with tension?

The issue? Clare doesn't need Cornelia. What she needs is for her mother to be well. That isn't going to happen. Neither is Cornelia going to be a substitute. Count on it, there will be conflict. In other words, de los Santos uses the scene's final lines to foreshadow. Why not?

Young-adult writer Meg Cabot had a major hit with her Princess Diaries series, but she is also the author of other series and stand-alones. In *How to Be Popular* (2006), Cabot tells the story of eleventh-grader Steph Landry, who, ever since she spilled a cherry Super Big Gulp on one of the in-crowd, has had a reputation as a klutz. Steph decides to do something about that, with help from an old book called *How to Be Popular*. Amazingly, it works. Soon Steph finds herself friends with the A-list girls, but at what cost?

A key step in Steph's evolution comes one day when a stalwart friend, Jason, can't drive her home from school. Steph will have to take *the bus*. Horrors! Rescue arrives in the form of dreamboat Mark Finley, who shames one of the A-list girls, Lauren Moffat, into giving Steph and her embarrassing B-list friend Becca a ride in her BMW. It's a big social step up for Steph. So, how would you open this scene? Cabot uses hyperbolic YA first person:

> I think I died and went to heaven.

Eleventh grade is far from heaven, if you ask me, but we get the point. Notice that at the beginning of this scene, Steph has not yet copped a ride in Lauren's chariot-like BMW. Cabot is creating anticipation, a form of tension, by framing the scene. We read ahead to see why she's so elated. This flashback structure happens so quickly we hardly notice. It's not a technique that will work for every scene, but it illustrates the importance of tension in line one.

By the end of the scene there are uneasy hints of the cost of Steph's new popularity. Still, Steph is happy—maybe irrationally so. How would you cap off this scene? Here's Cabot's choice:

> Jason freaking out and refusing to give me rides anymore
> might just be the best thing that ever happened.

The very best thing, *ever*? I wonder if that's true ... which is exactly what Cabot wants us to do at this moment.

First and last lines need not be fancy. Even a utilitarian line can work well if it yanks us straight into, or amplifies, a scene's main action. M.J. Rose built a sizable audience with her steamy series of thrillers about Dr. Morgan Snow, a Manhattan sex therapist. In *The Venus Fix* (2006), Rose relates another multilayered tale in which someone is killing webcam girls. Simultaneously, Morgan copes with her uneasy relationship with police detective Noah Jordain and her daughter Dulcie's budding Broadway acting career.

Midway through the novel, Rose needs to ratchet up the stakes in the daughter subplot. Dulcie can audition for the lead in a television adaptation of the play she's in, but the audition entails going to L.A. Morgan is opposed; Dulcie is defiant. One night Morgan goes to see her daughter's Broadway performance. After the show, Dulcie disappears. During the scene Morgan learns that Dulcie has gone to stay with her father, Morgan's ex, but didn't warn her in advance.

It's a routine middle scene, moving things along a step: daughter disappears, defies mother, turns up, but of course a mother-daughter problem is apparent. How would you start this scene? Rose selects a detail to signal that Dulcie has deviated from routine:

> The black town car was not where it always was.

It's basic, that line, but it does the job. Rose hardly needs to elaborate Morgan's apprehension. Her anxiety is easy to guess. The line gets right to its essence. By the end of the scene a couple of cell phone calls have established that Dulcie is with her dad. Morgan marches to his apartment—on foot, taxis being impossible to find at curtain hour. How would you close this off? Rose has snow symbolically begin to fall as theatergoers turn their faces to the sky:

> I was mystified by the storm, too: the one going on within my family.

I'm not sure why Morgan is puzzled by her daughter's acting out (let the kid get her big break, why don't you?), but Rose's last line nevertheless effectively caps the scene and gets us looking ahead.

What about your first and last lines? Suppose you did a first line/last line draft, doing nothing but honing the bookends of every scene in your manuscript. Would those little changes give your story a bigger and more effective shape?

I thought so. Is that a checkered flag I see waving?

THE TORNADO EFFECT

Novels need events. Things need to happen: little things, big things. Especially big things. Big events shake protagonists, change the course of lives, and stay in readers' memories.

What is a big event? Is it only the kind of thing that makes the six o'clock news? Can it be an interior shift; a realization of the truth, say, that has a seismic jolt? Having read I don't know how many manuscripts and novels over the course of my career, I've realized two truths of storytelling: 1) Most novels don't have enough big events; 2) What makes an event big is not its size but the scope of its effect.

To put it another way, a big narrative event is one that affects not just one's protagonist, but everyone in a story. Making an event big, then, is not so much a matter of dreaming up a natural disaster (useful as those can be) but rather measuring an event's impact on more than a few characters.

Mystery writer Nancy Pickard's stand-alone suspense novel *The Virgin of Small Plains* (2006) was a finalist for the Edgar, Dily, and Macavity awards and winner of the Agatha Award. Set in the town of Small Plains, Kansas, it's a complex story revolving around the murder of an unknown teenage girl seventeen years ago. Moved by the death of this nameless runaway, the town paid for her burial. The grave of "The Virgin," as she's known, is now a shrine that is said to heal.

Of course, the truth is more tangled. Two of the main players are Abby Reynolds and Mitch Newquist, who on the winter night of the Virgin's death, were a teenage couple. On that night, Mitch suddenly left town without a word, presumably having some culpability in the Virgin's death. Seventeen years later, Abby vows to learn who the Virgin was; meanwhile, Mitch returns to Small Plains. A storm of secrets is unleashed.

The book's climactic sequence also involves a storm: this being Kansas, a tornado. The sequence in which the tornado rips through Small Plains is an extended one, seen from a number of points of view. Mitch is one of those who sees it coming:

> He was facing southwest, looking straight into the leading edge of the blackest, biggest, baddest storm he had seen since he left his hometown. *My God, he thought, did I ever take these for granted? Did I used to think this was no big deal?* The line of black was huge, rolling for miles horizontally, and also up, up, up until he had to bend his neck back to see the top of it. He'd seen dramatic clouds in the city sky, but nothing had the overwhelming drama of this panorama in which he could view the whole front edge, and watch it marching toward him.
>
> It was close, he realized with an inner start.
>
> The wind was kicking up in front of it.
>
> He could see the lightning now, hear the rumble of thunder.
>
> It was spectacular. He didn't know how he had lived without seeing this for so many years. He felt as if it was made of sheer energy—which, he supposed, it was—and that all of it was starting to infuse him with something that felt exciting. Ions of excitement.

That passage would be enough to convey the tornado's power, but *The Virgin of Small Plains* is a big novel and Pickard wants a big impact. A second point of view on the twister is that of a young woman, Catie Washington, who is in the terminal stage of cancer. As the tornado approaches, she lies on the Virgin's grave:

> When she reached it, she turned over and lay spread-eagle, her face to the clouds.
>
> All around her, the branches of the trees danced and the trees themselves leaned one way and then the other. There was a howling all around her, and then there was a roaring like a train coming closer to her. She felt like a damsel tied to the tracks, but that's how she had felt for months in the path of the cancer that was killing her. This was no different: No one could rescue her.
>
> No strong, handsome man would come along to pick her up this time.
>
> This was her third go-round with chemotherapy for her brain tumors. Each of the first two times, she had "known" she would lick it. When the third diagnosis came in, she lost the will to fight. She would endure one more round of chemo, she told her doctors, but that would be it. In the other two rounds, she had fought to control the nausea, using acupuncture and medicine, using what-ever worked, and for a while, it had seemed to work.
>
> It wasn't working anymore, nothing was working anymore.
>
> She was in pain a lot of the time, and so very ill.
>
> Now, from under the black, black oily layer of clouds, she watched the funnel form high in the air, watched it dip down once, watched it rise, back up again, always moving in her direction.
>
> When it traveled over her, it was one hundred feet wide at the tip.
>
> She gazed up directly into the mouth of it, where she could see the revolution of the air and things—objects—

whirling around inside of it. The roar was deafening and terrifying. She felt her whole body being picked up as if she were levitating, and then being laid back down. And then some of the things inside of the funnel began to fall on her. She closed her eyes, expecting to the killed by them. But they fell lightly atop her and all around her.

When she opened her eyes, she discovered she was covered with flowers.

The unexpected and solace-giving rain of flowers is one of the novel's remarkable high points. There are other perspectives on the tornado, too: townspeople, the sheriff, and Abby, who owns the town's nursery and gardening center, which, as it happens, is the one place where the tornado touches down and where it picks up the flower petals that comfort Catie Washington.

In the immediate aftermath of the tornado's passing, Mitch and Abby meet for the first time in seventeen years. Is the tornado a symbol? Certainly, but it's also an event that unlocks the town's secrets. It turns out that Mitch did know the Virgin, but his involvement with her was not as expected. Who really killed her and why Abby's father battered her corpse's face with a golf club on the night of her death (an event Mitch witnessed and which sent him on the run for his own protection) takes a little longer to learn.

What gives this sequence the force of a tornado? Is it Pickard's selection of this common plains phenomenon for her climax? Is it her descriptions? Is it the healing rain of flowers on Catie Washington? Is it how it brings Mitch and Abby together?

I would argue that it is not one aspect of the tornado or its effect that gives Pickard's sequence its power; rather, it is the cumulative impact of all of them. A tornado is just a tornado. To create the tornado effect on the plot, Pickard had to put a number of Small Plains residents in a whirl.

What is the Big Event in your current manuscript? How many people does it change? How many of those changes do you portray? To create the Tornado Effect, you will need to portray all of them. It's extra work but the extra impact will be worth it, don't you think?

PRACTICAL TOOLS

Outer & Inner Turning Points

Step 1: Pick a scene. Identify its outer turning point, the exact minute when things change for your protagonist or point-of-view character.

Step 2: Wind the clock back ten minutes. Write a paragraph saying how your protagonist or point-of-view character sees herself at this moment, before the turning point.

Step 3: Wind the clock ten minutes beyond the outer turning point. Write a paragraph saying how your protagonist or point–of-view character sees herself at this moment.

Step 4: Note three visible or audible details of the turning point in Step 1. Make one an oblique detail; i.e., something that would only be noticed upon a close look or a replay of the tape.

Step 5: Combine the results of Steps 2, 3, and 4 into a passage in which you delineate and detail your protagonist or point-of-view character's inner turning point.

Discussion: Have you ever changed in a moment, such as when, say, shattering news came via telephone? At such a moment you realize that your life will never be the same. But if we readers are observing you from outside, how would we know that? We wouldn't. An inner turning point can only be captured by going inside to detail the nuances of the change.

Stripping Down Dialogue

Step 1: From your manuscript, pick any two-character passage of dialogue. Choose an exchange that is a page or so in length.

Step 2: Strip out any attributives (*he said, she said*) and any incidental action.

Step 3: Rewrite this dialogue entirely as an exchange of insults.

Step 4: Rewrite this dialogue as a rapid-fire exchange of lines that are a maximum of 1–5 words.

Step 5: Rewrite this dialogue as an exchange in which one character speaks only once and the other character responds with a non-verbal gesture (say, an eloquent shrug).

Step 6: Without referring to your original version, rewrite this dialogue incorporating the best of the results from the above steps.

Discussion: In reconstructing the passage, do you notice the dialogue itself getting tighter? Are you using fewer attributives? Are you cutting incidental action that chokes up the passage? Good. It is the spoken words that give dialogue its punch. Everything else gets in the way.

Setting Goal & Setting Back

Step 1: Write down what it is in this scene that your protagonist or point-of-view character wants.

Step 2: Create three hints in this scene that your protagonist or point-of-view character will get what he wants. Also, build three reasons to believe that he *won't* get what he wants.

Step 3: Write the passages that express the results of Steps 1 and 2. In rewriting the scene in the next exercise, incorporate those passages. Eliminate as much else as possible.

Discussion: Just as stripping down dialogue helps punch up a scene, reducing a scene to a few strong steps toward or away from a goal also lends force and shape. Many authors wander through scene drafts, groping for the point. You can do it differently. Instead, start with the point and enhance from there.

Scenes That Can't Be Cut

Step 1: Pick any scene and work through the three exercises above.

Step 2: Close the original draft of the scene on your computer, or turn over your manuscript. Do not refer to your original draft.

Step 3: Write a new first line for the scene. Write a new last line, too.

Step 4: Write down five details of the setting. Go for details not normally noticed, such as:

- boundaries (walls, fences, horizon)
- quality of light
- temperature

- smell
- prominent objects in this place

Step 5: Without referring to your original version, rewrite the scene. Start with your new first line, and end with your new last line. Use the oblique setting details you just noted. Incorporate the inner and outer turning points, leaner dialogue, and steps toward or away from the goal that you created earlier.

Discussion: Is this rewritten version of your scene better than the original? I'm not surprised. Scenes that are written in the normal flow of accumulating pages may be fine but often will lack force. Constructing the key elements first can, by contrast, give a scene shape, tautness, and power.

The Tornado Effect

Step 1: Choose a major plot event.

Step 2: For each point-or-view or major character in your novel, write a passage that details the effect of this event. How does it change each character? How do they see themselves or others differently afterward?

Step 3: Write the event not from one point of view, but from all. In each passage, incorporate the results of Step 2.

Discussion: The Tornado Effect is a powerful tool that can magnify the significance of already large plot events. For it to work, though, there must be an actual, transforming effect on each character who experiences it.

ov— CHAPTER FOUR —vo

THE WORLD OF
THE NOVEL

In certain fiction, the setting lives from the very first pages. Such places not only feel extremely real, they are dynamic. They change. They affect the characters in the story. They become metaphors, possibly even actors in the drama.

Powerfully portrayed settings seem to have a life of their own, but how is that effect achieved? *Make your setting a character* is a common piece of advice given to fiction writers, yet beyond invoking all five senses when describing the scenery, it doesn't seem that anyone can say exactly how to do it.

Do you ever skip description in a novel? I do, too. Obviously, merely describing how things look, sound, taste, feel, and smell is not, by itself, going to bring a location to life. Something more is required. Is it a setting that is unusual, exotic, or unexpected? If so, our job would be easy. We merely would have to find a spot on the face of the Earth where a novel has not previously been set. The Gobi Desert?

Unfortunately, the Gobi Desert won't do when your novel is about pioneering the American West, coming of age in 1950s Minnesota, suburban angst, or vampires. If those are your subjects you will have to find new ways to bring to life Durango, Lake Wobegon, Levittown, or sexy urban nightclubs. Others have visited your setting before, too, and may even have colonized it.

Does anyone dispute that the tidewater Carolinas are the kingdom of Pat Conroy? After *The Prince of Tides* (1986) or *Beach Music* (1995), who would be crazy enough to set a novel in that unique territory with its Charleston gardens, Gullah dialect, and marshes of waving cattails? Yet Conroy is far from the only contemporary novelist who has effectively set novels in the coastal Carolinas. Sue Monk Kidd, Mary Alice Monroe, and Dorothea Benton Frank are just a few who come to mind. That Conroy got there first hasn't hurt those authors' sales, or even diminished their settings.

The trick is not to find a fresh setting or a unique way to portray a familiar place; rather, it is to discover in your setting what is unique *for your characters*, if not for you. You must go beyond description, beyond dialect, beyond local foods to bring setting into the story in a way that integrates it into the very fabric of your characters' experience.

In other words, you must instill the soul of a place into your characters' hearts and make them grapple with it as surely as they grapple with the main problem and their enemies. How do you do *that?* It takes work but the basic principles of powerful settings are not exceptionally hard to grasp.

Let's look at some examples.

LINKING DETAILS AND EMOTIONS

As a child, did you have a special summer place? A family beach house, or a lake cabin? One that's been in the family for years, rich in history, stocked with croquet mallets, special iced tea glasses, and a rusty rotary lawn mower?

For me the special summer place was my Great Uncle Robert's farm on a hillside near Reading, Pennsylvania. "Uncle Locker," as we called him, was, as far as I knew, born old. He loved his John Deere tractor but didn't particularly like children, especially not after my younger brother dropped the tin dipping cup down the front yard well.

Uncle Locker raised sheep. He stocked the lower pond with trout. He had connected a Revolutionary War-era log cabin with a Victorian-era farmhouse, erecting a soaring brick-floored, high-windowed living room between them. In that living room was a candy dish that each day magically refilled itself with M&M's. (I suspect now that it was my Great Aunt Margaret who was the magician.)

In the evenings Uncle Locker would read the Reading newspaper on the glassed-in porch, classical symphonies crackling on his portable transistor radio as summer lightning flashed across the valley. That, today, is my mental image of perfect contentment. When I hear a radio crackle in a storm, I relax. I miss my Uncle Locker with a sharp pang.

Now, let me ask you this: Without looking back over what you just read, what do you remember best about what I wrote? Was it a detail, like the dipping cup, the M&M's, or the lightning? Or was it the feeling of contentment that, for me, accompanies an approaching storm? Whatever your answer, I would argue that you remember what you remember not because of the details themselves or the emotions they invoke in me, but because *both* those details and personal feelings are present.

In other words, it is the combination of setting details and the emotions attached to them that, together, make a place a living thing. Setting comes alive partly in its details and partly in the way that the story's characters experience it. Either element alone is fine, but both working together deliver a sense of place without parallel.

Father Andrew Greeley, an Irish-American Roman Catholic priest, is a durable novelist with some sixty novels to his credit, including *The Cardinal Sins* (1981), the science-fiction novel *God Game* (1986), and mystery novels featuring the Irish-American Roman Catholic priest (later bishop) "Blackie" Ryan. Needless to say, Father Greeley has had to deal with a lot of settings, though Chicago and Ireland recur frequently in his work. In one of his novels, though, a lake surrounded by summer homes is the main locale.

Summer at the Lake (1997) is about three friends the Irish-American Roman Catholic priest "Packy" Keenan, university administrator Leo Kelly, and the woman whom as young men they both loved, Jane Devlin. Now turning fifty, these three return to the lake where one summer their lives and almost-loves were disrupted by a tragic car crash that was no accident, that may have been intended to kill Leo and certainly led to Jane marrying (unhappily) the driver of the ill-fated auto.

Learning that Jane, now divorced, will once again visit the lake, Leo also returns to meet her again, to learn the truth behind the accident, and finally, he hopes, to lay to rest the ghosts of the magical and mysterious summer that was his life's turning point.

Half way through the novel, Leo contemplates the lake, or, rather, the homes surrounding it:

> ... All I can recall are images of the Lake, images perhaps shaped by nostalgia for the summer of 1948 when Jane and I loved and lost one another.
>
> Our side of the Lake, as I came to call it, though nothing in it was mine except my friends, had been settled first, at our end before the turn of the century. Indeed some of the sprawling Victorian homes with their gables and turrets and porches and balconies dated to the first summer settlements of the late 1880s and early 1890s before the Columbian exposition in 1893. Each of the Old Houses, as they were called by everyone, boasted a neatly manicured lawn rolling down the hill to the Lake and a freshly painted gazebo and pier—usually with a motor launch of some sort, steam first, then internal combustion (idle during years of the War). On the road side of the house there would usually be a park of trees, all carefully maintained and landscaped and protected by a wrought-iron fence and gate with the family name scrolled always on the gate and sometimes on the fence too. Art deco swimming pools, with pillars and porches and fountains and classic statues graced some of the homes—though not the Keenans'. (Tom Keenan: Who needs a pool when you have a lake that's warm for three months?)
>
> ...
>
> Then I thought the homes were the most elegant houses in the world, the kind of places I read about in English mysteries or ghost stories. Later I would realize

that they were in horrendous bad taste (and the people who lived in them for the most part new rich). Still later I would agree that they are interesting museum pieces from the Gilded Age and the Mauve Decade.

Is there anything more evocative of summer than Victorian homes with their wide verandas, wide lawns, gingerbread trim, and bright colors? The promise of badminton, lawn parties, and lacy parasols has probably seduced more homeowners into the money pit than any other style of architecture.

In the above passage Greeley invokes Victorian elegance with encyclopedic detail, skipping quickly over the "gables and turrets and porches and balconies" in favor of dates and a catalogue of decorative styles. His images are, to my eye, a bit generic: "wrought-iron" gates and fences, "classic" statues. Although I love American domestic architecture and enjoy spotting it the way some people identify trees or birds, to me this part of the passage feels dry.

What makes an impression on me is not Greeley's knowledge of Gilded Age style but Leo Kelly's changing perception of the "Old Houses" around the lake. Once splendid and romantic, in later life they seemed to him tacky, and still later academically "interesting." This progression of feelings about the lake houses mirrors Leo's own life: evolving from a young middle-class guest at a rich resort, to a jilted would-be lover, to a detached university functionary.

A summer home of the Arts and Crafts era is the focus of Susan Wiggs's *Lakeside Cottage* (2005). In this tale of returning home—in this case a summer home—Seattle journalist Kate Livingston brings her mildly difficult son Aaron for a restorative summer at the once brimming family cottage, now left to Kate alone by her dispersed family. There Kate takes in a teenage runaway and resists (sort of) her growing attraction to a secretive neighbor, JD Harris, a medic who is hiding a heroic self-sacrifice that led to national celebrity and the destruction of his privacy, poor guy.

As Kate and Aaron arrive at Lake Crescent in Washington State's Olympic Peninsula, Kate harks back to the treasured family summers of years past:

Some practices at the lake house were steeped in tradition and ancient, mystical lore. Certain things always had to be done in certain ways. S'mores were just one of them. They always had to be made with honey grahams, not cinnamon, and the gooey marshmallow had to be rolled in miniature M&M's. Nothing else would do. Whenever there was a s'mores night, they also had to play charades on the beach. She made a mental list of the other required activities, wondering if she'd remember to honor them all. Supper had to be announced each evening with the ringing of an old brass ship's bell suspended from a beam on the porch. Come July, they had to buy fireworks from the Makah tribe's weather-beaten roadside stand, and set them off to celebrate the Fourth. To mark the summer solstice, they would haul out and de-cobweb the croquet set and play until the sun set at ten o'clock at night, competing as though life itself depended on the outcome. When it rained, the Scrabble board had to come out for games of vicious competition. This summer, Aaron was old enough to learn Hearts and Whist, though with just the two of them, she wasn't sure how they'd manage some of the games.

Susan's memories of summer traditions are as sweet as her family's s'mores. (What is it about M&M's?) The daily dinner bell, solstice croquet, rainy-day Scrabble … don't you wish you had been invited to spend an August with Kate's clan?

The details in this passage stand out because they are made highly specific: S'mores not just any old way but the Livingston way, charades not in the living room but on the beach, croquet played not simply at length but until sunset on the year's longest day. These details are not generic. They are the particular memories of a protagonist who has lived them.

But how does Kate Livingston feel about these memories? When she looks back on past summers, how do they appear to her now? Bathed in a rosy glow, I would say. This sweet nostalgia is nice, but also exactly what we expect Kate to feel. What happens when less expected emotions are plumbed?

Barbara Delinsky's *Lake News* (1999) is another story of returning to a summer home for healing. In this case, the place is Lake Henry in New Hampshire. Two wounded protagonists come back: Lounge singer Lily Blake, who has been devastated by the publicity surrounding an untrue accusation of an affair with a high church official, and John Kipling, a burned-out Boston journalist. Lily hates reporters; John is now running the local newspaper. See the conflict coming?

As *Lake News* opens, John Kipling has been back in Lake Henry for several years. Early one autumn morning before work, John paddles a canoe out on the lake to visit a family of loons that will soon start their winter journey south.

> Like everything else at the lake, dawn arrived in its own good time. The flat black of night slowly deepened to a midnight blue that lightened in lazy steps, gradually giving form to the spike of a tree, the eave of a cottage, the tongue of a weathered wood dock—and that was on a clear day. On this day, fog slowed the process of delineation, reducing the lake to a pool of milky glass and the shoreline to a hazy wash of orange, gold, and green where, normally, vibrant fall colors would be. A glimpse of cranberry or navy marked a lakefront home, but details were lost in the mist. Likewise the separation of reflection and shore. The effect, with the air quiet and still, was that of a protective cocoon.
>
> It was a special moment. The only thing John Kipling would change about it was the cold. He wasn't ready for summer to end, but despite his wishes, the days were noticeably shorter than they had been two months before. The sun set sooner and rose later, and the chill of the night lingered. He felt it. His loons felt it. The foursome he watched, two adults and their young, would remain on the lake for another five weeks, but they were growing

restless, looking to the sky lately in ways that had less to do with predators than with thoughts of migration.

...

In time, the loon closest to him stretched his neck forward and issued a long, low wail. The sound wasn't unlike the cry of a coyote, but John would never confuse the two. The loon's wail was at the same time more el-emental and more delicate.

This one was the start of a dialogue, one adult call-ing the other in a succession of haunting sounds that brought the distant bird gliding closer. Even when they were ten feet apart, they continued to speak, with their beaks nearly shut and their elongated throats swelling around the sound.

Goose bumps rose on his skin. This was why he had returned to the lake—why, after swearing off New Hampshire at fifteen, he had reversed himself at forty. Some said he'd done it for the job, others that he'd done it for his father, but the roundabout truth had to do with these birds. They signified something primal and wild, but simple, straightforward, and safe.

I urge you to read that passage again. It is impressive first of all because Delinsky begins her novel with a big no-no of openings: a description of the scenery. How does she get away with that when less experienced writers would be slapped down by their critique groups? Delinsky's opening is beautifully written, but also notice the subtle tension with which she infuses her images:

Like everything else at the lake, dawn arrived in its own good time.

Analyze that line. It conveys a feeling of the natural rhythm of the lake, yet there is also a note of apprehension, almost impatience, introduced with the phrase "in its own good time." Like there is any other time frame? Well, yes. John lives at a faster pace than the lake itself. Man and nature are at odds. Quicker than our brains can grasp the discord, we're subconsciously ill at ease. We speed ahead to the next line looking, faintly, for relief.

Look at how Delinsky continues to compile tension:

> He wasn't ready for summer to end …
>
> He felt it. His loons felt it. … they were growing restless, looking to the sky … with thoughts of migration.
>
> This was why he had returned to the lake … [why] he had reversed himself at forty …

Reversed himself at forty? Why exactly? After the tiniest of pauses, Delinsky tells us. Question and answer. Tension raised and relieved without us even being aware of it. Micro-tension (see chapter eight) is the secret behind page-turning fiction, and Delinsky uses it here to make a no-no opening riveting.

Next, take a look at the scenery itself. Is it generic? It would be except that Delinsky filters it through a morning fog, not quite letting us see the usual lakeside sights of autumn leaves, dock, or house but merely a hint of their colors. How would you sum up the mood of a lake on a foggy morning? Delinsky dubs it a "protective cocoon."

No sooner has she presented us with some unusual visuals than Delinsky immediately introduces feelings:

> It was a special moment. The only thing John Kipling would change about it was the cold. He wasn't ready for summer to end …

Now, this regret over the passing of summer is nothing out of the ordinary. If that were the only emotion in the passage, it would be unremarkable. Delinsky, however, does not leave it at that. Have still another look at that last paragraph:

> Goose bumps rose on his skin. This was why he had returned to the lake—why, after swearing off New Hampshire at fifteen, he had reversed himself at forty. Some

said he'd done it for the job, others that he's done it
for his father, but the roundabout truth had to do with
these birds. They signified something primal and wild,
but simple, straightforward, and safe.

Look at how much we learn about John Kipling in these few lines:
he once hated the lake but came back at forty, there's a cloud in his
past, plus he owed something to his father. No wonder John likes
the loons. Compared to all that messy stuff the loons are simple. He
longs for what is uncomplicated. Family, flight, fog, cold, longing,
and contentment just out of reach … What is Delinsky up to here?
Is she setting the scene? Yes, but more than that she is building a
metaphor for her protagonist's precarious inner state.

What grabs you more in Delinsky's passage, the specific images
or the strong emotions? For me, the author makes both work together.
The elements are not cobbled together but instead form a unity of man
and nature, lake and loneliness, longing and peace. Scenery openings
generally have me reaching for the next book on my pile, but in *Lake
News* Delinsky rapidly brings the world of the story alive.

MEASURING CHANGE OVER TIME

There are other ways to bring setting alive. One of them is to measure
the change in a place over time. Of course, most places don't change
much—only the people observing them do.

Kristin Hannah's *On Mystic Lake* (1999) is yet another heading-
home-to-heal novel. Once more the lake in question is on Washington State's Olympic Peninsula, which I figure will soon have a
lock on ever-so-special childhood places. In this case, however, the
wounded heroine of the story, Annie Colwater, is a native of the
suburbs of Los Angeles; indeed, the middle of the novel is framed
by two sequences set there.

In the first part of the novel, Annie, immediately after her
seventeen-year-old daughter's departure for a semester in Europe,
is devastated to learn that her husband wants a divorce. Don't be
shocked, but he has taken up with a younger woman at the office. It's

a humdrum set up, yet Hannah deftly uses the very ordinariness of Annie's world as a starting point for building tension. In this passage near the novel's beginning, she details springtime in L.A.:

> It was March, the doldrums of the year, still and quiet and gray, but the wind had already begun to warm, bringing with it the promise of spring. Trees that only last week had been naked and brittle seemed to have grown six inches over the span of a single, moonless night, and sometimes, if the sunlight hit a limb just so, you could see the red bud of new life stirring at the tips of the crackly brown bark. Any day, the hills behind Malibu would blossom, and for a few short weeks this would be the prettiest place on Earth.
>
> Like the plants and animals, the children of Southern California sensed the coming of the sun. They had begun to dream of ice cream and popsicles and last year's cutoffs. Even determined city dwellers, who lived in glass and concrete high-rises in places with pretentious names like Century City, found themselves veering into the nursery aisles of their local supermarkets. Small, potted geraniums began appearing in the metal shopping carts, alongside the sundried tomatoes and the bottles of Evian water.
>
> For nineteen years, Annie Colwater had awaited spring with the breathless anticipation of a young girl at her first dance. She ordered bulbs from distant lands and shopped for hand-painted ceramic pots to hold her favorite annuals.
>
> But now, all she felt was dread, and a vague, formless panic. ... what did a mother do when her only child left home?

Shows you how much I know. L.A. always feels pretty much the same to me; but then again, I grew up in New England. Who knew that the change of seasons could be measured by visions of Popsicles and cutoffs? By showing me the minute seasonal changes that a SoCal native would notice, Hannah nails spring as seen by Annie Colwater. But that's not all. This spring, Annie's usual "breathless anticipation" is replaced by dread. The contrast is jarring—in a good way.

In the middle of *On Mystic Lake*, Annie heads home to Mystic Lake, her gruff-but-wise father, and a rendezvous with an old almost-flame, now a local police officer, Nick Delacroix. Nick has grown bitter, distant, and boozy due to the suicide of his manic-depressive wife, Kathy, the third leg of their teenage triumvirate. His morose mood is especially damaging to his six-year-old daughter, Izzy. Izzy has stopped talking, has been suspended from school, and wears black gloves because her fingers are disappearing one by one, or so she thinks. She eats and dresses with two fingers of her right hand, the only two digits that are left.

At Nick's request, Annie begins to babysit Izzy while he's at work, and slowly Izzy begins to come around. (The moment when she can again see her lost fingers is one of the novel's many tear-jerking high moments.) Harder to rehabilitate is Nick. His alcoholism grows worse and eventually he bottoms out. As painful as his decline is, worse still is the news that Annie is pregnant at forty, and not by Nick.

When Annie's remorseful husband himself shows up, dumped by the office hottie, and shortly before their daughter is due to return from Europe, Annie is persuaded to return to L.A. to honor her vows, have their baby, and give their marriage a second chance.

And so Annie returns to L.A. Readers at this point probably are, as I was, screaming, *Don't go!* But Hannah is too good a storyteller to make Annie's choices easy. The wayward husband makes a real effort. Life is comfortable and familiar. Even L.A. itself creates opportunities for healing. In this passage late in the novel, Hannah again paints a change of seasons in Southern California, this time the turning to autumn:

> Autumn brought color back to Southern California. Brown grass began to turn green. The gray air, swept clean by September breezes, regained its springtime

blue. The local radio stations started an endless stream of football chatter. The distant whine of leaf blowers filled the air.

It was the season of sharp, sudden changes: days of bright lemon heat followed by cold, starlit nights. Sleeveless summer shirts were packed away in boxes and replaced by crew-neck sweaters. The birds began one by one to disappear, leaving their nests untended. To the Californians, who spent most of their days in clothes as thin as tissue and smaller than washrags, it began to feel cold. They shivered as the wind kicked up, plucking the last dying red leaves from the trees along the road. Sometimes whole minutes went by without a single car turning toward the beach. The crossroads were empty of tourists, and only the stoutest of spirit ventured into the cool Pacific Ocean at this time of year. The stream of surfers at the state beach had dwindled to a few hardy souls a day.

It was time now to let go. But how did you do that, really? Annie had spent seventeen years trying to protect her daughter from the world, and now all of that protection lay in the love she'd given Natalie, in the words she'd used in their talks, and in the examples she'd provided.

Leaf blowers, crew-neck sweaters, empty roads heading to the beach ... Hannah uses these details to delineate the change in her protagonist's perception of a place. There is emotion, as well; specifically, Annie's inadequacy in knowing how to protect her now nearly grown daughter and Annie's inability to let go, even now as the turning season demands it.

These two passages on either end of Hannah's novel are one of the ways in which she creates a sense of dynamic movement—movement that doesn't depend on plot. By measuring change by minute degrees she not only heightens the tension in Annie's dilemma but also amplifies the world of the story in ways that make it inseparable from her heroine.

Is the setting a character in *On Mystic Lake*, or is it the character of Annie Colwater whose perceptions make L.A. feel alive? I'd say it's the storytelling skill of Kristin Hannah that makes the question moot. Character and setting meld into one.

HISTORY IS PERSONAL

Historical novelists think a lot about what makes the period of their novels different than ours. They research it endlessly. Indeed, many historical novelists say that is their favorite part of the process. When the research is done and writing begins, though, how specifically do they create a sense of the times on the page? *With details* is the common answer, but which details, exactly, and how many of them?

And what if the period of your novel is not terribly far back in history? If your story is set in the 1970s, is it enough to mention Watergate, or do you need to be even more specific about disco, VWs, horizontally striped polo shirts, and oil shocks? How about contemporary stories? Does one need to convey a sense of the times when the times are our own?

To start to answer those questions, read the Op-Ed pages in the newspaper. Does everyone see our times in the same way? No. Outlooks vary. That should also be true for your fictional characters. What is your hero's take on our times? As in so many aspects of novel construction, creating a sense of the times first requires filtering the world through your characters. For examples, let's travel to Venice.

Joseph Kanon's richly layered debut mystery novel, *Los Alamos* (1997), won the Mystery Writers of America Edgar Award for Best First Novel. He followed with *The Prodigal Spy* (1998), *The Good German* (2001), and the tragic and complicated *Alibi* (2005).

Alibi is set in Venice in late 1945, immediately after the close of World War II. Rich Americans are returning to Europe, among them widow Grace Miller, who migrates south to Venice, having found Paris too depressing. Grace invites her son Adam, the novel's hero and narrator, who has been newly released from his post-war service as a Nazi hunter in Germany. As the novel opens, Adam tells of his mother's return to the expatriate life:

> After the war, my mother took a house in Venice. She'd gone first to Paris, hoping to pick up the threads of her old life, but Paris had become grim, grumbling about shortages, even her friends worn and evasive. The city was still at war, this time with itself, and everything she'd come back for—the big flat on the Rue du Bac, the cafés, the market on the Raspail, memories all burnished after five years to a rich glow—now seemed pinched and sour, dingy under a permanent cover of gray cloud.
>
> After two weeks she fled south. Venice at least would look the same, and it reminded her of my father, the early years when they idled away afternoons on the Lido and danced at night. In the photographs they were always tanned, sitting on beach chairs in front of striped changing huts, clowning with friends, everyone in caftans or bulky one-piece woolen bathing suits. Cole Porter had been there, writing patter songs, and since my mother knew Linda, there were a lot of evenings drinking around the piano, that summer when they'd just married. When her train from Paris finally crossed over the lagoon, the sun was so bright on the water that for a few dazzling minutes it actually seemed to be that first summer. Bertie, another figure in the Lido pictures, met her at the station in a motorboat, and as they swung down the Grand Canal, the sun so bright, the palazzos as glorious as ever, the whole improbable city just the same after all these years, she thought she might be happy again.

There are several things to note in this highly atmospheric opening. First, Kanon weaves an undercurrent of tension through these two paragraphs, a tension that derives from his mother's longing for ... well, what? Paris is dissatisfying. Venice, seemingly untouched by the war, is full of sunlight and memories. A mood of nostalgia would be enough here, but Kanon himself is not satisfied with a mere rosy glow. Venice is "improbable" and Grace's lift of spirit is tinged with doubt: "She thought she might be happy again."

That word "might" is a calculated choice. Do you get the feeling that Adam's mother will not re-create in Venice the happiness of the pre-war party of the 1920s and 1930s? You are correct. Grace is courted by a distinguished Italian doctor, Gianni Maglione, whom Adam immediately dislikes—with good reason, as it turns out. When Adam begins a love affair with Claudia Grassini, a Jewish woman who survived the camps by becoming a Fascist's mistress, he is drawn into a tragic conflict. Claudia accuses Dr. Maglione of wartime collaboration and, worse, condemning her own father to death at Auschwitz. Adam's mother wishes to leave the past buried, but Adam, given his background and love for Claudia, cannot leave it alone.

Kanon's opening also effectively evokes Europe in the immediate aftermath of the war. Paris is "grim" and "grumbling." Grace's Paris is specific, too: Kanon mentions not just the city's streets, cafés, and markets, but Grace's flat on the "Rue du Bac" and the market on the "Raspail." For all I know, Kanon could be completely making up those places. It doesn't matter. It is their specificity that brings this Paris of food shortages and long memories alive.

Venice, by contrast, is full of false sunlight and sweet memories. These memories themselves are highly specific: afternoons on the Lido, striped changing huts, Cole Porter. Kanon plucks from his research a few choice tidbits that hint at a life of gay carelessness and privilege. His narrator's casual familiarity with them contributes to the passage's reality. But it's not only that. The details and the mood, Grace's naïve longing and Adam's cynical foreknowledge all roll together into a couple paragraphs that create a unique moment in time.

Renaissance Venice attracts many novelists. The story of Christi Phillips's debut novel, *The Rossetti Letter* (2007), springs from an historical footnote: In 1618, a Spanish conspiracy to overthrow the city was exposed in a letter written by little-known courtesan Alessandra Rossetti. Meanwhile in the present, graduate student Claire

Donovan is writing her thesis on Rossetti; however, her ambition is threatened by the news that a well-known British historian, Andrew Kent, will be publishing a book on the same subject. Claire wangles a plane ticket to Venice by chaperoning a troubled teenage girl. There she plans to hear Andrew Kent lecture and thus learn if her thesis is doomed.

As in A.S. Byatt's *Possession* (1990), Phillips spins her tale of academic obsession in both present and past. In the past, we follow courtesan Rossetti's unfolding story of love and betrayal. It begins with Rossetti delivering the fateful letter that will expose the Spanish Conspiracy:

> They turned into the Rio di San Martino, then into a narrow waterway that circled west toward the Piazzetta dei Leoncini. In their wake, small waves gently slapped against stone foundations smothered in clumps of thick, glistening moss. She could reach out and brush the damp stone with her fingertips is she desired, so close were the buildings, and she inhaled their familiar grotto scent with a kind of reverence. Traveling through Venice at night always filled her with a rising excitement, but tonight her anticipation was tinged with fear. Alessandra tried not to think about what waited for her at the end of her journey, which was quickly approaching.
>
> …
>
> The Piazza was bright with torchlight, alive with music and revelry, but she could not join in the general high spirits; the sinister maw that waited for her in the dark courtyard of the Doge's Palace filled her with dread. The *bocca di leone*, the lion's mouth, was a special receptacle created by the Venetian government to receive letters of denunciation. Into this bronze plaque went accusations of theft, murder, or tax evasion—the last a particularly heinous crime according to the Great Council, the Republic's ruling assembly of two thousand noblemen. Alessandra had never imagined, until recently, that she would ever avail herself of it. Behind

the *bocca di leone*'s grotesque, gaping mouth lurked every terror hidden within the depths of the palace, the prison, and the Republic itself; surely unleashing that terror was a fearsome act not to be done with indifference.

By now I'm sure you can spot for yourself the mixture of specific details of place, as well as the courtesan's taut emotions, that together make this historical moment vivid and real. Take another look at Phillips's passage and pick them out.

Also, note the level of historical detail that Phillips mixes in. There's very little. She explains that the Great Council is Venice's governing body and that the "bocca di leone" (wonderful image) is the mailbox for rat-out letter writers. That's it. Everything else in this passage is a detail that would be the same in the present day. This suggests to me that a sense of the era does not depend on digging up tidbits that only existed way back when.

A striking example of seeing the times through a particular point of view can be found in Sarah Dunant's *In the Company of the Courtesan* (2006), another novel about a Venetian courtesan, albeit in the slightly earlier year of 1527. Fleeing a sacking of Rome, Fiammetta Bianchini resurrects her business in Venice. The novel is narrated through the eyes of her business manager, Bucino Teodoldo, who happens to be a dwarf. Bucino's perspective on Renaissance Venice is quite literally different than anyone else's:

> My God, this city stinks. Not everywhere—along the southern wharves where the ships dock, the air is heady with leftover spices, and on the Grand Canal money buys fresh breezes along with luxury—but everywhere we are, where crumbling houses rise out of rank water and a dozen families live stacked one on top of another like rotting vegetables, the decay and filth burn the insides of your nostrils. Living as I do, with my nose closer to the ground, there are times when I find it hard to breathe.
>
> The old man who measures the level of the well in our *campo* every morning says that the smell is worse

because of the summer drought and that if the water falls any lower, they will have to start bringing the freshwater barges in, and then only those who have money will be able to drink. Imagine that: a city built on water dying of thirst.

Is Bucino right that Venice had a sharper stink to the short than to the tall? I doubt it. Still, his keen sensitivity about his stature along with his cutting wit gives this otherwise familiar lament about Venice a special odor. "Imagine that: a city built on water dying of thirst."

Creating a sense of the times, then, is not just about details, or even coupling them with emotions; the times are also enhanced by infusing a character with strong *opinions* about both the details and emotions.

SEEING THROUGH CHARACTERS' EYES

Let's dig deeper into the relationship between character and time/place. Is there a technique more powerful than infusing a character with a strong opinion about his place or time? Yes. Infusing *two* characters with that.

Novelist Thomas Kelly focuses on working-class heroes and gritty New York settings. His novel *Payback* (1997) features two Irish-American brothers, one a mob enforcer, the other a foundation digger, pitted against each other before the backdrop of the 1980s building boom. *The Rackets* (2001) is about a disgraced City Hall advance man who returns to the old neighborhood to grapple with corruption, unions, and city politics. Kelly himself is a former construction worker and teamster, so you can see the origin of his passion for this milieu.

In *Empire Rising* (2005), Kelly builds his panoramic, multiple point-of-view novel around the construction of the Empire State Building in the 1930s. One principle point of view is that of Irish-American steelworker Michael Briody. In the novel's opening scene, Briody is chosen to pound in the first rivet at the building's groundbreaking ceremony, a piece of political theater for which the waiting workers have little patience. On the site once stood a hotel, the demolition of which gives Briody pause during the self-congratulatory speeches:

> Briody is not surprised that none of the swells on stage mention the six men who died demolishing the old hotel. Not surprised in the least. He considers their ugly endings, the crushed and broken bodies spirited away like just more rubble, their names already forgotten. Their stories untold. He shifts his weight from foot to foot, is anxious to start work. His fellow workers watch with dull stares. They have no interest in the staged spectacle. They mutter and joke under their breath until one of the concrete crew makes a loud noise, like a ripe fart, and the superintendent swivels his fat head around and glares at them as if they were recalcitrant schoolboys. They fall silent. They want the work. The next stop is the breadline.

The tension in this paragraph is, to my eye, nicely restrained: impatience mixed with a downtrodden cynicism unique to Depression workers who are one step away from starvation. What is Briody's opinion of the ceremony? Kelly hardly needs to tell us; he simply lets Briody's passing regard for the dead workers who preceded him imply how he feels.

A short while later in the story, Kelly introduces another principle point-of-view character, Johnny Farrell, a lawyer and bagman (bribe collector) for Mayor Jimmy Walker. Johnny is king of his world, but all is not right with it. Johnny's wife is from a rich and very proper family. She disdains his work and the people with whom he must associate. One Sunday morning they argue as his wife bundles their children off to her Episcopal church. After she departs, Johnny reflects on the differences in their upbringings:

> Farrell kissed the children goodbye and watched as Pamela shepherded them into the waiting car, insisting that they ride the four blocks to the Church of the Resurrection rather than walk because she liked to make an impression. He thought for a moment of his own childhood

in the Bronx, how his mother used to drag them through the crowded neighborhood streets to St. Jerome's, all those immigrants seeing the church as a way to keep their past alive, and for a moment standing in his Fifth Avenue apartment so far from the warrens of his youth he could smell the incense and hear the Latin intonations and feel his mother's rough hand holding his. The woman had lived in fear. And that fear had instilled in him a hunger, an ambition, and a need to never settle for anything, and now this is where that need had brought him—an elegant and spacious home among the city's elite where his own children were total strangers to him. He grabbed his coat and hat and headed out into the day.

What would you say this passage is about? Scene setting? No. It's about the different values of Pamela and Johnny Farrell, as well as Johnny's rueful realization that the fulfillment of his ambitions has a bitter side. Yet notice the period details that the author weaves in: the Church of the Resurrection, the Bronx, immigrants, long-gone Fifth Avenue mansions. I would say that Farrell's feelings about his family and childhood are intimately connected to New York City.

Another way in which to deepen the sense of place and time is to let a point-of-view character observe an aspect of that place or time that we would not ordinarily expect her to notice.

Kevin Baker's *Strivers Row* (2006) is the third in a trilogy of novels about New York called City of Fire. The first volume, *Dreamland* (1999), is set in 1910 and revolves around the city's violent underbelly, particularly Coney Island. *Paradise Alley* (2002) portrays the Civil War-era Draft Riots of 1863. *Strivers Row* is a novel about Harlem during World War II, a time when the Harlem Renaissance is slowly giving way to the poverty, police harassment, and racial tension of later decades.

This time of transition is seen through the lives of two African-American men: the light-skinned minister Jonah Dove (his similarity to Adam Clayton Powell Jr. is notable) and activist Malcolm Little, who later became Malcolm X. We associate Malcolm X with the fiery activism of his maturity, but at one time he was a new arrival. Baker portrays this naïve Malcolm Little in a long sequence at the novel's beginning.

In the passage below, Malcolm Little gets his first glimpse of Harlem from the window of a taxicab:

> But Malcolm had already stopped listening, staring out at the amazing sidewalk scene emerging all around them. Suddenly there was color everywhere, as if someone had just switched the screen to technicolor, like in *The Wizard of Oz*, which he had seen six times back in Michigan. Men wearing green, and yellow, and red sports shirts. Men wearing porkpie hats, and Panamas, and fedoras, men in white and lemon-lime and peach ice-cream suits—even men wearing sharper zoots, he had to admit, than what he had on himself.
>
> And *women*. He was sure that he had never seen so many beautiful women in his entire life. There were women everywhere, at least two for every man, not counting the clusters of soldiers and sailors gaping and gesturing at them on every street corner. Women wearing gold and ruby-red glass in their ears, and open-toed platform heels that made them sway with every step. Women in tight violet and red and blue print dresses, held up only by the thinnest of shoulder straps over their smooth, brown backs. Women striding up from the subways, stepping regally down from the trolleys and the elevated, and women, everywhere he looked, strolling out of smoking storefronts, as if their smoldering presence had touched them off.

What a riot of color! Baker's palette is a chaotic contrast to the severe black-and-white documentary of the 1940s that most of us carry in our heads. More surprising still is Malcolm X leering at the smoldering, swaying women of Harlem in their tight print dresses. He didn't mention that in his seminal Black Power speech "The Ballot or the Bullet"!

THE FIRE IN FICTION

One of the things we mean when we speak of *richness* in a novel is the depth with which an author creates the setting of his story. But what does *depth* mean? It means showing us more about a place than we would get on our own. How is that done? In a practical sense, that comes from details that take us by surprise and perspectives that are not our own.

Those can only come from characters whose eyes and understanding are not merely a mirror of their author's.

CONJURING A MILIEU

What if your novel isn't exactly about a particular time and place, but rather is set in a milieu? What if you are writing about the world of professional baseball, undersea salvage, nuclear terrorists, or bird watchers? Such stories may span many settings. A *roman à clef* may span many decades. In stories with such a variety of times and locales, how can you effectively bring the world of the novel alive?

A look at some recent novels about the world of books may help us learn.

In conjuring a milieu, invoking an air of mystery and importance can be useful. This effect is handled nicely in Carlos Ruiz Zafón's cult hit *The Shadow of the Wind* (2001), a novel set in Barcelona. It concerns Daniel Sempere, who at the age of ten discovers a novel, *The Shadow of the Wind*, by little-known author Julián Carax. The novel is a rarity, in part due to the disfigured man who has been burning copies of it. At the novel's outset Ruiz Zafón has Daniel's bookseller father introduce him to a magical rare bookshop where he will first encounter Carax's novel:

> Night watchmen still lingered in the misty streets when we stepped out of the front door. The lamps along the Ramblas sketched an avenue of vapor that faded as the city began to awake. When we reached Calle Arco del Teatro, we continued through its arch toward the Raval quarter, entering a vault of blue haze. I followed my father through that narrow lane, more of a scar than

a street, until the gleam of the Ramblas faded behind us. The brightness of dawn filtered down from balconies and cornices in streaks of slanting light that dissolved before touching the ground. At last my father stopped in front of a large door of carved wood, blackened by time and humidity. Before us loomed what to my eyes seemed the carcass of a palace, a place of echoes and shadows.

"Daniel, you mustn't tell anyone what you're about to see today. Not even your friend Tomás. No one."

A smallish man with vulturine features framed by thick gray hair opened the door. His impenetrable aquiline gaze rested on mine.

"Good morning, Isaac. This is my son, Daniel," my father announced. "Soon he'll be eleven, and one day the shop will be his. It's time he knew this place."

The man called Isaac nodded and invited us in. A blue-tinted gloom obscured the sinuous contours of a marble staircase and a gallery of frescoes peopled with angels and fabulous creatures. We followed our host through a palatial corridor and arrived at a sprawling round hall, a virtual basilica of shadows spiraling up under a high glass dome, its dimness pierced by shafts of light that stabbed from above. A labyrinth of passageways and crammed bookshelves rose from base to pinnacle like a beehive woven with tunnels, steps, platforms, and bridges that presaged an immense library or seemingly impossible geometry. I looked at my father, stunned. He smiled at me and winked.

"Welcome to the Cemetery of Forgotten Books, Daniel."

The Gothic atmosphere in this passage is as thick as the fog enveloping Barcelona's famous pedestrian street, La Rambla. Daniel's father's dire warning, "You mustn't tell anyone what you're about to see today," would perhaps be enough, but Ruiz Zafón then piles on a labyrinth of twisting passages, a "basilica" of shadows and light, a "beehive" of tunnels, steps and bridges all leading to an "immense" library

THE FIRE IN FICTION

of "impossible geometry," the Cemetery of Forgotten Books. By now you should have the idea that this temple of rare books is special.

Ruiz Zafón's novel earned comparisons to A.S. Byatt's *Possession* (1990), Gabriel García Márquez's *One Hundred Years of Solitude* (1967), Umberto Eco's *The Name of the Rose* (1980), Arturo Pérez-Reverte's *The Club Dumas* (1993), Victor Hugo's *The Hunchback of Notre Dame* (1831), and William Hjortsberg's *Falling Angel* (1978). It's a Grand Guignol thriller, a love story, an historical, and a mystery. It's long, twisty and complex. Above all things, though, it is a novel about a novel and before anything else Ruiz Zafón establishes the sacred status and magical pull of books upon his story's characters. He shows us the special status that books have to them and, consequently, to us.

A similar family obsession is at the heart of Hal Duncan's *Vellum* (2005), which follows a search by Reynard Guy Carter for *The Book of All Hours*, also known as *The Vellum*, said to be a blueprint for all creation written by the scribe of God. When found, *The Vellum* proves to be a portal to a parallel reality where, among other things, angels and demons battle for control of the order of everything.

Duncan's *Vellum* is rich with many characters and storylines, tracing the history of the ancient-yet-advanced civilization of Kur through Egyptian, Babylonian, and East Indian myths. There are also bitmites, cyber-avatars, and warring bands of fallen angels. Before he introduces us to all of this, though, Duncan must first establish the mythic importance of *The Vellum* to Carter and his family. This Duncan does by, paradoxically, denying its importance in a passage of reverse psychology:

> "The Book of All Hours," my father had said. "Your grandfather went looking for it, but he never found it. He couldn't find it; it's a myth, a pipe dream. It doesn't exist."
>
> I remember the quiet smile on his face, the look all parents have at some time, I suspect, when they see their children repeating their own folly, a look that says, yes, we all think like that when we're your age, but when you're older, believe me, you'll understand, the world doesn't work that way. I'd come to ask him about these

fanciful stories I'd been told, about the Carter family having ancient secrets, not just skeletons in the closet, but skeletons with bones engraved with mystic runes, in closets with false walls that hid dark tunnels leading deep, deep underground.

"But Uncle Reynard said that when grandfather was in the Middle East—"

"Uncle Reynard is an incorrigible old fox," said my father. "He tells a good tale, but you really have to … take what he ways with a pinch of salt."

I remember being shocked, confused; I was young, still young enough that it had never occurred to me that two adults whom I trusted absolutely might believe entirely different things. My father and his brother, Reynard—my namesake uncle—they knew everything after all, didn't they? They were grown-ups. It had never occurred to me that the answers they gave to my questions might be entirely incompatible.

"Of course, you should listen to your father," Uncle Reynard had said. "Honestly, you shouldn't believe a word I say. I am *utterly* untrustworthy when it comes to the Book."

And he held my gaze with complete sincerity … and winked.

"Almost as bad as the Cistercians," he said.

After discouragement like that, it's not surprising that Carter seeks *The Vellum* even harder than before—and finds it.

Lev Grossman's brainy thriller *Codex* (2004) involves a similarly legendary work of medieval literature which comes to light when an up-and-coming investment banker named Edward Wozny is hired by the mysterious Duchess of Bowmry to catalogue her library. Needing a break, Edward agrees to this temporary career switch. Charged with finding a particular codex (a bound manuscript), Edward enlists the help of quirky-but-cute medieval scholar Margaret Napier, who explains to him the importance of this codex:

THE FIRE IN FICTION

"So Gervase wrote two books, and maybe a few poems," Edward said, "and he had a lousy job working for a minor nobleman. Why is he so important?"

Margaret arched her thin, dark eyebrows quizzically.

"What makes you think he's important?"

Edward hesitated, puzzled.

"I guess I just assumed—you're saying he's not important?"

Edward caught a faint flash of something in her eyes.

"He's a significant minor figure," she said, calmly enough, and took another sip of coffee.

All right, he thought. *We'll come back to that.* He wanted another glass of wine, and he signaled the waiter and tapped his glass.

"And this other book, the one I'm looking for? Where does the *Viage* fit in?" He tried to imitate her pronunciation.

"The *Viage* is another matter entirely," she said. "If, for the sake of argument, we take seriously the possibility that it is genuine—and I suppose that doing so is one of the conditions of my employment—it would of course have real importance. There were only three really important writers in the medieval England: Chaucer, Langland and the Pearl Poet. Together they essentially invented English literature. A fictional narrative of significant length from that period, written in English and not Latin or French, by a scholar of Gervase's general sophistication … its value would be inestimable. And of course," she added pragmatically, "the book itself could have some monetary value, as an artifact."

"How much?"

"Hundreds of thousands. Maybe millions."

Expert characters are useful devices for explanation in many types of novel. Here, Grossman uses Margaret not only to explain the MacGuffin (the object that everyone is after), but also to set the stakes. The Codex, if found, would be a major literary discovery and a financial windfall. As important as that, though, is the allure that the Codex exerts on scholars—and eventually on Edward too, who slips into addiction to a weirdly realistic computer game that mimics his search for the Codex and may be connected to it in ways not immediately obvious.

Rare books are also involved in John Dunning's mystery series featuring Cliff Janeway, an ex-policeman turned book dealer. In *The Sign of the Book* (2005), the fourth title in the series, Janeway investigates the murder of a collector of first editions at the request of his girlfriend, Denver criminal attorney Erin D'Angelo. The case grows complicated as Janeway learns that the victim was Erin's first love and also that the confessed killer, the collector's wife, is likely not guilty.

Dunning takes a different approach to creating the milieu of rare books. Instead of a establishing the importance of a particular special book to Janeway, Dunning reveals Janeway's perspective on the rare book trade itself, mainly that he feels it has changed for the worse thanks to the Internet:

> The next day I made some bold predictions.
> In a few years much of the romance would disappear from the book trade forever.
> The burgeoning Internet, as it would later be called, would bring in sweeping change. There would be incredible ease, instant knowledge available to everyone: even those who have no idea how to use it would become "experts." Books would become just another word for money, and that would bring out the hucksters and fast-buck artists.
> No bookseller would own anything outright in this brave new book world. One incredibly expensive book would have half a dozen dealers in partnership, with the money divvied six ways or more when it sold. "I might as well be selling cars," I said.

Janeway not only knows books but the book trade. His nostalgia for the way it used to be combines with bitterness over the way it has changed. Janeway's opinion is strong and grounds the reader in the rare book business. We know where we stand. The world of rare books is alive for us even as its romance is dying.

The lesson for us is that a milieu exists not in a time or place, but in the mind and hearts of the characters who dwell in it. Their memories, feelings, opinions, outlook, and ways of operating in their realm are what make it real.

SETTING AS A CHARACTER

Sometimes the setting itself may participate in the story. Blizzards, droughts, and other natural phenomena are obvious ways to make the setting active. But there are certainly more.

Find in your setting specific places that have extra significance, or places where events recur. You know, those spots that are legendary. Maybe in your hometown there was a quarry turned into a swimming hole, where boys tested their nerve, girls lost their virginity, and the cops regularly busted potheads or fished bodies from the water. Such a place was legendary, right? What about where you live now? What's the spot that everyone knows but isn't on any tour?

In my neighborhood in New York City that's the 72nd Street entrance to the Dakota apartment building where John Lennon was murdered in 1980. No plaque or statue marks the spot, but every neighborhood resident brings visitors by to point it out. When giving out-of-towners a personal city tour I also like to show them an unremarkable bar in Greenwich Village that is called the Stonewall Inn. It was a riot there in 1969 (some of the rioters in drag) that began the gay rights movement in America.

New York City is chock-a-block with special places, needless to say. One of them is the boardwalk on Coney Island. It has been featured in countless movies, songs, and novels, but one of my favorite uses is in a recent novel in Reed Farrel Coleman's gritty series of New York mystery novels featuring ex-cop turned P.I. Moe Prager. *The James Deans* (2005) won the Shamus, Barry, and Anthony Awards. In *Soul Patch* (2007), Coleman focuses on Coney Island. The novel begins with a meditative prologue that slowly zooms in, cinema style, on the boardwalk a number of years before the action of the story, to a group of four men:

> At the steps that led down to the beach, one of the four men decided he was having second thoughts. Maybe he didn't want to get sand in his shoes. No one likes sand in his shoes. The man standing to his immediate right waited for the rumble of the Cyclone—several girls screaming at the top of their lungs as the roller coaster cars plunged down its steep first drop—before slamming his leather covered sap just above the balking man's left knee. His scream was swallowed up by the roar of the ocean and the second plunge of the Cyclone. He crumpled, but was caught by the other men.
>
> …
>
> It was much cooler under the boardwalk, even at night. The sea air was different here somehow, smelling of pot smoke and urine. Ambient light leaking through the spaces between the planks imposed a shadowy grid upon the sand. The sand hid broken bottles, pop tops, used condoms, and horseshoe crab shells. Something snapped, and it wasn't the sound of someone stepping on a shell.

The Drifters's song "Under the Boardwalk" just doesn't sound the same to me now. As *Soul Patch* unfolds, an old friend of Moe Prager's, the NYPD chief of detectives, gives him a tape of an interrogation of an informant who was said to know who really murdered a drug lord of the early 1970s, Dexter Mayweather. Soon enough the chief of detectives himself turns up dead, an apparent suicide. It's up to Moe to dig up the truths of the past and present.

What is it that gives the boardwalk at Coney Island its mythic significance in this passage? The Cyclone? The smell of pot smoke and urine? There are other places that have those things. It is rather that something violent—and symbolic—happens there. Without that, the boardwalk is just a place to get a decent hot dog. To make a place iconic, make something big happen there. Something bigger than cotton candy.

As I mentioned at the beginning of this section, it is also possible to give natural phenomena a plot function, as well. Mystery novelist Nancy Pickard did just that in her stand-alone suspense novel *The Virgin of Small Plains* (2006), which we also discussed in chapter three. Remember the tornado described by two different characters in those passages? That's a perfect example of a natural phenomenon at work in the plot. But Pickard has others at work as well.

As you might recall from the plot description, twenty years before the action of the story a nameless teenaged girl was found in the small town of Small Plains, Kansas, beaten to death, her face unidentifiable. The crime was never solved. The citizens of Small Plains took up a collection and gave the girl a grave and a headstone. This grave has now taken on mystical power. The Virgin, as she's known, is said to heal. Pilgrims come as if to Lourdes.

The Virgin of Small Plains takes a perfectly flat landscape and finds in it an amazing variety of moods and meanings. Toward the beginning Abby Reynolds, a principle point-of-view character and owner of the town's plant and shrub nursery, is working in the graveyard. Abby's life was upended on the night when the Virgin was found (her high school boyfriend, Mitch Newquist, disappeared that night) and now something in the Kansas prairie stirs in her a resolve:

> When Abby couldn't see Verna's car anymore, she stood up and scanned the horizon.
>
> She could never look out over such a span of prairie without thinking about the Indians who used to live there. Her mother, who had loved facts and dates and history, had made her aware of them from the time she was old enough to look for arrowheads in the dirt. And now Abby found herself thinking about another time and another crime that nobody talked about, just like Verna Shellenberger didn't seem to want to talk to her about the murder of the Virgin.

Once, the Osage and Kansa tribes had roamed forty-five million acres, including the patch of ground on which she stood. They had shared it with thirty to seventy-five million bison. If she used her imagination, she could almost hear the pounding hooves and see the dark flood of animals pouring over the fields. But the Indians had been chased and cheated down to Oklahoma, including a forced exodus in 1873. The bison had been killed. Abby had friends who owned a bison ranch, and she had toured it, had stared into the fierce eyes of an old bison bull. In search of native grasses to plant and sell, she had also walked onto the land of Potawatomi, Iowa, and Kickapoo reservations that remained in the state. She had a natural affinity for underdogs, and she thought she had at least some small sense of what it must be like to feel helpless in the path of history. She couldn't solve those million crimes, by she thought that maybe she could help solve one crime.

On her way out of the cemetery, Abby whispered a few words to her mother, and then she touched the Virgin's gravestone.

"If you tell me who you are," she promised the dead girl, "I'll make sure that everybody knows your name."

How the horizon, arrowheads, bison, and the forced exodus of the Indians should combine to fuel in Abby a resolve to learn the truth about the Virgin—"she had at least some small sense of what it must be like to feel helpless in the path of history"—is a non-linear progression and irrational motive that nevertheless feels exactly right. Abby is a Kansas woman connected to the land; more, she knows its meaning.

What does the setting of your current novel mean to the characters in it? How do you portray that meaning and make it active in the story? The techniques of doing so are some of the most powerful tools in the novelist's kit. Use them and you will not only give your novel a setting that lives, but also construct for your readers an entire world, the world of the story.

PRACTICAL TOOLS

Connecting Character to Place

Step 1: Select a setting in your novel. Note details that are particular to it. Include what is obvious but also include details that tourists would miss and only natives would see.

Step 2: How does your protagonist *feel* about this place? Go beyond the obvious emotions of nostalgia, bitterness, and a sense of "connection." Explore specific emotions tied to special times and personal corners of this place.

Step 3: Weave details and emotions together into a passage about this place. Add this to your manuscript.

Discussion: It is impossible to powerfully capture a place via objective description—at least, to capture it in a way that readers will not skim. Only through the eyes and heart of a character does place come truly alive. Who in your novel has the strongest feelings about his setting? That character will be a good vehicle for bringing this place alive.

Changing the Landscape

Step 1: Pick an important setting in your story. Choose a moment when your protagonist or another point-of-view character is there. Using specific details and emotions, create that character's sense of this place following the steps above.

Step 2: Bring that character back to this place one week, or one year, later. Again, follow the steps above.

Discussion: Are the two passages that you created in this exercise different? They should be. Measuring the minute differences in a character's perception of a place over time is another way to bring that place alive. Remember, places generally don't much change, but people do.

Time and Sentiment

Step 1: What is your novel's era? If it is our own, give it a label.

Step 2: Write out your protagonist's opinion of her times. What does she like about them? What does she think is wrong about them?

Step 3: Note three details that are particular to this time. Go beyond the obvious details of news events, popular music, clothing, and hairstyles. Find details that your protagonist would notice.

Step 4: Weave the above results into a passage that captures your protagonist's sense of the times.

Discussion: How do you view our times? Are you optimistic? Pessimistic? One thing's for sure: you have an opinion. The same is true of your characters. The times live in the brightly hued sentiments of your cast. For a strong sense of how people saw historical eras in which they lived, check out contemporaneous essays, editorials, and speeches. (For instance, find online Malcolm X's speech "The Ballot or the Bullet" mentioned in this chapter. It captures a highly specific moment and mood in Black American history.) For a multidimensional sense of the times, examine an era from several characters' points of view using the steps above.

Conjuring a Milieu

Step 1: What is your novel's milieu? Give it a label.

Step 2: Write out your protagonist's outlook on this milieu. What does he feel is best about it? What does he believe is the worst about it? What makes it magical? What makes it hell?

Step 3: Note three observable details that are particular to this milieu, things that only an insider would see.

Step 4: Weave the above results into a passage that captures your protagonist's view of this milieu.

Discussion: Do you know your novel's milieu with an expert's depth of experience? If so, great. If not, there is research. Experts often are glad to share their knowledge and insights. Books, articles and Web sites can be helpful too. It doesn't take many details to conjure a milieu, but a milieu will spring to life most effectively when those details are not known to most people.

Setting as Character

Step 1: In the world of your novel, select a place of significance, or that you wish to make significant.

Step 2: What has already happened here? Note one or more past events associated with this place that people remember.

Step 3: In what way is this place mysterious or magical? Or, possibly, what makes it completely ordinary?

Step 4: What is your protagonist's personal connection to this place? Write it out. Make it specific. How was this place seminal in her personal history? What does she love about this place? Why is she afraid of this place? What stands out about this place? What makes it different from any other place like it?

Step 5: Does an important plot event occur at this place? Find a second event that can occur here too.

Step 6: Sorry if this sounds obvious but … incorporate the above results into your manuscript—right now.

Discussion: A place is just a place. It isn't alive. It doesn't do anything. Only people do things. In other words, making setting a character isn't really about animating that locale. It is a matter of *you* building a history for it, making big things happen there, giving characters strong feelings about it, and, *in their minds*, making it a place that is magical. That, in turn, brings it to life in the readers' minds.

CHAPTER FIVE

A SINGULAR VOICE

Do you have style?

My agency's office in New York City is close to the Fashion Institute of Technology, a college for the rag trade. There also are many photographers' studios and modeling agencies in the neighborhood. In the suite next to ours are the offices of a trendy, high-end fashion magazine. Now, I am not on any worst-dressed lists (that I know of) but I am surrounded by daily reminders of my limited fashion sense.

I wonder how these stylish people do it. It's their business, true, but clearly their flair for personal expression through clothing comes not from their closets but from inside. So it is in fiction. *Voice*, that fuzzy literary term that embraces everything from prose style to sensibility to seriousness (or silliness) of purpose, is in the first place a matter of who you are.

Some authors have a plain prose style. That is said often of John Grisham, James Patterson, and Nicholas Sparks. They are strong storytellers and bestsellers so I dare say they are not much bothered about it. Other writers are known almost entirely for their way with words. Reviewers swoon over their "lapidary" prose (I had to look it up) and their "closely observed" take on their subjects, which I sometimes think is code for *not much happens*. Prose stylists can sell well too, which, for me, implies that fiction's punch and appeal is achieved in part by writing with force.

Now, by that I do not mean just words as bullets; I mean that impact can be felt from the many ways in which the author's outlook comes across. Having something to say, a theme, is important (we'll examine that in chapter nine) but just as powerful can be how you say it, or how your characters say it.

What's your narrative style? I don't care about your choice particularly, but I *do* care whether or not you have a distinctive way of telling your tale. That is part of your power. Let's look at different ways in which voice can shout out.

GIVING CHARACTERS VOICE

In your circle of friends, who is the most outrageous? Do you have an acquaintance who will blurt out anything, wears horrible bow ties or skin-tight jump suits zipped down to the naval, flies to Borneo on a whim, flirts with your mother, shoots cactus tequila, believes in astral projection, named a cat Richard Nixon, does calculus for pleasure, drives a hot pink hearse, got arrested once in Omaha? No? Wouldn't it be fun? It would be great to meet some outrageous characters in manuscripts, too, but I rarely do.

Most characters I meet are ordinary Joes and Janes. (Well, in romance novels they might be named Cyan and Blake.) It isn't that all characters must be outrageous. That would be exhausting; more to the point it isn't right for most stories. On the other hand, why do characters have to be uninteresting? Did someone pass a law while I wasn't looking?

Any character can stand out without being a ridiculous caricature. It may only be a matter of digging inside to find what makes him different and distinct from you and me. It can be as simple as giving him his own unique take on things.

Criminals definitely look at things in a different way. (Or do they?) Since *Fifty-Two Pick Up* (1974), Elmore Leonard has brought us inside the world of crooks, killers, and con men, mostly in Detroit.

THE FIRE IN FICTION

Leonard's ear for street dialogue is unmatched. In *Killshot* (1989), he spins the story of real estate agent Carmen Colson and her iron-worker husband Wayne, who accidentally happen upon an extortion scheme run by two killers and enter the Federal Witness Protection Program, only to find that it isn't much of a place to hide.

Leonard opens *Killshot* in the point of view of one of the bad guys, a half-Ojibway, half-French-Canadian hit man named Armand "Blackbird" Degas. Blackbird gets a phone call in his Toronto fleabag hotel offering him a hit. He hondles for a better price, musing about the way punks talk to each other:

> The phone rang. He listened to several rings before picking up the receiver, wanting it to be a sign. He liked signs. The Blackbird said, "Yes?" and a voice he recognized asked would he like to go to Detroit. See a man at a hotel Friday morning. It would take him maybe two minutes.
>
> In the moment the voice on the phone said "De-troi-it" the Blackbird thought of his grandmother, who lived near there, and began to see himself and his brothers with her when they were young boys and thought, This could be a sign. The voice on the phone said, "What do you say, Chief?"
>
> "How much?"
>
> "Out of town, I'll go fifteen."
>
> The Blackbird lay in his bed staring at the ceiling, the cracks making highways and rivers. The stains were lakes, big ones.
>
> "I can't hear you, Chief."
>
> "I'm thinking you're low."
>
> "All right, gimme a number."
>
> "I like twenty thousand."
>
> "You're drunk. I'll call you back."
>
> "I'm thinking this guy staying at a hotel, he's from here, no?"
>
> "What difference is it where he's from?"

"You mean what difference is it to *me*. I think it's somebody you don't want to look in the face."

The voice on the phone said, "Hey, Chief? Fuck you.
I'll get somebody else."

The guy was a punk, he had to talk like that. It was
okay. The Blackbird knew what this guy and his people
thought of him. Half-breed tough guy one time from
Montreal, maybe a little crazy, they gave the dirty jobs
to. If you took the jobs, you took the way they spoke to
you. You spoke back if you could get away with it, if they
needed you. It wasn't social, it was business.

That could pretty much be Leonard's own philosophy of voice.
Punks. They have to talk like that. It's business. Leonard's business
is to get it down the way it sounds, unadorned, fragmentary, all
muscle, subtle in the way two fingers poking hard against your chest
is subtle. Street shit.

What's the lingo of the lawyers in your courtroom thriller? Do
the cowboys in your romance talk like real ranch hands, or do they
sound more like English literature majors? Everyone's got a style of
talking. You use words that I wouldn't and vice versa. (Hey, I'm from
New York, fuckin' get over it.)

Characters' outlook can be as distinctive as their way of talking.
Their opinions speak for the story and, in a way, for the author. Why,
then, are many fiction writers reluctant to let their characters' speak
up? Often when I have finished reading a manuscript I cannot tell
you much of anything about what the protagonist believes, loathes
,or even finds ridiculous. People have opinions. Authors are people.
What happens to them while writing to muzzle their views and
dampen their voices?

Nick Hornby, in novels such as *High Fidelity* (1995) and *About
a Boy* (1998), has established himself as a wry and witty observer
of British shortcomings and discontent. In *How to Be Good* (2001),
he introduces Katie Carr, a doctor who is married to a major mal-
content, David, who trumpets himself in his newspaper column as
"The Angriest Man in Holloway." Fed up, Kate has an affair with

an unexpected consequence: David has a deep and sudden religious conversion and decides to give up his anger in favor of being good.

Being good, it turns out, is massively inconvenient and irritating. Be careful what you wish for. At any rate, David's new focus causes Kate to examine many aspects of her life and question what it really means to be good. At one point she reflects on the pervasive English delight in cynicism:

> I got sick of hearing why everybody was useless, and ghastly, and talentless, and awful, and how they didn't deserve anything good that had happened to them, and they completely deserved anything bad that had happened to them, but this evening I long for the old David—I miss him like one might miss a scar, or a wooden leg, something disfiguring but characteristic. You knew where you were with the old David. And I never felt any embarrassment, ever. Weary despair, sure, the occasional nasty taste in the mouth, certainly, flashes of irritation almost constantly, but never any embarrassment. I had become comfortable with his cynicism, and in any case, we're all cynical now, although it's only this evening that I recognize this properly. Cynicism is our shared common language, the Esperanto that actually caught on, and though I'm not fluent in it—I like too many things, and I am not envious of enough people—I know enough to get by. And in any case it is not possible to avoid cynicism and the sneer completely. Any conversation about, say, the London mayoral contest, or Demi Moore, or Posh and Becks and Brooklyn, and you are obliged to be sour, simply to prove that you are a fully functioning and reflective cosmopolitan person.

As shocking as it may be to discover that Demi Moore causes eye-rolling in England, there's no doubt that Katie is a woman of definite opinions, capable of missing her husband's sourness. She is one who reflects on the inner life of her countrymen and women. Or is she? Come to think of it, the passage above was actually written by Nick Hornby. It is not Katie who has a voice, in point of fact, but her author.

What kind of opinions do your characters have? How do they express them? You can develop the way they talk, or their outlook and opinions, or both. In doing so you will be developing not just characters more interesting to read about but a voice of your own that speaks with greater force and authority.

That's my opinion and, you know, whatever, I'm fuckin' sticking to it.

DETAILS AND DELIVERY

Some novelists imagine it is best to have a narrator as neutral as a TV news anchor, a universal American into whom all readers can project themselves. I wonder. Is it a commercial strategy or an avoidance of the work of making a hero truly different? Even the most ordinary people have a life that's unique. The details that make it so are a secret source of what critics glibly refer to as voice.

Take me: I had the most white-bread upbringing imaginable—in the 1960s, in East Coast suburbs with brand new housing subdivisions and schools with trailer-park temporary classrooms for the Baby Boom overflow. My childhood memories are of scorching summers without air conditioning in just-finished houses where the lawn was still topsoil; stubby trees in the yard held up by thin cables; moving boxes in the garage; the afternoon jangle of the Good Humor ice cream truck bells; the hot rubber taste of water gulped from a garden hose; the new plastic smell of blow-up wading pools; the shriek and riot at eight o'clock in the evening (the sky blazing orange) when the can was kicked and fifty neighborhood kids were all at once freed from jail.

See? It isn't hard. Details are plentiful. If you don't have them in your head, the library has them in books. Details are an automatic voice all by themselves. They might seem to limit a novel's appeal, but in fact they bring it to life.

Jonathan Lethem broke into the mainstream with his memory novel *Motherless Brooklyn* (1999), in which Lionel Essrog, an orphan

THE FIRE IN FICTION

with Tourette's syndrome, recalls his Brooklyn childhood and in particular his relationship with neighborhood tough guy and fixer, Frank Minna. As adults, Minna and his minions become a de facto detective agency and limo service, until Minna is killed and Lionel himself must turn detective. One Christmas, Minna brings Lionel to his mother's apartment:

> Carlotta Minna was an Old Stove. That was the Brooklyn term for it, according to Minna. She was a cook who worked in her own apartment, making plates of sautéed squid and stuffed peppers and jars of tripe soup that were purchased at her door by a constant parade of buyers, mostly neighborhood women with too much housework or single men, young and elderly, bocce players who'd take her plates to the park with them, racing bettors who'd eat her food standing up outside the OTB, barbers and butchers and contractors who'd sit on crates in the backs of their shops and wolf her cutlets, folding them with their fingers like waffles. How her prices and schedules were conveyed I never understood—perhaps telepathically. She truly worked on an old stove, too, a tiny enamel four-burner crusted with ancient sauces and on which three or four pots invariably bubbled. The oven of this herculean appliance was never cool; the whole kitchen glowed with heat like a kiln. Mrs. Minna herself seemed to have been baked, her whole face dark and furrowed like the edges of an overdone calzone. We never arrived without nudging aside some buyers from her door, nor without packing off with plateloads of food, though how she could spare it was a mystery, since she never seemed to make more than she needed, never wasted a scrap.

Bocce, OTB, sautéed squid, and a mother with a face baked like a calzone … this can't be anywhere but Brooklyn. What creates the narrator's unique voice is not his grammar or outlook but the details he chooses to convey. Elsewhere in the story, Lionel's Tourette's gives him a different perspective than normal, but for the moment his unique voice is made up of nothing but the particulars of Brooklyn in 1979.

Sometimes it is not the details but a manner of expression that creates a sense of voice. In a departure from earlier novels such as *Reservation Road* (1998), John Burnham Schwartz turned in *The Commoner* (2008) to the cloistered and crushingly formal world of Japan's Chrysanthemum Throne. In 1959, a young woman, a commoner who in this novel is called Haruko, was asked by the Crown Prince to be his consort. Although she was well raised, the gulf between Haruko's life and that of the court causes her father anxiety, which he expresses to the Prince's representative:

> "There is in the Imperial Palace—how shall I put this— the old guard. The nobility. You yourself are such a worthy man. It is my understanding that such people make up nearly all of that world, and certainly all of the positions of relevance. Now, I'm the first to admit that I don't know much about any of this. I am a simple businessman—which, I suppose, is precisely my point. If I myself, out in the world fifty years, don't know anything about the ways and customs of imperial life, then how could Haruko? She would be utterly lost, humiliated. More than that, and I mean this sincerely, Doctor, she would be a humiliation to the Crown Prince and the entire Imperial Family. She would be a humiliation to Japan. And yet here you are—honorably, respectfully, on behalf of His Highness— asking us to agree to give her up for a role for which we sincerely believe her to be unfit. A problem that, of course, has little to say about the other kind of loss being asked of us, one that you yourself, as you say, would feel only too painfully. To lose a daughter to another household is comprehensible; to lose her to another world defeats the mind, to say nothing of the heart. And, once she has committed herself, it is for life. She will never be able to leave that world. She will be sealed in forever."

Such strained formality. Such depth of humility. How very Japanese. But take another look at that passage. Except for the words "Imperial Palace," "Imperial Family," "Crown Prince," and "Japan" itself, what words, images and details in this speech are specifically Japanese? Well, none.

The cultural authenticity here comes from the father's extreme self-effacement. Also consider, if you would, although I may be pushing too hard, I know, the number of commas, of parenthetical phrases, and the high and noble language in this passage, which so exquisitely—to a point of painfulness—expresses a father's anguish; and, perhaps, his duty, which of course is to refuse the high honor on the basis of his family's low position, as is expected of him.

In other words, a character's voice, and by extension your own, can arrive through syntax as well as through the details you deploy in what he says, does, observes, and experiences.

DIFFERENT WAYS OF RELATING A STORY

There are many ways to tell a story, many points of view from which to look. What sort of storyteller are you? Are you a benevolent observer, reporting what happens to your characters with objective neutrality? Or are you an active participant: pulling strings, stacking the deck, letting your reader know how you feel, and calling attention to your themes?

What about point of view? Do you lurk in the third person or vocalize in first person? Do you stick to your protagonist's point of view, widen to others, or explore unexpected perspectives?

There is nothing wrong with any particular choices. What bugs me is that many writers do not seem to have made a choice in the first place. Most manuscripts wander along in the way that it first occurred to their authors to write them. They do not confront me, insist that I listen, or seek to surprise me with a different way of seeing. They feel flat.

Choices of first vs. third person, or present tense vs. past tense, are fundamental to how a novel reads. There's no right way, just the way that works best and feels best to you. The subject has been covered in many other books.

What concerns me more is the straightforward and chronological approach of virtually all manuscripts. That's not bad in itself, but it does make for a certain sameness. Stories gear up, get going, plod dutifully through the middle, and finish. Getting to the end can be more a duty than a necessity.

There are so many ways to relate what happens and so many perspectives to bring. Why not take advantage of some of those options?

Matt Ruff's genre-bending novel *Bad Monkeys* (2007) centers on Jane Charlotte, a member of an evil-battling organization named The Department for the Final Disposition of Irredeemable Persons (or "Bad Monkeys" for short). They kill nasty people. The novel is Jane's personal story, related after her capture in a long psychotherapy session at the Las Vegas County Jail. Early on she tells how as a kid she sought out the school janitor for drugs but instead discovered that he was a serial killer:

> *You thought you might have better luck with the janitor?*
>
> Sure. I mean, four o'clock in the afternoon, the guy goes into an abandoned part of the building. What for? Not to mop floors. And he wasn't carrying any tools, so he couldn't be doing repairs. So what's that leave?
>
> *Any number of things, I'd imagine. But I take it you were hoping for vice?*
>
> You bet I was. And we're talking about a young guy with long hair and a Jesus beard. So what kind of vice was he likely to be into.
>
> *But it wasn't what you thought.*
>
> No, actually, it was what I thought. It's just, it was also *more* than what I thought.

The question-and-answer pattern of Ruff's novel not only allows him to add extra layers of tension to Jane's highly suspect account of herself, but also gives him a chance to convey more of Jane's personality. There are long stretches without interjected questions, allowing the story to gain momentum. Over time, though, the therapist interjects doubt about Jane's account. Unreliable narrators are a staple of postmodern fiction, but the transcript format that Ruff employs undercuts his antiheroine in a fresh way.

Another striking narrative strategy introduced itself in Mohsin Hamid's *The Reluctant Fundamentalist* (2007). The narrator of this post-9/11 novel is Changez, a young Pakistani who is thoroughly Americanized, a Princeton graduate, a highly paid employee of a New York valuation firm, a social success with a rich and beautiful (though damaged) girlfriend. Then the towers fall. Changez's reaction is the opposite of most: he sympathizes with the attackers. His alienation is instantaneous and made no easier by his slacking, his visit home, or his beard, which he insists that others accept.

What makes Hamid's novel especially unusual is that Changez relates his story in one long monologue delivered to an American stranger (an operative?) whom he approaches in a café in Lahore:

> Excuse me, sir, but may I be of assistance? Ah, I see I have alarmed you. Do not be frightened by my beard: I am a lover of America. I noticed that you were looking for something; more than looking, in fact you seemed to be on a *mission*, and since I am both a native of this city and a speaker of your language, I though I might offer you my services.
>
> How did I know you were American? No, not by the color of your skin; we have a range of complexions in this country, and yours occurs often among the people of our northwest frontier. Nor was it your dress that gave you away; a European tourist could as easily have purchased in Des Moines your suit, with its single vent, and your button-down shirt. True, you hair, short-cropped, and your expansive chest—the chest, I would say, of a man who bench-presses regularly, and maxes out well above two-twenty-five—are typical of a certain *type* of American; but then again, sportsmen and soldiers of all nationalities tend to look alike. Instead, it was your *bearing* that allowed me

to identify you, and I do not mean that as an insult, for I see
your face has hardened, but merely as an observation.
Come, tell me, what were you looking for?

This direct-to-the-reader address gives Hamid's novel an immediacy and intimacy that a simple first-person point of view would not accomplish. It is urgently important to Changez that the man to whom he is speaking *understands* him. More to the point, it is important to Mohsin Hamid that his readers understand why even an Americanized Muslim might feel something other than horror and outrage at the actions of terrorists. There's more than one way to see 9/11, Hamid is pointing out; to reach us, he tells his story in an alternate way, too.

Is your focal character someone sort of like you? That's not a bad way to go. It certainly makes the writing easier. It can also give heroes and heroines a numbing familiarity. Why? I'm not sure, but as I've noted before, a great many protagonists do not come alive as distinctive people.

Perhaps authors are afraid to make their characters stand out, appear foolish, look exaggerated, or in some other way put off readers. That can be especially true when protagonists are heavily autobiographical. Who wants to portray oneself in a light that is anything but kind and flattering?

That's a shame because paradoxically heroes and heroines can be the most winning when they are the most different. Mark Haddon in his novel *The Curious Incident of the Dog in the Night-Time* (2003) chose as his narrator Christopher Boone, a boy who is autistic. Christopher has a savant quality. He relaxes by doing math problems, but he cannot understand other people's cues or use intuition. He fits the world and the way it works into formulae and physical laws.

When he is falsely accused of killing a neighbor's poodle, Christopher undertakes to learn who actually did the deed:

This is a murder mystery novel.
Siobhan [a social worker at his school] said that I
should write something I would want to read myself.

Mostly I read books about science and maths. I do not like proper novels. In proper novels people say things like, "I am veined with iron, with silver and with streaks of common mud. I cannot contract into the firm fist which those clench who do not depend on stimulus." What does this mean? I do not know. Nor does Father. Nor does Siobhan or Mr. Jeavons. I have asked them.

Siobhan has long blond hair and wears glasses which are made of green plastic. And Mr. Jeavons smells of soap and wears brown shoes that have approximately 60 tiny circular holes in each of them.

But I do like murder mystery novels. So I am writing a murder mystery novel.

There is no mistaking Christopher's literal and linear mind for a normal boy's. He writes things down as he sees them, focusing on details and missing the context. He cannot interpret, he can only observe, which in a way makes him a perfect detective and successor to Sherlock Holmes, one of whose famous remarks is the origin of the novel's title.

You would think that seeing the world from the perspective of an autistic savant would be exhausting, but instead it is exhilarating. Granted, Haddon gives us a structure, a mystery, onto which to hold and through which to filter Christopher's unfiltered narration. As solid as that strategy is, it's not a gimmick. Christopher is more than accessible; he is alive and so is Haddon's novel in ways that it would not have been had he chosen a safer way to write it.

When thinking about voice it is easy to focus on words, as if painting pretty pictures, capturing moments, and building metaphors is all there is to it. I'm not opposed to any of that, but the more I read the more I feel that skillful use of words and an author's ability to get down a fleeting illusion of reality can cover up a novel's core emptiness.

Not all beautifully written novels have a voice, or much of one. Potboiler plots may be exciting, but also may have little flavor. It is when the words on the page demand that I, the reader, take notice that I begin to hear the author's voice. It isn't words alone that do that, I find, but rather the outlook, opinions, details, delivery, and original perspectives that an author brings to his tale.

Above all, a singular voice is not a lucky accident; it comes from a storyteller's commitment not just to tell a terrific story but to tell it in a way that is wholly his own.

PRACTICAL TOOLS

Giving Characters Voice

Step 1: Find something in your story about which your protagonist has a strong opinion. Sharpen that opinion. Magnify it. Let your protagonist rant, sneer, demur, avoid, laugh at, feel deeply, care less about, or in any way feel even more strongly about whatever it is.

Step 2: What are outward, external, observable details of the world in general that only your protagonist finds interesting?

Step 3: Find a passage of exposition in your novel; that is, a passage in which we are privy to the thoughts and feelings of a character. Whether you are working in the first person or third person, rewrite this passage so that it is more like how your protagonist or point-of-view character talks.

Step 4: Take the same passage from step 3 and rewrite it in a way that is the exact opposite of how your protagonist or point-of-view character would speak.

Discussion: Opinions expressed in a natural way, details coupled with a characteristic syntax … it doesn't matter which approach you choose, only that you choose an approach. Developing a voice as a novelist in part means giving your characters voices that are uniquely theirs.

Narrative Voice

Step 1: Pick any page in your manuscript.

Step 2: Rewrite the page. Strip out all opinions, remove all conflict. Choose generic nouns and common verbs. Delete all color and description. Eschew slang. Make the characters bland. Make the action mild. Have as little as possible happen on this page.

Step 3: Rewrite this page again. This time write it like Cole Porter, all upper crust formality, understatement, and wit.

Step 4: Rewrite this page again. This time write it like Joe Palooka, all slang and dumbfound disbelief. Make sure that your narrator or point-of-view character takes everything that happens or is said personally. Make him easily offended.

Step 5: This time write it like a politician, all generalities and evasion while at the same time emphasizing popular principles and sentiment.

Step 6: This time write it like a foreign tourist, all awe and bewilderment.

Step 7: This time write it like a banker, all caution, thoughtful consideration, and weighing of options.

Step 8: This time write it like an old-timer full of wisdom.

Step 9: Now rewrite this page as it will appear in print.

Discussion: As you can see, there are many ways to create a narrative voice. It is a matter of choosing it and then using the associated vocabulary, attitude, outlook, and diction. Is neutral your flavor? Objective narration is fine, but first experiment with alternate approaches. You may find that a different voice will better serve your story.

Alternate Narrative Perspectives

Step 1: Choose any page from your manuscript.

Step 2: Rewrite this page in any of these voices and tenses:

- Second person, future tense (*you will go, you will see*)
- Collective past tense (*we went, we saw*)
- Objectified present tense (*it goes, it sees*)

Step 3: Rewrite this page from different points of view:

- Someone who doesn't speak, but who reacts strongly to everything
- A person with a disability; e.g., color blindness
- A person with a super power
- An object in the room; e.g., the ceiling or the carpet

Step 4: Rewrite this page in reverse chronological order, then as a journal, finally from a great distance.

Discussion: The object of this exercise is not to make your novel experimental, but to raise your awareness of the choices you make in telling your story. What if you told it from the point of view of a murdered girl in heaven or the point of view of a dog? Alice Sebold's *The Lovely Bones* (2002) and Garth Stein's *The Art of Racing in the Rain* (2008) took those approaches and sold big. Frame-and-flashback timelines and unreliable narrators are nice but all too common. How can you tell your story in a way that's never been done before? It takes courage to violate expectations, but sometimes the reward is a new level of success.

CHAPTER SIX

MAKING THE IMPOSSIBLE REAL

Do you believe in vampires? No, seriously. You don't, right?

Here's another question: Do you read vampire novels? Whether or not you do, a great many readers enjoy them. To do so they suspend their disbelief. They must. How do authors get them to do that?

The same question can be asked about novels in which justice is done, love triumphs, and lone protagonists save the world. In real life those things don't always happen, or at least not easily and despite the high odds posed in a well-plotted novel. Even character-driven stories such as sagas, coming-of-age novels, and women's and literary fiction present events that are not everyday occurrences. What happens in all fiction is to some degree preposterous and yet readers go along.

Or not.

Have you ever felt that a novel you were reading got ridiculous? When fiction feels far-fetched we cease to enjoy it; indeed, we may even hurl it across the room. Then again, there are those novels in which the very premise defies logic and yet we breathlessly turn the pages. Even realistic fiction can put its characters through things that would send ordinary human beings into therapy, yet we identify with those characters and praise the author's powers of observation and ability to capture the "truth" of human experience.

How do those authors pull that off? We may speak of them *getting away with* something, but I do not believe that any fiction writers get a free pass. When novels work, they build a feeling of believability. For us to enter into the story and experience it, they must. For us to buy in we must be sold.

What, then, are the methods by which a story is made to feel real? More than that, how can we construct the high level of dramatic events that make a novel a powerful and transformative experience—and at the same time do so in a way that has our readers never doubting and even cheering all the way?

To find out what makes the impossible feel real, let's absorb lessons from some of the most outlandish stories on the shelves today: thrillers built around conspiracies, cloning, killer viruses, genetic engineering, and the supernatural.

THE SKEPTICAL READER

Are you paranoid? No, I mean seriously and deeply paranoid to the point that your friends think you're obsessed and you've wondered if you might need professional help? Do you know way too much about the grassy knoll, Skull and Bones, the Masons, Majestic 12, or MK-Ultra? If so, congratulations. You have the makings of a conspiracy novelist.

You're in good company, too. Michael Innes, Graham Greene, Don DeLillo, Richard Condon, Robert Ludlum, and Dan Brown are just a few whose conspiracy-driven novels have entertained millions. Margaret Atwood, Thomas Pynchon, Ishmael Reed, and Philip K. Dick also have given conspiracy fiction a literary pedigree.

Whether your purpose is commercial or high-minded, clearly it pays to believe that the cartoon character Pogo got it wrong when he famously declared in 1970, "We have met the enemy and he is us." Oh no, no. It's actually us against *them*! There's a lot to be paranoid about, too. Just watch the news.

Judging by queries that arrive at my agency, though, there are certain fears that in our times provoke extra degrees of paranoia.

Control of government by a self-selected few, the far reach of ancient secret societies, cloning and genetic engineering, and supernatural beings such as vampires, werewolves, and shape-shifters all seem to preoccupy us.

Why these dangers and not communists, nuclear bombs, cults, giant meteors, aliens, or any of the other unsettling worries that have preoccupied us in the past? Obviously, paranoid fears are topical. They reflect what is new and unknown. Well, I suppose except for vampires. They've been around for a while, in entertainment at least, which may explain why they've morphed from scary monsters to sex objects.

But we'll get to that.

Let's begin with this principle: We are afraid of the dark. In other words, we are afraid of nothing. There's not a thing under the bed at night that wasn't there during the day. The closet still holds our clothes and smelly sneakers and nothing else. So it is with conspiracies, clones, computer brains, and supernatural beings. They're not real.

No, sorry, they're not. Let's not get into an argument about this. Real conspiracies are, historically speaking, exceedingly rare and mostly unsuccessful. We cannot clone human beings and are unlikely to do so for a very long time. Computers cannot think. Heck, they can't even infer that the crack of a bat and the roar of a crowd mean a home run.

And vampires? Please. Have your dentist implant prosthetic fangs, if you want, but get over it: You won't live forever.

People know this. Readers, generally speaking, are not paranoid. Despite the efforts of religious extremists, our times remain rational and scientific. It is important for suspense novelists to accept this. Why? Because their first task is to convince readers that the improbable is not only possible, not only likely, but actually is happening.

That is not as easy as it sounds. If you don't believe me, drop by my office any Wednesday afternoon during our weekly query meetings, when we comb through query letters and partial manuscripts. Paranoid conspiracy stories turn up every week. Many have similar premises to already successful novels, movies, and TV shows, but they don't work.

They fail to frighten. The failure lies not in the selection of a terrifying possibility. After all, many other novelists have already kept us awake with Masonic cabals, computers run amok, and Hitler clones. No, the real failure is to overcome our rational resistance. *It can't happen.* That is a reader's first assumption. A thriller writer's first responsibility is to convince us, *yes it can.*

How? Essentially, you must pulverize every particle of reader resistance. Every single rational objection must be obliterated, one at a time. Every bit of help for the hero must be taken away; every obstacle for the villain must be overcome. *No problem*, you are thinking. I'm here to tell you that virtually all thriller manuscripts fail to meet those challenges.

Even established bestsellers find it difficult to frighten us with the improbable. That is why they have developed certain narrative strategies to help. Three recur in successful suspense fiction. What are these magic formulae?

First, ignore the reader and instead make believers out of the story's characters. Second, focus strongly on the human villains. Third, convince the reader of the improbable by overwhelming her with brute force pseudo-facts, and simultaneously by eliminating every reason why this scary whatever-it-is wouldn't happen in the real world.

All of these are ways of getting around a reader's natural skepticism. I emphasize, again, that these techniques are not simple or easy to apply. They require an extreme level of commitment. Be warned. If you want to frighten readers, deeply and for real, then you are in for more work that you've ever imagined—and more pages too. Did you ever notice that most thrillers are fat? There's a reason.

That said, let's dig in to examples of how winning suspense strategies have been applied in some successful contemporary novels. It doesn't matter whether you are putting over conspiracy, cloning, computers, or any other fear. The techniques are the same as they are for serial killers, courtroom skullduggery, medical horrors, and monsters.

MAKING CHARACTERS AFRAID

Do you want your readers to be afraid? Sure, me too. Let's try it. Are you ready? Here it comes: Be afraid! Be *very* afraid!

There. Are you terrified? No? A little nervous maybe? If you aren't quaking in your shoes right now then you are experiencing resistance, or possibly even defiance. *You trying to make me afraid? Ha. Keep trying.* In other words, announcing to readers that a story will be scary does not by itself invoke fear. In fact, it may rouse the opposite. It will now be twice as hard to make readers tremble.

Let's try a different approach. Ready? *Cold terror chilled Steve to the bone.* Heh, heh. Got you that time, didn't I. No? Well, why not? Steve's fear has chilled him to the *bone*, for Pete's sake. More frightened than that you cannot get.

Needless to say, my simplistic approach isn't going to get you to feel Steve's fear. You don't know anything about him. You aren't connecting with his life, experience, and emotions. You don't identify with him. Furthermore, my thudding cliché "chilled to the bone" has no impact. Its effect has dulled over time. In order to get you to feel Steve's fear I will first have to get you involved with Steve and then get you to experience Steve's terror in a way that is fresh.

John Case, in his thriller *The Genesis Code* (1997), faces these very problems. Something profound has happened: a famous fertility doctor in Italy has conducted an experiment at his clinic that could *change the course of human history!* Hmmm. Do you already feel resistant to that premise? Sure. Case knows that, so in his opening chapters he does not explain the doctor's work but instead details the effect it has on several important characters.

The first is the doctor's chess partner and confessor, Father Azetti. On hearing the doctor's deathbed account of his experiments, Father Azetti is shaken. He realizes that he must tell someone. He sets out for Rome. That would be good enough to set the plot in motion. Five pages would do it.

But Case is too experienced a novelist to let it go at that. He makes sure that we get to know Father Azetti. As the opening unfolds, we learn everything from what Father Azetti likes for lunch to his sad history as a politically active priest in South America whose wings were clipped by the Vatican—clipped, in fact, by the very Cardinal whom he must now visit. He's barely got enough money to get there, too.

In the following passage, Father Azetti waits on a train platform for the first of several local trains he must take:

> Father Azetti had nearly an hour to wait before the train to Perugia arrived. In Perugia he would take the shuttle to the other station, and wait another hour for the train to Rome. Meanwhile, he sat on a small bench outside the train station in the Todi, baking in the heat. The air was heavy with dust and ozone, and the black robes of his order pulled the sunlight toward him.
>
> He was a Jesuit, a member of the Society of Jesus. Despite the heat, he did not relax his shoulders or let his head droop. He sat erect. His posture was perfect.
>
> Had he been an ordinary parish priest in a small town in the Umbrian countryside, the entire matter of Dr. Baresi's confession would probably have gone no further. Indeed, if he'd been a simpler priest, it was unlikely that he'd have *comprehended* the doctor's confession, let alone its implications. And if he had understood, he wouldn't have had the faintest idea what to do with the information or where to go with it.
>
> But Giulio Azetti was no ordinary priest.
>
> …
>
> Seated on the platform, Father Azetti mediated upon the *dimensions* of the sin confessed to him. Simply stated, it was an abomination—a crime not only against the Church, but against the cosmos. It offended the natural order, and contained within itself the end of the Church. And not only the Church.
>
> …
>
> Father Azetti shook his head ever so slightly and let his eyes rest on the dusty weeds that grew in the cracks of

concrete near the train bed. Just as the seeds that had fallen in those cracks contained within themselves the promise of this destructive vegetation, so, too, the sin confessed by the doctor, if unaddressed, contained … what?

The end of the world?

Notice how many different tasks Case accomplishes in this passage. There is no action, per se. Father Azetti is sitting and waiting. That should be deadly dull. But Case makes waiting a tense experience by detailing Azetti's inner fear. Azetti, with his dignified posture and sense of purpose, also becomes heroic. Case wants to be sure we care about him.

Eventually Azetti makes it to Rome, there to wait in the outer office of Cardinal Orsini, who oversees the Vatican's Congregation for the Doctrine of the Faith (the CDF), the Curia or department charged with investigating heresy. Azetti waits there for a month, sleeping on a train station bench at night and growing smellier by the day. Eventually the Cardinal deigns to see him. The confession that Azetti reports has an even stronger effect on Cardinal Orsini:

In the days that followed, Cardinal Orsini worried.

He worried about Man. He worried about God. And he worried about himself. What was he to do? What could *anyone* do? The implications of Dr. Baresi's confession were so profound that for the first time in his life Orsini felt that he'd been asked to shoulder a burden that was too heavy for him. Obviously, the matter should be taken directly to the Pope, but the Pope was barely conscious half the time, his lucidity flickering in and out like a weak radio signal. An issue like this … it could kill him.

Thus, the torch is passed up the ladder of authority. Worry increases. This buildup is not quick. Case spends thirty-one pages on these early plot developments. Wait, isn't the idea to keep thriller plots moving fast? Yes, yet Case is crafty. The premise underlying his story is going to be a hard one to swallow. Therefore, he first builds our belief in his characters.

Having laid his groundwork, Case next launches events in America. In an upscale suburb of Washington, D.C., a house explodes. The single mother and a small child inside are dead, but an autopsy shows that they were killed before the explosion. The dead woman's brother is the novel's protagonist, Joe Lassiter, head of a high-tech investigation agency. Joe takes a leave of absence to find out who killed his sister and why. Now, let me ask you, how many pages would you spend on this set-up phase of the novel? Two or three chapters?

Case gives it more than one hundred pages. Why so many? He is investing us deeply in Joe Lassiter. We are shown his methodical working method, the loyalty of his staff, his bond to his dead sister. Only a third of the way through this long novel does Lassiter finally land in Rome where we meet the novel's villain, the leader of the sinister Catholic organization Opus Dei (yes, it's the same Opus Dei as in Dan Brown's *The Da Vinci Code*), which is one by one murdering eighteen select children around the world, including Joe's nephew.

What makes those eighteen children special? It turns out that the world-renowned Dr. Baresi specialized in a fertility solution known as "gamete intrafallopian transfer." Got that? Case spends a number of pages detailing this procedure to make sure we know it's genuine. (It means a donor egg and a father's sperm are combined, then implanted in a mother's uterus.)

Dr. Baresi also became obsessed with religious relics. Now, most relics are medieval fakes, but Baresi investigated thousands and concluded that eighteen had some possibility of being genuine. Salvaging DNA from those, he impregnated eighteen women. One or more of the resulting children may carry the DNA of Jesus.

At this point you may be groaning, but remember that in the novel that kicker is not disclosed for nearly three hundred pages. *Three hundred pages of groundwork!* What hooks us, in other words, is not the shocker that the son of Jesus walks the Earth. To that our reaction is a snide *Yeah, right!* But Joe Lassiter and others believe it to be so, and because we now believe in Case's characters, our skepticism is overcome ... or at least enough for us to read ahead to see what will happen to Joe Lassiter, Father Azetti, and others.

Another novel involving the Vatican, Richard Doetsch's debut thriller *The Thieves of Heaven* (2006), pursues a similar strategy. This time, let's start with Doetsch's ridiculous premise and work backwards to discover how he prepares us to accept it.

Ready? Three hundred pages into *The Thieves of Heaven* we learn that Satan is hanging around in our times in the guise of—what else?—a billionaire German industrialist and collector of macabre religious art who goes by the name Finster. Finster has hired a reformed American thief, Michael St. Pierre (*St. Peter*, get it?), to steal two ancient keys from the Vatican. These keys are literally the keys to the gates of Heaven, given by Jesus to Peter. With these keys in his possession, Satan gets to go home and, better still, control access to eternity.

Are you sweating bullets contemplating this awful scenario? Nah, me neither. We don't buy it. If Doetsch had started off with this information he'd face impossible-to-overcome degrees of reader skepticism. So he holds it back. Instead he begins by introducing his protagonist, the former master thief Michael St. Pierre. There's a lot to know about him. Michael got caught on what was supposed to be his final job because he paused in his escape to rescue a woman (spotted through a window with his night vision goggles) who is being tortured by a serial killer.

Having established Michael's credentials as a thief with a heart, Doetsch zooms ahead to show us Michael's life following a three-and-a-half year stretch in prison. Remarkably, Michael's beautiful and spirited wife, Mary, has stuck by him. She's a schoolteacher. He has opened a security hardware business. They're struggling but happy. She's religious; he is not. Michael has a steadfast best friend in Paul Busch, who also happens to be his parole officer.

Now, hold on. This is all backstory and setup. Stuff like that bogs down most openings. It's unnecessary junk that the author thinks we need to know to understand his characters, but actually is for the author's benefit not ours. So how does Doetsch get away with it? He does so by making each scene genuinely narrative; that is, by presenting a problem (*bridging conflict* in my terminology) and keeping us constantly wondering what will happen with line-by-line micro-tension. (We'll discuss that in depth in chapter eight.)

After fifty pages of Michael's bridging conflict—*fifty pages!*—Doetsch finally puts the main problem in place: Michael and Mary don't have health insurance. She's briefly between jobs; he's starting out. They decide to save money for the three months before Mary's new benefits kick in. Unfortunately, during this window they learn that Mary has aggressive ovarian cancer. Treating it will cost $250,000. To pay for it, Michael has no choice but to break his solemn vow to Mary, and the conditions of his parole, by thieving. Enter Finster, who wants Michael to steal a pair of keys from the Vatican.

Fifty pages of setup is excessive—or is it? In the hands of a lesser writer those fifty pages would be dull and obstructive. Agents and editors would reject with comments like *slow to get underway*. What is meant by *slow*, however, is really lack of tension. Tension is the technique that makes any action necessary and riveting, even ordinarily slack passages such as travel, mulling over prior events, drinking tea or coffee, or relaxing in a nice hot bath.

Allow me to digress for a moment on this business of thriller openings. It's highly important and too little understood.

Beginners' beginnings indulge in scenery descriptions, arrival, setup, backstory, and all manner of low-tension material, but unintentionally. More experienced writers know better. They get the plot going. A frequent choice, especially in thrillers, is a grabber prologue in which an anonymous killer slaughters a hapless victim. *Seize their attention and don't let it go!*

Right?

The problem with slamming a killer on stage and hitting the readers with immediate violence is that we have no reason to care. We know nothing about these characters and, worse, are inured to violence. Real life violence is unforgettable and life changing. Violence in movies, on TV, or in novels is ho-hum. Even if visually fresh, we're still not emotionally invested.

Don't get me wrong: I'm not recommending fifty pages of backstory and setup for most novelists. But for thriller writers who grasp the methods of micro-tension and are committed to using them all the time (trust me, that is less than one percent of all fiction writers), there is enormous benefit in getting readers deeply involved with characters before trying to put over a premise that they will resist.

Okay, thanks. Back to *The Thieves of Heaven*.

Does Doetsch succeed? I'd say so. The middle third of his novel is a highly researched and effectively detailed account of Michael's theft of the keys to Heaven. (It turns out he must steal them not once but three times.) Doetsch also effectively weaves in Michael's atheism, which stands in for any reader skepticism. Michael's motive is to save his wife, who does believe, so no matter what your own orientation you have a way to enjoy the story without having to accept an unwelcome postulate. The conflicts of the secondary character Paul Busch are also developed, as are Mary's cancer struggle and her faith in Michael. A secondary villain also gets page time: the serial killer who was the cause of Michael's arrest.

Talk about packing a plot! Doetsch makes sure there's plenty to occupy readers who may not be willing to buy that Satan is a German billionaire. Michael doesn't either, or at least not for a long while. Finally, though, deep into the novel he realizes what Finster really is and the horrible mistakes he's made. He even persuades his buddy Paul.

Does Michael, or more properly Doetsch, persuade us? By then it doesn't matter. We're afraid because Michael is afraid.

Are you willing to commit to the same level of character building, constant tension, research, and multiple-point-of-view plotting? You are? I accept your willingness but pardon my cocked eyebrow. The proof is on the page.

FOCUS ON VILLAINS

As I mentioned earlier, there's another way to overcome reader skepticism about scenarios that, in reality, are unlikely if not impossible. It involves convincing a reader to fear not what's happening but who is doing it.

Again, this is not as easy as it sounds. Cardboard villains are a staple of the slush pile. Such baddies go about their mean-spirited business for no other reason than that they are evil. Uh, right. I am willing to believe that pure evil exists, I guess, but most of the time bad actions have a comprehensible basis no matter how hard they may be to discern. In any event, villains whose motives we can understand are much scarier than those whose motive is merely *Mwoo-ha-ha-ha!*

One of our most reliable thriller writers is Greg Iles. In his novel *The Footprints of God* (2003) he took a detour from his usual story patterns to spin a chiller about a supercomputer poised to take over the world, maybe even *wipe out humanity!* Yeah, I know. Give me a break. I can't even get Wi-Fi to work at Starbucks and you're telling me an electronic super-brain is going to take over the world and eradicate human life?

Again, the challenge for Iles is to overcome reader skepticism. He does this in several ways. First, he begins his action *in medias res*—in the middle of the action. As *The Footprints of God* opens, Andrew Fielding, a senior scientist on a secret NSA research project called Trinity, has died apparently of heart failure. One of his colleagues, the novel's hero David Tennant, doesn't buy that. He thinks it was murder. And he's right.

Let's back up. Trinity is an effort to use a new supercomputing technology to create a computer that cannot just think like a human but do so millions of times faster. Building a brain from the ground up is too difficult, though, so the plan is to scan the brains of the senior scientists on the project with an incredibly powerful new MRI technology and thus install an *existing* brain in the computer's memory banks. You can see where this is going? Yep, conflict: whose brain is going to live forever? That is the multibillion-dollar question that drives much of the plot.

Iles has anticipated our skepticism, luckily, and makes sure that we have little time to reflect. His hero, an ethicist assigned to the project by the President, is on the run as the novel opens. (The President, unfortunately, is in China and cannot be reached.) Right from page one, David Tennant fears for his life. Why? Not because of the big brain that even now is stretching tentacles into all the world's databases. No, the threat to David's life is far scarier: It's human.

Now, I'll bet you didn't know that some scientific projects are so secret and sensitive that researchers not only are sworn to secrecy but work under threat of physical termination. This happens right here in the United States. Amazing, huh? Well okay, only in thrillers and Iles is experienced enough to know he's got to sell us on this premise. That is why he lavishes considerable page time on Trinity's security enforcer, Geli Bauer. Geli was hired under a contract that requires her to follow all orders without question, including killing anyone that she is instructed to whack.

Are you buying that? Iles doesn't expect you to, which is why he takes seven chapters, a total of sixty-one pages, to build up Geli as the perfect instrument to enforce the wishes of Trinity's mastermind, Peter Godin (*God*-in, get it?). We learn the scope of Geli's authority, her Army background, her kill-on-command contract, her facial scar, her father (a hawkish general out of *Dr. Strangelove*), and more. We see her in action. She is single-minded and unstoppable.

All that would make Geli no more than a cardboard baddie, so Iles goes further. Midway through the novel Geli gets a double dose of additional motivation courtesy of her nominal superior, John Skow. Skow reveals to her the full extent of Trinity's ambitions. Peter Godin is dying. If he expires before the Trinty computer is up and running, billions of dollars will have been wasted and Geli will be blamed. (She killed Andrew Fielding, you see, the only computer genius able to make Trinity work.) In case that is not enough to keep her going, Skow also informs Geli that Trinity's security is actually being supervised by her own father. Their hostile relationship insures that Geli will stay involved if only to keep battling with her heartless dad.

Did you follow all that? Never mind. The point is, Iles doesn't assume that we'll accept Geli Bauer's actions without question. He continues to humanize and reinforce her throughout the story. Her dynamic planning scenes take the place of the limp, low-tension aftermath scenes that a less experienced thriller writer would use to

THE FIRE IN FICTION

fill out the manuscript. Iles keeps his onstage villain active, motivated, and understandable.

What if you are writing a hybrid mystery-thriller, a story in which the identity of the villain is hidden? How do you plumb the depths of your bad guy if the most you've got to work with is an anonymous point of view? How can you get your readers involved with your villain without giving him away?

David Baldacci faced this challenge in his thriller *The Collectors* (2006), a sequel to *The Camel Club* mentioned in chapter two. The novel opens with two acts of violence: the assassination of the Speaker of the House and the locked-room murder of the director of the Rare Books Room at the Library of Congress. That archivist, though, leaves behind an astonishing rarity in his private collection: a hitherto unknown copy of the first book printed in America, the *Bay Psalm Book*. We are also quickly introduced to an Aldrich Ames-type traitor who is selling America's most sensitive secrets to the highest bidders.

This traitor, Roger Seagraves, is the novel's onstage villain, and accordingly, Baldacci spends many pages making sure that we see Seagraves meticulously at work as well as the reasons for his perfidious actions. But behind Roger Seagraves is a mastermind. This Mr. Big's identity is a mystery. Fine, but that presents Baldacci with a problem: How to make this mastermind powerful and frightening when we never meet him?

Indeed, no one's even sure there *is* a mastermind, or even anything awful afoot. Enter Baldacci's team of eccentric protagonists. The Camel Club is made up of four average-yet-extraordinary guys who have no particular mandate to act except that they are unusually perceptive and alert to trouble in the shadowy realms of politics and power in America.

As mentioned earlier, the leader of the Camel Club is a quirky-but-highly-committed man who calls himself Oliver Stone. He sometimes lives in a tent opposite the White House marked by a sign that proclaims simply *I want the truth*. The other members of the Camel Club are a loading dockworker, an obsessive-compulsive computer genius, and conveniently, a clerk at the Library of Congress. The clerk, Caleb Shaw, faints upon finding his dead director and winds up in a hospital. In Shaw's hospital room Oliver Stone debates with the dockworker, Reuben Rhodes, whether the archivist's death is significant or even suspicious:

> "The guy died from a coronary, Oliver. It happens every day."
>
> "But probably not for someone who'd just been given a clean bill of health by Johns Hopkins."
>
> "Okay, so he popped a blood vessel or fell and cracked his skull. You heard Caleb: The guy was all alone in there."
>
> "As far as Caleb knows, he was, but he couldn't possibly know for sure."
>
> "But the security camera and the pass card," Reuben protested.
>
> "All good points, and they may very well confirm that Jonathan DeHaven was alone when he died. But that still doesn't prove he wasn't killed."
>
> "Come on, who'd have a grudge against a librarian?" Reuben asked.
>
> "Everyone has enemies. The only difference is for some people you just have to look harder to find them."

It is nothing more than Stone's suspicion, then, that sets the Camel Club onto an investigation. What they will dig up, of course, is a nasty conspiracy that ties together the assassination of the Speaker, the death of the Rare Books Room director, and the forged (sorry) *Bay Psalm Book*.

Because Mr. Big's identity remains a secret until the novel's final pages, Baldacci doesn't try to build up his ultimate bad guy. Instead he builds up the Camel Club. Their incremental success, dangerous scrapes, and growing convictions convince us step-by-step that evil is at work. The villain becomes stronger, in other words, because the heroes prove him so.

We've now examined two methods for overcoming reader resistance to improbable premises, both involving buildup of characters instead of building up the scary scenario. There is also a third way.

VERISIMILITUDE: PSEUDOSCIENCE, GENUINE FACTS

If you have ever argued with a dyed-in-the-wool conspiracy nut, you know they cannot be budged. For your every doubt they have an answer. Facts and figures are massed in their favor. Never mind that what they believe is nonsense; it's *true*.

Then again, don't we all believe things that are at face value a bit illogical? Do you have some faith in astrology? Do you *pay it forward* because you believe in *karma*? Do you imagine that America is a pure democracy with equality and justice for all? If so, you probably can argue your case and marshal some evidence to support it. Then again, I can support the opposite view. For purposes of storytelling it doesn't matter whether either you or I are right. What matters is that we both can make a case in detail.

That is important in thriller writing because, while the case for human cloning or alien messages from outer space may not be persuasive to many readers, the case nevertheless needs to be made exhaustively if only to make the motivations and convictions of your characters believable. We may not buy your premise, but we'll buy that there are people who buy it.

How much justification do you need? Ask yourself this: How much would it take to convince you, personally, that Jesus actually has been cloned? I'll wager it would take quite a bit.

There's your answer.

In *The Judas Strain* (2007), James Rollins posits a virus that creates a sudden, worldwide pandemic. From his author's notes and the research in evidence throughout the novel, it's clear that Rollins believes such an outbreak is truly possible. So why hasn't it happened? The truth is, viruses don't spread that easily. Even bird flu didn't fly very far.

No matter. Rollins has got it covered. In *The Judas Strain* he again features the covert team called Sigma Force, familiar from his earlier novels, which fortunately for us is packed with scientists who can explain any crazy thing that Rollins dreams up. As the novel opens, Dr. Lisa Cummings has been dispatched to a cruise liner-turned-makeshift hospital in the Indian Ocean, where a powerful plague has surfaced from the depths. It is as mysterious as it is deadly.

The following is an excerpt from one of several long sequences in which Lisa discusses the plague with Dr. Henrick Barnhardt, a Dutch toxicologist whom Lisa, for tension purposes, does not much like. Joining in is Dr. Devesh Patanjali, "acquisitions officer" of the mysterious Guild, Rollins's baddie organization which has taken over the ship. Together these three ponder how the virus is turning ordinary bacteria in human bodies into biological death camps:

> Devesh continued. "These two plasmids—pX01 and pX02—are what turn ordinary *Bacillus* species into superkillers. Remove these two rings, and anthrax transforms back into an innocent organism, living happily in any garden. Put those same plasmids into any friendly *Bacillus* and the bug turns into a killer."
>
> Devesh finally swung around to face them. "So I ask you, where did these extraneous and deadly bits come from?"
>
> Lisa answered, intrigued despite herself. "Can't plasmids be shared directly from one bacterium to another?"
>
> "Certainly. But what I meant was, how did these bacteria *first* acquire these foreign bits of genetic material? What's their *original* source?"
>
> Henri stirred, moving closer to study the screens. "The evolutionary origin of plasmids remains a mystery, but the current theory is that they were acquired from viruses. Or more specifically *bacteriophages*, a category of viruses that only infect bacteria."
>
> "Exactly!" Devesh turned back to the screen. "It's been theorized that, sometime in the ancient past, a

> viral bacteriophage injected a peaceful *Bacillus* with this
> deadly pair of plasmids, creating a new monster in the
> biosphere and transforming a sweet little garden bug
> into a killer."
>
> Devesh tapped more rapidly, clearing the screen.
> "And anthrax isn't the only bacterium thus infected. The
> bacterium that causes the black plague, *Yersinia pestis* …
> its virulence is also enhanced by a plasmid."
>
> Lisa felt a prickling chill as realization dawned. …
>
> "Are you suggesting it's happening here again?" she
> mumbled. "This same corruption of bacteria."
>
> Devesh nodded. "Indeed. Something has risen
> again out of the depths of the sea, something with the
> ability to turn all bacteria deadly."

Plasmids? Bacteriophages? If your eyes glazed over during all that bio-speak, that's okay. You've got the basic message, which is that this outbreak is bad news for us since, as we quickly learn, 90 percent of the cells in our bodies are composed of bacteria. We're food for the Judas Strain.

If you don't believe that, hey, you can believe Dr. Cummings, Dr. Barnhardt, and Dr. Patanjali. They know what they're talking about—or seem to, anyway. Rollins has boned up on bacteriophages for us and wields his research like a hammer. *The Judas Strain* is wildly speculative, but by the time Rollins is through pummeling us we are ready to cry, "Killer Virus!" Anyway, why argue with him?

I hope you like research. If you do, that's good. You'll need tons of it no matter what kind of thriller you're writing. But wait, can't you just postulate the crazy idea behind your story and ask readers to go with it? After all, science-fiction and fantasy writers have been doing that for eons.

Sorry. SF and fantasy readers know that what they're reading isn't real. Thriller writers haven't got that luxury.

Maybe, to make the job easier, you could set your story in the near future? Maybe, but that cheat just robs a thriller of its veracity. Might as well whisper in your readers' ear, *Don't worry, this isn't going to happen.* They'll relax, which I think explains why near future thrillers rarely sell.

Still, maybe there's something to be said for launching in and simply smacking readers in the face with a scary mackerel. That was the choice of James Patterson in *When the Wind Blows* (1998), a novel in which he took a break from his Alex Cross series to build a thriller around ... well, you'll see. As the novel opens, a girl named Max is running in terror from a bad place called the School. *Men are chasing her!* As I read, I could hardly believe Patterson was indulging in such a generic opening.

Quickly Max reaches the perimeter of the School's grounds. Faced with a "huge, high fence" topped with "rows of razor-sharp concertina wire," and electrified to boot, Max is stuck:

> The hunters were almost there. She could hear, smell, sense their awful presence.
>
> With a sudden flourish, she unfurled her wings. They were white and silver-tipped and appeared to have been unhinged. The wings sailed to a point above her head, seemingly of their own accord. Their span was nine feet. The sun glinted off the full array of her plumage.
>
> Max started to run again, flapping her wings hard and fast. Her slippered feet lifted off the hardscrabble.
>
> She flew over the high barbed wire like a bird.

Wings? Patterson puts it on the page and we go along for the flight, at least for a little while. But Patterson knows the harvesting of babies, the activation of their atavistic and dormant genes, and the auctioning of the children later for billions apiece to international bio-tech companies—all done in perfect secrecy—will sooner or later feel pretty far-fetched.

And so we meet Dr. Frannie O'Neill, a veterinarian, who, along with rogue FBI agent Kit Harrison, finds Max and realizes her significance. When Frannie finally gets a chance to examine Max, she does so with a veterinarian's appreciation:

> "Would you take another deep breath," I said. Max nodded. She did as she was asked. She was being very

cooperative, and she was almost always polite. Max was a very sweet young girl.

I couldn't believe what I heard inside her chest. She didn't have the billow-type action of mammal lungs. Hers were relatively small, and from what I could hear, attached to air sacs, both anterior and posterior. What lungs! I could write a book on her lungs alone. Man, oh man! I was having a little trouble breathing now myself.

I couldn't be sure, but it followed logically that her bones were hollow, that some air sacs intruded into her bones.

"Thanks, Max. That's great."

"It's okay. I understand. I'm a freak." She shrugged her shoulders.

"No, you're just special."

I turned her to face me and placed my stethoscope over her heart. Jesus. It was at a resting rate of sixty-four beats a minute, but it was *booming.*

Max had the heart of an athlete, a great athlete. The organ was huge. I figured it weighted a couple of pounds. She had the heart of a good-sized horse.

Patterson keeps his science light but he doesn't neglect it, any more than he neglects keeping Max, Frannie, and Kit in constant danger, or than he neglects developing his villains. Whether you think Patterson's writing is simplistic or expertly tuned to contemporary tastes, he does the job. *When the Wind Blows* was a number one bestseller on many lists.

The same level of research turned into pseudo-expert authentication is a technique essential not only for science-based thrillers but also for suspense scenarios that spring from the realms of the historical, financial, legal, espionage, medical, military, paranormal, police, political, psychological, or any other sphere of the human adventure.

Put it this way: If we're supposed to be scared, someone has to explain why, and in detail.

SCARY MONSTERS

What more is there to say about vampires? I ask you, haven't we had enough? The number of vampire series out there is staggering. We have vampire hunters, vampire heroes, bad vampires, tormented vampires, and above all, sexy vampires. Why are they so popular? Is it the idea of living forever, post-9/11?

Whatever the reason, vampires are overdone. So let's focus on werewolves. Werewolves, too, are easy to find on the shelves and, like vampires, they present a conundrum for authors. As with all monsters that have become overly familiar, they raise a question: Are we supposed to fear them or love them? What's the winning approach? Scary or sympathetic?

I propose that it doesn't matter. Whatever your take on monsters, the first task is to make them believable and then to make your story tense. Howling at the moon alone won't do it, either. Too many writers have run with the pack ahead of you.

Carrie Vaughn, in her successful original paperback Kitty series, chose the sympathetic route. Her series heroine is Kitty Norville, a closet werewolf in a world where werewolves coexist uneasily with vampires and witches. When she's not running on four legs, Kitty is a Denver radio deejay. She broadcasts a phone-in show called "The Midnight Hour," on which she doles out advice to the troubled and lovelorn undead.

Kitty's show is popular enough to achieve syndication—straight people think it's a howl—but the attention it draws doesn't please everyone. The local vampires threaten her. Kitty's pack leader is not happy about it, either. Kitty knows she is providing an important public service, though. That's evident from the anguished calls she gets on the air.

Kitty's first program at the beginning of *Kitty and the Midnight Hour* (2005) illustrates the depth of need in the undead community. After a couple of joke calls, requests for Pearl Jam songs, and questions about whether vampires are real, Kitty gets the call she's been waiting for:

Then came the Call. Everything changed. I'd been toeing the line, keeping things light. Keeping them unreal. I was trying to be normal, really I was. I worked hard to keep my real life—my day job, so to speak—away from the rest. I'd been trying to keep this from slipping all the way into that other world I still hadn't learned to live in very well.

Lately, it had felt like a losing battle.

"Hi Kitty." His voice was tired, flat. "I'm a vampire. I know you believe me." My belief must have showed through in my voice all night. That must have been why he called me.

"Okay," I said.

"Can—can I talk to you about something?"

"Sure."

"I'm a vampire. I was attacked and turned involuntarily about five years ago. I'm also—at least I used to be—a devout Catholic. It's been really … hard. All the jokes about blood and the Eucharist aside—I can't walk into a church anymore. I can't go to Mass. And I can't kill myself because *that's* wrong. Catholic doctrine teaches that my soul is lost, than I'm a blot on God's creation. But Kitty— that's not what I feel. Just because my heart has stopped beating doesn't mean I've lost my soul, does it?"

Now there's a good one for you. How would you answer that question? Kitty delivers a discourse on Satan in Milton's *Paradise Lost*, and Satan's big mistake, which was not pride or rebellion but failing to believe that God would forgive him. She counsels faith over rage at one's fate, and striving for an honorable life. The caller is comforted.

A Catholic vampire having a crisis of faith? That's pretty heavy for a popcorn read. It's also logical. Vaughn assumes that her creatures are real and that their problems are ones they'd actually face in our world. Kitty's call-in shows make it easy to slip into Vaughn's alternate Denver and the conflicts that its supernatural denizens face.

Verisimilitude is carried a step further in Max Brooks's *World War Z* (2006), which followed on his prior cult hit *The Zombie Survival Guide* (2003). *World War Z* purports to be an oral history of humanity's ten-year struggle against an army of zombies. It is full of faux-documentary trappings—including an introduction by the disgruntled archivist Max Brooks, who collected accounts of the war from around the globe—plus interviews, footnotes, and more.

It's not the scholarly trappings, though, that give *World War Z* its authenticity; rather, it's the varied and all too human vignettes that Brooks has "recorded." The initial section of the novel chronicles warning signs and early encounters with the zombies. A doctor in Chongqing, China, recounts a night when some residents of the obscure hamlet New Dachang come to his hospital requesting help with an emergency:

> What could I say? The younger doctors, the kids who think medicine is just a way to pad their bank accounts, they certainly weren't going to go help some "nongmin" just for the sake of helping. I guess I'm still an old revolutionary at heart. "Our duty is to hold ourselves responsible to the people."* Those words still mean something to me ... and I tried to remember that as my Deer** bounced and banged over direct roads the government had promised but never quite gotten around to paving.
>
> I had a devil of a time finding the place ...
>
> ...
>
> I found "Patient Zero" behind the locked door of an abandoned apartment across town. He was twelve years old. His wrists and feet were bound with plastic packing twine. Although he'd rubbed off the skin around his bonds, there was no blood. There was also no blood on his other wounds, not on the gouges on his legs or

---

* From "Quotations from Chairman Maozedong," originally from "The Situation and Our Policy After the Victory in the War of Resistance Against Japan," August 13, 1945.
** A prewar automobile manufactured in the People's Republic.

arms, or from the large dry gap where his right big toe had been. He was writhing like an animal; a gag muffled his growls.

At first the villagers tried to hold me back. They warned me not to touch him, that he was "cursed." I shrugged them off and reached for my mask and gloves. The boy's skin was as cold and gray as the cement on which he lay. I could find neither his heartbeat nor his pulse. His eyes were wild, wide and sunken back in their sockets. They remained locked on me like a predatory beast ...

Take another look at that passage. The young boy's bloodless-yet-alive condition is made more chilling by the doctor's cold assessment. That objective tone would be enough to achieve the desired effect, but Brooks also takes time to humanize the doctor, even to make him heroic, with the doctor's rueful admission of his old-fashioned Red idealism.

We feel for this doctor just as we do for so many of Brooks's one-time-appearance characters. To put it another way, Brooks is not asking us to buy his zombies (though his slow buildup of them is persuasive) but instead banks on bonding us in sympathy with his eyewitnesses to the Zombie War. If you think about it, isn't that the same technique used by the conspiracy novelists cited earlier? Don't try to convince your readers of the improbable premise; instead convince your characters.

A focus on villains can also aid in putting over improbable—scratch that, *impossible*—monsters. That technique is just one of an array of methods employed by the prolific Sherrilyn Kenyon in her *Dark-Hunter* novels. If you haven't read any of this interwoven series, get ready to immerse in an alternate America crowded not only with us plain old mortals but also with Dark-Hunters, Apollites, Daimons, Were-Hunters, Dream-Hunters, Charontes, Squires, and Oracles. And will someone please explain to me the Chthonians?

Never mind. I'll wait. For now it's enough to know that Dark-Hunters are shape-shifters whose job it is to track down and kill the evil Daimons, who start out as less-objectionable Apollites but later, in their twenty-seventh year, make the ugly choice to prolong their lives by stealing human souls. (Paying attention? There's going to be a quiz.) All of this derives, somehow, from Greek mythology and makes for stories in which our drab human society is but a thin soap opera compared to the titanic struggles of the immortals around us. Fortunately, a few humans are clued in.

In the tenth *Dark-Hunter* novel, *Dark Side of the Moon* (2006), the lucky crossover human is a disgraced political reporter, Susan Michaels, who is reduced to writing for a Seattle rag, the *Daily Inquisitor*, which specializes in articles about killer moths, alien babies, and other paranormal drivel. Susan is destined to perform an act of animal rescue, the animal in this case being hunky Dark-Hunter Ravyn Kontis, who when we first meet him is in the form of a cat.

Ravyn has been snagged by Apollites in Seattle's Pike Market with the help of a slinky streetwalker whom he hoped would pet him, the jerk. Over in Kenyon's version of hell, Kalosis, the Apollites and Daimons rejoice over Ravyn's capture. As they celebrate in baths of Apollite blood, we learn of the plans of their leader, Stryker, to bring about the final salvation of his unfairly (as he sees it) cursed subjects:

> Like the other Spathis gathered here, Stryker envisioned a better world. A world where his people weren't condemned to die at the tender age of twenty-seven. A world where they could all walk in the daylight that he'd taken for granted as a child.
>
> And all because his father [Apollo] had knocked up a whore and then gotten pissed when the Apollites had killed her off. Apollo had cursed them all ... even Stryker, who had been the ancient god's most beloved son.
>
> But that was eleven thousand years ago. Ancient, ancient history.
>
> Stryker was the present and the Daimons before him were the future. If everything went as planned, they would one day soon reclaim the human realm that had been taken from them. Personally, he'd have rather started

> with another city, but when the human official had come to him with a plan for the humans to help rid Seattle of Dark-Hunters it had been a perfect opportunity to start aligning the race of man with the Apollites and Daimons. Little did the humans know that once the Dark-Hunters were cleared, there would be no one to save their souls. It would be open season on all mankind.

How sweet for the Apollites that Stryker is a visionary, not to mention a good guy. He is. I mean, all he wants for his people is a little sunlight and fresh air … well immortality, too, at the expense of our human souls. That's forward thinking, though, wouldn't you say? Why can't we get that kind of leadership out of Washington, D.C.?

Kenyon's slangy, tongue-in-cheek narrative style helps bring her cosmology down to human level. Do you find her approach cartoonish? Maybe so, but you have to admit that Stryker's motives are accessible, even sympathetic. By slipping us easily into his head, Kenyon also eases us into a world of her own devising.

What about simply launching into a supernatural scenario and forcing the reader to go with it? Can that work? Sure. It can even be fun. Julie Kenner's demon-hunting suburban soccer mom (*Carpe Demon* [2005] and sequels) may owe a lot to Buffy but her sprightly tone unfailingly seduces. Charlaine Harris in her Sookie Stackhouse fantasy-mysteries (*Dead Until Dark* [2001] and sequels) gives the supernatural a fried-green-tomatoes Southern twang.

The king of humorous horror, though, is undoubtedly Jim Butcher, whose series about down-at-heels Chicago wizard-detective Harry Dresden has soared high on the *New York Times* best seller list and spun off tthe Sci-Fi Channel TV show *The Dresden Files*. Harry's sardonic narration never fails to amuse even if guts are flying and ghouls are dying. Butcher, indeed, gives the supernatural its sting with that very juxtaposition.

In the ninth novel in Butcher's Dresden Files, *White Night* (2007), Harry Dresden is once again brought in by the Chicago police to consult on a series of murders with occult overtones. Someone is killing the witches of Chicago, all mild-mannered Wiccans of modest magical talents. As Harry investigates, he begins to suspect that the murders are related to a larger conflict between the White Council, the ruling body of paranormal practitioners, and the Vampire Courts, the analogous institution for the undead.

Indeed, it looks like someone is trying to frame a Grey Cloak (that is, a Warden or law enforcer of the White Council) for the murders. In the following passage, Harry discusses the warlock-vampire war with his cute police department contact Lieutenant (temporarily demoted to Sergeant) Karrin Murphy:

> ... "So," [Murphy] said, filling time. "How's the war going?" She paused for a beat, and said, "God, what a question."
>
> "Slowly," I said. "Since our little visit to Arctis Tor, and the beating the vampires took afterward, things have been pretty quiet. I went out to New Mexico this spring."
>
> "Why?"
>
> "Helping Luccio train baby Wardens," I said. "You've got to get way out away from civilization when you're teaching group fire magic. So we spent about two days turning thirty acres of sand and scrub into glass. Then a couple of the Red Court's ghouls showed up and killed two kids."
>
> Murphy turned her blue eyes to me, waiting.
>
> I felt my jaw tighten, thinking back on it. It wouldn't do those two kids any good, going over it again. So I pretended I didn't realize she was giving me a chance to talk about it. "There haven't been any more big actions, though. Just small-time stuff. The Merlin's trying to get the vamps to the table to negotiate a peace."
>
> "Doesn't sound like you think much of the idea," Murphy noted.
>
> "The Red King is still in power," I said. "The war was his idea to begin with. If he goes for a treaty now, it's only going to be so that the vamps can lick their wounds, get their numbers up again, and come back for the sequel."

> "Kill them all?" she asked. "Let God sort them out?"
>
> "I don't care if anyone sorts them or not. I'm tired of seeing people they've destroyed." My teeth ground together. I hadn't realized I was clenching my jaw so hard.

Let me ask you something: In the passage above, what stands out? What got your attention? Was it the backstory review of training wardens, the ghoul attack, the Red King and peace negotiations? Or was it Harry's not-so-buried anger? I'll bet, as it was for me, it's the emotion that has impact.

There's plenty of action in *White Night*, including a series of gory ghoul attacks. Butcher writes violence effectively yet Harry's matter-of-fact narration doesn't aim to shock us, surprise us, or creep us out (much) with visuals. Butcher knows we've seen in all on TV. Instead, the horror comes largely from inside Harry; that is, from his feelings.

Later in the novel, Harry goes on a rampage after ghouls kidnap a pair of sixteen-year-old twins and chow down on them:

> I kicked the ghoul's wildly thrashing lower body into the blackness of the mine shaft. I turned to the upper half.
>
> The ghoul's blood wasn't red, so he burned black and brown, like a burger that fell into the barbeque just as it was finished cooking. He thrashed and screamed and somehow managed to flip himself onto his back. He held up his arms, fingers spread in desperation, and cried, "Mercy, great one! Mercy!"
>
> Sixteen years old.
>
> Jesus Christ.
>
> I stared down for a second. I didn't want to kill the ghoul. That wasn't nearly enough to cover the debt of its sins. I wanted to rip it to pieces. I wanted to eat its heart. I wanted to pin it to the floor and push my thumbs through its beady eyes and all the way into its brain. I wanted to tear it apart with my fingernails and my teeth,

and spit mouthfuls of its own pustuled flesh into its face as it died in slow and terrible agony.

The quality of mercy was not Harry.

I called up the Hellfire again, and with a snarl cast out the simple spell I use to light candles. Backed by Hellfire, directed by my fury, it lashed out at the ghoul, plunged beneath its skin, and there it set fat and nerves and sinews alight. They burned, burned using the ghoul for tallow, and the thing went mad with the pain.

Gee, do you think Harry is pissed off? Okay, what is the most horrific part of that passage: the descriptions of the burning, bisected ghoul ("like a burger that fell into the barbeque"), or Harry's own rage ("I wanted to ... push my thumbs through its beady eyes")? Both aspects of the passage are graphic, but really isn't it Harry's anger and actions that are the most awful?

What pulls us through *White Night* and all the novels in the *Dresden Files*, I'd argue, is not any macabre fascination with the occult but the innate appeal of Harry Dresden. What makes Harry compelling? His sardonic humor, of course, but also his high personal stakes. Each plot problem matters profoundly and personally to Harry, and therefore it matters to us. What horrifies him horrifies us.

In all the examples above, notice that what makes monsters scary is what makes them human. Indeed, the trick of frightening readers has always been to first make the world of the story highly believable, then gradually add what is weird. From Wilkie Collins to H.P. Lovecraft to Shirley Jackson to Stephen King to Joe Hill, what is scary is not the buildup of what is supernatural but the buildup of what is real.

Don't get me wrong. Any type of suspense novel must accomplish a lot and successfully deploy many techniques: heroic heroes, high stakes, ticking time bombs, relentless pressure, endless new obstacles, escalating consequences, taut writing, and more. All of that has been covered in any number of good books on thriller construction. What concerns me, and what I see missing in so many manuscripts, is passion.

How is passion expressed in a thriller? Is it exhaustive knowledge of the underlying threat? Certainly. But that by itself is not enough. That kind of passion we can get from any conversation with a conspiracy nut in a bar.

Passion in a suspense novel means giving a protagonist the author's own paranoia, either gradually or right away. It means constructing a villain out of compelling motives and high convictions. It means pouring research-gleaned details into the story both to feign verisimilitude and to build believable character motives.

If what you feel genuinely is paranoia, great. Use it. But don't confuse paranoia with passion. Passion is patient and hardworking. It's crafty. It doesn't rest until every last consumer is turning the pages without ceasing.

We have been talking about thrillers, but the techniques in this chapter have important applications in every kind of fiction. Even contemporary realism lifted straight from your own life will, at some point, strain credulity.

How can you counteract that? In the same ways we've been discussing. First, give your protagonist real reasons to act. Second, motivate your antagonist convincingly and at length. Third, and above all, find what is improbable in your story and remove every shred of reader objection and answer every reason why these improbable things don't happen in real life.

When readers are drawn into a story, especially one that can't really happen, it is not a lucky accident. It's because the author has worked hard to make the impossible feel real.

PRACTICAL TOOLS

Effect vs. Cause

Step 1: Identify the most improbable event in your novel.

Step 2: What about this event makes your protagonist the most afraid? What does your protagonist do in response?

Step 3: Escalate and add steps to your protagonist's response. What is the most extreme length to which your protagonist can go?

Step 4: What is a level of response beyond *that*? Take your protagonist to that level.

Discussion: In many manuscripts the protagonist's motivation is shallow. We do not believe that protagonist is driven to action, and often the action to which the protagonist is driven is less than it could be. Pump up the motivation. Pump up the response. You may feel afraid of going too far. In fact, in most manuscripts the protagonist does not do enough.

The Highly Motivated Villain

Step 1: Who is your novel's principle antagonist?

Step 2: What is the biggest wrong that your antagonist must do?

Step 3: List twelve reasons why someone in real life would not do that, or would be prevented by others from doing that.

Step 4: Work out twelve reasons why, in this case, your antagonist is motivated to do the worst, and also why others are unable to prevent it.

Step 5: Incorporate the above results into your manuscript. Do not cheat. Add the extra pages. Put it all in.

Discussion: It takes extra effort, not to mention pages, to fully motivate an antagonist. It also requires the author to go to the uncomfortable place where the antagonist can be understood. But it is worth the journey. Similarly, in manuscripts there often is little to get in the antagonist's way. That produces weak tension. Knocking down real obstacles step by step raises tension and makes improbable actions increasingly plausible.

Building Believability

Step 1: What is the most improbable event in your novel?

Step 2: List twenty reasons why in the real world this event would not occur. What prevents it? Who stops it?

Step 3: Did you really list twenty reasons? Come on now. Dig deeper. Assume that this improbable event can and will fail to occur. List every last reason why that will be so.

Step 4: For each point, work out why and how in this case each obstacle fails to prevent the improbable event.

Step 5: Incorporate the above results in your manuscript.

Discussion: Even when thrillers are not based on speculative elements, the terrible disaster that looms often fails to frighten.

We know it won't really happen. If it could, then in the real world it would happen. But it doesn't. The effect of removing obstacles to the event is to lower readers' resistance to the idea of this awful calamity. The farther you go in removing obstacles, the more your readers will believe. How far is required? Much farther than most authors go.

Note: This principle applies to novels other than suspense. Every story involves something unlikely. Making it believable is an essential technique of mastery.

Scary Monsters

> **Step 1:** Is there a monster in your novel?
>
> **Step 2:** Create three ways in which your monster is very human.
>
> **Step 3:** Motivate your monster. Find six good reasons for your monster to act. ("Evil" is not a motivation.)
>
> **Step 4:** Find three reasons why your monster does *not* want to act. Make them strong reasons. Include, then overcome, each one.

Discussion: It's rare in manuscripts to meet a scary monster. Mostly they are evil, powerful, and unstoppable. That's fine, but if that evil isn't motivated, that power isn't earned, and the monster's obstacles aren't real, then evil will feel thin and the monster won't panic anyone. That's as true of human monsters as it is of the supernatural kind.

CHAPTER SEVEN

HYPERREALITY

Are you having a nice time? I'm glad. Isn't it great when you hit one of those days, or even a whole stretch of your existence, when you just cruise along, no particular worries, everything going pretty well? How wonderful to be able to drop phrases like *same-old, just routine,* and *nothing new.*

At times like those, problems are in perspective, drama queens don't draw you in, you remember to exercise, you say no to dessert, and you speak to your kids and co-workers in thoughtful and measured tones. Life is in balance. Your outlook is sunny.

If that describes you right now, stop working on your manuscript immediately. You could be in terrible danger. Why? You may be seeing the world and its woes in a way that is calm and rational. Nothing could be worse, at least for your fiction. Effective storytelling doesn't minimize problems, it exaggerates them. To the passionate novelist, everything isn't smaller than it really is—everything is bigger.

The world of a story is a hyperreality. In a passionately told tale, characters are larger than life, what's happening matters profoundly, the outcome is important in the extreme, and even the words on the page have a DayGlo fluorescence. A certain verisimilitude is required, of course, otherwise a story would not feel real. But that's a trick. In a passionate story the particulars of life are magnified.

A depressingly large share of manuscripts that I read fail to heighten much of anything. Protagonists, places, and problems don't stand out. There's a sense of *same-old* to them that's not a good thing. If I want *same-old* I can phone my brother-in-law. From a novel I want an experience more unusual, or at least more vivid, than the humdrum beat of a regular day.

In practical terms, what constitutes a hyperreality? How does it get on the page? To find out, it will be useful to have a look at the methods of our top satirists. Satire by definition exaggerates. That's how it works. Luckily, the techniques of satire have applications in every story. And if it is satire that you specifically are aiming for, then it will be good to study the systems of the very best.

But first let me tell you why most satiric manuscripts fall flat.

THE SECRETS OF SATIRE

Life is full of irony, isn't it? Sometimes you have to laugh. If you didn't, you'd scream. In fact, at times the world is so absurd the only thing to do is to write about it.

Others have felt that way too. From Daniel Defoe to Mark Twain to Kurt Vonnegut to contemporary practitioners like Steve Aylett, Douglas Coupland, Jeff Noon, and Chuck Palahniuk, satire saturates our literature. Laughing at others is essential. Making fun of ourselves, it seems, is even more necessary.

Whether you have spent decades on Capitol Hill or gone no further than college, you, too, probably feel a need to poke fun at the world. How do I know? Because I receive countless manuscripts that intend to satirize. Queries also frequently pitch us stories that are "by turns tragic and hilarious."

So why am I not laughing?

Sadly, comedic manuscripts almost never live up. The biggest problem is that they aren't funny. They rarely deliver even chuckles, never mind the whoops of laughter that their authors intend to provoke. Why not? It is not because their authors are humorless trolls. Most are funny people. The problem is that their humor comes through on the page only a little.

It's one thing to crack a joke or be occasionally witty; it's another thing altogether to be funny for four hundred pages. But that is what it takes. Humor is cumulative. Laughter builds. Have you ever enjoyed a comedian's routine? When do you laugh the hardest, at the beginning or at the end? Toward the end, of course, because the comedian's outrageous outlook takes a while to overwhelm you.

So it is with fiction. For humor to come through in a novel it needs to be bigger and more relentless than most authors realize. You can crack yourself up at the keyboard but barely raise a smile on your readers' faces. To slay those readers you need to hammer their funny bones like Noah nailing the Ark.

The malnourishment of comic manuscripts is a shame, too, because the methods of mirth are so plentiful. They're even free. Here are a few of them, on me:

- hyperbole
- wit
- biting comment (think insults)
- ironic juxtaposition and reversal
- escalation of the mildly ridiculous
- being extremely literal ("Who's on first?")
- funny name and word choices
- deadpan delivery of dumb remarks
- deliberate misunderstanding
- unlikely points of view
- extreme personas or voices
- stereotyping

There are a thousand ways to be funny but it is hyperbole that I wish all fiction writers would master. It's a universal leavening. It is a crucial element that can punch up description regardless of the type of novel you are writing

If I describe the pancakes served at a diner as *humungous*, you get the idea. But if I instead have your waitress, Dixie, slam down a platter of whole grain banana-peach pancakes that are *the size of Firestone Extreme Service truck tires*, doesn't that have more visual impact? That's hyperbole.

Those novelists who intend to be hilarious need not use only hyperbole but a whole grab bag of comic techniques. Where to start? Almost anything can be made funny, but recognize that humor depends in part on the readers' familiarity with your subject. You can't effectively riff on something if your audience is completely ignorant of it. Thus, it's useful to target first some things that everyone has in common.

FUNNY PEOPLE, FUNNY PLACES

Some people should not be taken seriously. Think wine stewards, spiritual gurus, or productivity teams. Certain places also make us grin: Chuck E. Cheese, nude beaches, Baptist karaoke bars.

Yeah well, okay, maybe nude beaches make us wince.

Regardless, is making a person or a place a screaming riot simply a matter of choosing a ripe target? No. Even naturally funny subjects have got to be mined for their humor. By the same token, any person, place, or thing is funny if you know how to look at it. Take your hometown. For you, is it bathed in nostalgia or is it a memory more like Alcatraz?

In Jonathan Tropper's *The Book of Joe* (2004), hero Joe Goffman's hometown is Bush Falls, Connecticut. It's also the subject of Joe's autobiographical novel, a bestseller and scathing exposé of small town sins. Joe expects never to go back. If he does he certainly won't be welcome. But when Joe's father has a stroke, Joe is forced to return to the place where he was raised:

> Bush Falls is a typical if small version of many middle-class Connecticut towns, a planned and determinedly executed suburbia where the lawns are green and the collars predominantly white. Landscaping in particular is taken very seriously in Connecticut. Citizens don't have coats of arms emblazoned above their front doors; they

have hedges, fuchsia and pachysandra, flower beds and emerald arborvitae. A neglected lawn stands out like a goiter, the telltale symptom of a dysfunctional domestic gland. In the summer, the hissing of the cicadas, invisible in the treetops, is matched by the muted machine-gun whispers of a thousand rotating sprinklers, some dragged out of the garage after dinner, others installed beneath the lawns and set on timers. Soon, I know, the sprinklers will be put away for the season, replaced by rakes and leaf blowers, but for now they remain heavily in evidence as I drive down Stratfield Road, the main artery connecting the residential section of Bush Falls with its commercial district.

Did the passage above have you howling? Me neither. It isn't meant to be riotous, just a wry take on a white-collar suburban town. For me, that intention takes hold with the line, "Landscaping in particular is taken very seriously in Connecticut." Of all the things one can take seriously in this world, landscaping? It's the conjoining of the words "seriously" and "landscaping" that makes this humorous.

Developing his theme, Tropper lands another nice line with, "A neglected lawn stands out like a goiter." If he had chosen "sore thumb" instead, the line would not work. What would you have chosen to stand out? An elephant? An outdoor albino wedding? The first is too common and the second stretches too far. Neither one evokes ugly, either. Goiter is smack on. It's both true and over the top, like all good hyperbole.

Can you pick out other hyperbole in Tropper's passage? My favorite is "the muted machine-gun whispers of a thousand rotating sprinklers." Sprinklers are a suburban necessity. Describing their sound as "machine-gun" (but at a whisper) is ridiculous but exactly right. Here Tropper's exaggeration gives the image an especially nasty edge of meaning. Could the line better convey Joe's contempt for his hometown?

Along with hometowns, college is a frame of reference that authors can mostly count on sharing with their readers. In Tom

Perrotta's *Joe College* (2000), the university in question is Yale and the hero is Danny, a junior coping with typical undergraduate woes. Not least of these is his crush on smart and beautiful Polly, who of course already has a boyfriend, in this case a professor. One evening after walking Polly back to her dorm, they find the professor waiting. Danny must yield her. Perrotta handles Danny's sense of humiliation at this delicate moment this way:

> My face felt hot, like I was standing too close to a fireplace. I gave a shrug of what was supposed to be mature resignation and headed off down College Street as thought it were all the same to me, as though I'd expected the night to end like this all along. It seemed important not to look back or give too much thought to what they might be doing or saying, so I tried to distract myself by whispering the word "fuck" over and over again, in unison with my footsteps, and thinking about how cool I would be in the leather bomber jacket I was sure I would someday own.

Where exactly in that passage does the humor lie? It's in the third sentence when Danny blithely tries to distract himself with … well, what? Here is the turnabout. We expect something mundanely diverting, but instead Danny mutters *fuck* to himself repeatedly. Had Perrotta begun the paragraph with that detail, it wouldn't be funny. Instead, he sets up our expectation and then reverses it, a classic comedy technique.

Elsewhere in the novel, Danny gets a chance to dance with Polly. What kind of dancer do you think Danny is? You're right: the worst. Since you already expect that, making Danny's gyrations goofy is going to be difficult. To milk the moment for its humor, Perrotta becomes wildly hyperbolic:

> It was strange and awful at the beginning, a bad dream made flesh. I was the Dork-in-Chief, the Anti-Dancer, the Fred Astaire of Spaz. My arms moved and my legs moved, but these movements had little to do

> with the music, and even less to do with fun. They were
> abrupt and jerky, the flailings of a defective marionette.
> I needed oil. The beat was a distant rumor. If I'd been
> in water I would have drowned. To make matters worse,
> everyone else on the dance floor suddenly seemed im-
> probably fluid and limber, full of tricky spins and Soul
> Train swivels. I mean, they were Yalies. Molecular Biol-
> ogy and Biochemistry majors. People who petitioned
> to take seven courses in one semester so they wouldn't
> have to choose between Introductory Sanskrit, Medi-
> eval Architecture, and that senior seminar on *Finnegans
> Wake*. Where had they learned to dance like this? Gro-
> ton? Choate? Some special summer camp my parents
> hadn't heard about?

Perrotta's hyperbole here is grounded in his narrator's sense of humiliation. Feeling like a jerk is a universal experience. The fun lies in pumping up the emotion so that it inflates like a blimp. Bad enough to be a spaz on the dance floor, but on a dance floor full of *Yalies*? Ouch. Notice, too, how much time Perrotta spends developing Danny's I'm-a-bad-dancer diatribe. In satiric fiction it doesn't hurt to pile it on.

What about your manuscript? Are your similes merely apt? Are your metaphors mild? How do you paint emotions? Try feeding them amphetamines. Rev them up like a motorbike, maybe to a point where they become ridiculous. That's the idea. When infected with a case of the blahs, a novel doesn't need less, it needs more. It doesn't need small, it needs big.

The right medicine may be a dose of hyperbole.

SENDING UP SOCIETY

It's hard to compete with the great social satirists of our day, such as Tom Wolfe, but it can be done. What does it take? Again, I believe it begins not with choice of subject but with a will to point out what is puerile, peculiar, and pernicious in our world, and then to do so with gleeful malice and at great length. Satire is not a simple tone to adopt; it's a mission to embrace. Satiric novelists are, to me, less like occasional wits and more like Marines.

Does America seem to you controlled by corporations? If not actually running the country they certainly control the majority of many people's days. The cube farm must be a noxious place to work because corporate satires are easy to find in my agency's slush pile. Unfortunately, few of them work.

One corporate satire that does work is Max Barry's *Jennifer Government* (2003), which posits a future where the functions of government have been surrendered completely to corporations. This privatization is so extreme that schools are sponsored by companies and people adopt their corporation's names as their own. Barry's novel is set in the "Australian Territories of the USA," and it is there that hapless shoe company employee Hack Nike is sucked into a devious scheme. His company has created massive demand for a new athletic shoe by refusing to sell it. The next step is to make purchase of the shoe more difficult still by assassinating some shoppers who try to buy it. What a brilliant idea!

Unaware at first of this dimension of the campaign, Hack signs a contract to join the marketing team. Only later does he read the fine print and find out that he's supposed to do the shooting. Naturally, Hack wants to escape his contract. Following his girlfriend's sensible advice he brings his problem to the police, who also are now a corporation. At the station house a detective talks with Hack:

> "So what's your problem?" He flipped open a note-book.
>
> Hack told him the whole story. When he was done, Pearson was silent for a long time. Finally Hack couldn't take it anymore. "What to you think?"
>
> Pearson pressed his fingers together. "Well, I appreciate you coming forward with this. You did the right thing. Now let me take you through your options." He closed the notebook and put it to one side. "First, you can go through with this Nike contract. Shoot some

people. In that case, what we'd do, if we were retained by the Government or one of the victim's representatives, is attempt to apprehend you."

"Yes."

"And we *would* apprehend you, Hack. We have an eighty-six percent success rate. With someone like you, inexperienced, no backing, we'd have you within hours. So I strongly recommend you do not carry out this contract."

"I know," Hack said. "I should have read it, but—"

"Second, you can refuse to go through with it. That would expose you to whatever penalties are in the contract. And I'm sure I don't need to tell you they would be harsh. Very harsh indeed."

Hack nodded. He hoped Pearson wasn't finished.

"Here's your alternative." Pearson leaned forward. "You subcontract the slayings to us."

The police making hits? Why not? The police are well suited to solve Hack's problem, or so he thinks. But look closely, going beyond that funny development to notice the care with which Barry sets it up. For half a page it looks like the cop is going to help Hack in the way we expect. "We would apprehend you … So I strongly recommend you do not carry out this contract." Hack's anxiety grows. The cop offers three options: 1) bad, 2) worse, 3) ironic reversal.

It's a classic joke structure, leading you by steps to expect one thing then springing on you something logical but out of left field. You would think we'd grow inured to that pattern but we don't. Bar jokes work in the same way. With every new variation of a-priest-an-Irishman-and-a-duck-walk-into-a-bar they hook us over and over again, as does Barry.

Another approach to sending up social institutions is through parody. Where satire sends up social mores, parody sends up a literary form. Parody also automatically shoots down whatever happens to be the targeted genre's subject matter.

To show you what I mean, let's look at a prison story. In the following passage, a young and diminutive political prisoner named Hassan is recovering from a gunshot wound, but nevertheless receives hard treatment from his American jailers:

> The door of the cell clicked open and a plump female jailer entered, complaining to Agent Mike that the jail had no clothing on hand that would fit a traitor and murderer as puny as this one, and that something had to be specially ordered, which took most of the goddamn day and which the little piece of shit didn't deserve. "Put it on!" she shouted, throwing a set of gray clothes at the boy. The outfit fell from his grasp to the floor. "Pick it up!" she shouted now.
>
> It seemed to take an excruciatingly long time for him to remove his hospital gown and pull on the little T-shirt and pants, and indeed Agent Mike grumbled, "Christ—finally," when Hassan was done. Glancing down at the outfit, the boy didn't think he could be any more humiliated than this. A row of figures was stenciled on the front.
>
> "That's *yer number*," said the jailer, enunciating angrily as if the suspect might not understand, or might pretend not to understand, these simple words. "From *now on*. Don't *forgit* it."

Grim stuff, wouldn't you agree? We know without being told that Hassan is in for a bad time at this jail. Now let's take a look at the way that passage originally was written in Clifford Chase's *Winkie* (2006), in which the title character is a sentient teddy bear abandoned in a cabin and hauled in when the FBI raids the woods looking for a mad bomber:

> The door of the cell clicked open and a plump female jailer entered, complaining to Agent Mike that the jail had no clothing on hand that would fit a traitor and murderer as puny as this one, and that something had to

THE FIRE IN FICTION

be specially ordered, which took most of the goddamn day and which the little piece of shit didn't deserve. "Put it on!" she shouted, throwing a set of gray baby clothes at the bear. The outfit fell from his grasp to the floor. "Pick it up!" she shouted now.

It seemed to take an excruciatingly long time for him to remove his hospital gown and pull on the little T-shirt and pants, and indeed Agent Mike grumbled, "Christ—finally," when Winkie was done. Glancing down at the baby outfit, the bear didn't think he could be any more humiliated than this. A row of figures was stenciled on the front.

"That's *yer number,*" said the jailer, enunciating angrily as if the suspect might not understand, or might pretend not to understand, these simple words. "From *now on.* Don't *forgit* it."

Quite different when the political prisoner is a teddy bear, isn't it? But have another look. Generating humor around this toy depends first on building the believable context for the unlikely element. In Chase's scene, the sneering contempt of the prison matron and the excruciating exchange of hospital gown for prison garb are simple devices but effective for creating irony, considering that this extreme hostility is directed at a cuddly stuffed animal.

Later in *Winkie,* Chase subjects the bear to harsh interrogation and a mock trial. Both are spun out at length and in great detail; the longer and more detailed, the funnier it gets. In other words, the humor isn't in the teddy bear itself. Hilarity springs from the bear's too-real situation. The unfortunately familiar details of torture and secret trials are what make this a parody. The bear is merely a device for making hypervigilism against terrorism look ridiculous.

Political satire exploits one of the richest veins of irony that we've got, so why aren't more novelists mining it? Perhaps because politicians are already too close to self-parody? I'm not sure, but there's no doubt that Christopher Buckley is perhaps our finest political satirist. His novel *Boomsday* (2007) tackles a dry subject—the coming retirement of the Baby Boom generation and the financial drain it will place on America—in a way that is a nonstop hoot.

The heroine of *Boomsday* is not a Boomer but a Gen X public relations whiz kid named Cassandra Devine, who writes a popular blog on which she vents her frustrations. Most recent of these is her anger over higher taxes being imposed on her generation in order to finance the Boomers' retirement. As Cassandra sees it, her future is being mortgaged so that Boomers can retire in comfort and improve their golf games.

On her blog, Cassandra urges rebellion. Attacks on retirement communities follow. Gatehouses are stormed. Golf courses are burned. Cassandra gets in trouble but she is unrepentant. She dreams up an even more outlandish idea, which she uses her promotional skill to push. The media quickly picks up on it:

> "From Washington, tonight, a *novel* proposal on how to solve the Social Security crisis. For that story, we go now to our correspondent, Betsy Blarkin."
>
> "Thanks, Katie. Cassandra Devine, the twenty-nine-year-old blogger who calls herself Cassandra, is back in the news. Last month, she urged young people not to pay taxes and to storm the gates of Boomer retirement communities.
>
> "At a press conference today, she unveiled a plan that, she says, would solve the problem by making the *government* solvent.
>
> "Her solution? The government should offer incentives to retiring Boomers—to kill themselves."
>
> "'*Americans are living longer. Okay, but why should my generation spend our lives in hock subsidizing their longevity? They want to live forever—we're saying, let them pay for it.*'"
>
> "Under Devine's plan, the government would completely eliminate estate taxes for anyone who kills themself at age seventy. Anyone agreeing to commit suicide

at age *sixty-five* would receive a *bonus*, including a two-week, all-expenses-paid 'farewell honeymoon.'

"'*Our grandparents grew up in the Depression and fought in World War Two. They were the so-called Greatest Generation. Our parents, the Baby Boomers, dodged the draft, snorted cocaine, made self-indulgence a virtue. I call them the Ungreatest Generation. Here's their chance, finally, to give something back.*'"

"Devine has even come up with a better term for suicide: 'Voluntary Transitioning.' I spoke with her earlier today after her press conference. …

"Ms. Devine, do you expect anyone to take this proposal of yours seriously?"

"*Well, Betsy, you're interviewing me on network television, so I'd say that's a good start. If you're asking why am I proposing that Americans kill themselves in large numbers, my answer is, because of the refusal of the government, again and again, to act honestly and responsibly. When Social Security began, there were fifteen workers to support one retiree. Now there are three workers per retiree. Soon it will be two. You can run from that kind of math, but you can't hide. It means that someone my age will have to spend their entire life paying unfair taxes, just so the Boomers can hit the golf course at sixty-two and drink gin and tonics until they're ninety. What happened to the American idea of leaving your kids better off than you were? If the government has a better idea, hey, we're all for it. Put it on the table. Meanwhile, we're putting this on the table. And it's not going away.*"

"A number of experts that we spoke to, including Karl Kansteiner of the Rand Institute in Washington, actually *agreed* that such a measure, however drastic, would in fact solve the Social Security and U.S. budget crisis."

"*The average American now lives to seventy-eight, seventy-nine years old. Many live much longer. We cur-*

rently are experiencing what could be called a surplus of octogenarians, nonagenarians, and even centenarians. If the government didn't have to pay benefits to these elders, say, past the age of seventy, the savings would be vast. Enormous. Indeed, tempting. Certainly, it is not a solution for, shall we say, the faint of heart."

"Others, like Gideon Payne of the Society for the Protection of Every Ribonucleic Molecule, call Devine's idea 'morally repugnant.'"

"Have we finally reached the point where we are advocating mass murder as a national policy? This entire plan, this scheme, is an abomination in the eyes of the Almighty. I tremble for my country. This woman should be ashamed."

"Cassandra Devine doesn't appear in the least ashamed. Indeed, she seems quite determined. Katie?"

"Thank you, Betsy Blarkin in Washington, for that report. Finally, tonight, Wal-Mart announced that it has obtained permission to open a one-hundred-and-fifty-thousand-square-foot megastore on the Mall, in Washington. ..."

Students of English literature will recognize in Cassandra's plan echoes of Jonathan Swift's seminal satire of the eighteenth century, the essay "A Modest Proposal," in which he proposed solving the problem of the population explosion in Ireland by eating babies. Cassandra's plan has the similar satire value, but did you also notice Buckley's deft parody of an evening news broadcast? He combines in this passage the techniques of both satire *and* parody to make a point. It isn't Boomers who are at fault; it's the U.S. government, which repeatedly ducks the coming crisis.

If you are writing a satire, studying the lengths to which these novelists go is essential. I have quoted a few choice passages above, but the novels cited generate satire over their entire lengths. They are funny for hundreds of pages. If your current manuscript is a satire, how will you sustain the hilarity? I promise you, it is more work than you imagine.

FUNNY VOICES

As I mentioned at the outset of this chapter, there are a thousand ways to be funny. Another of them can embed itself in one of the most common of elements of fiction writing: the narrative voice.

It's easiest to examine this as applied to a first-person narrator. It isn't necessarily true that a narrator needs to be a stand-up comedian, although chic-lit is full of smart-mouthed heroines, of course, as is (strangely) a genre at the opposite end of the spectrum, vampire-hunter novels. Odd and offbeat narrators can supply plenty of wry lightness even in a heavy story. Think Holden Caulfield or Forrest Gump.

Gary Shteyngart made a sparkling debut with his novel *The Russian Debutante's Handbook* (2002) but also turned in a strong sophomore title, *Absurdistan* (2006). *Absurdistan* is the story of a large (in many senses) Russian man, Misha Vainberg, who was educated in America and even has an American girlfriend, but who finds himself trapped in Russia and unable to get a new visa after his father in St. Petersburg kills an Oklahoma businessman and then turns up dead himself.

In an attempt to influence the Immigration and Naturalization Service, Misha pens his appeal, the novel, opening it in his typical vainglorious-yet-melancholy fashion:

> This book, then, is my love letter to the generals in charge of the Immigration and Naturalization Service. A love letter as well as a plea: *Gentlemen, let me back in!* I am an American impounded in a Russians' body. I have been educated at Accidental College, a venerable midwestern institution for young New York, Chicago, and San Francisco aristocrats where the virtues of democracy are often debated at teatime. I have lived in

New York for eight years, and I have been an exemplary American, contributing to the economy by spending over US$2,000,000 on legally purchased goods and services, including the world's most expensive dog leash (I briefly owned two poodles). I have dated Rouenna Sales—no, "dated" is the wrong term—I have *roused* her from the Bronx working-class nightmare of her youth and deposited her at Hunter College, where she is studying to become an executive secretary.

Now, I am certain that everyone at the Immigration and Naturalization Service is deeply familiar with Russian literature. As you read about my life and struggles in these pages, you will see certain similarities with Oblomov, the famously large gentleman who refused to stir from his couch in the nineteenth-century novel of the same name. I won't try to sway you from this analogy (I haven't the energy, for one thing), but may I suggest another possibility: Prince Myshkin from Dostoyevsky's *The Idiot*. Like the prince, I am something of a holy fool.

You have to wonder if Vainberg is being serious in addressing himself to the INS in such bombastic terms; hopefully not. Even so, his comparisons of himself to the antiheroes of Russian literature and his boasting about expensive dog collars he has purchased lend credibility to his claim of being a "holy fool." Do you get the feeling that outrageous things are going to happen to Vainberg? You would be right. His semi-crazy voice has already got our expectations in line.

Novelists who work with first-person narrators have a natural advantage when creating funny voices, but third person can work, too.

Our lord of low comedy is undoubtedly Carl Hiaasen. His sendups of Florida low-lifes, crooks, and politicians have delighted readers for a dozen outings. In *Skinny Dip* (2004), he builds a caper around the revenge scheme of heiress Joey Perrone, whose husband pushes her off the stern of a cruise ship. Never mind why. It has to do with his role in an environmental scam. Trust me, it's wacky. Anyway, you don't have to go beyond the first page for a dose of Hiaasen's signature voice:

> At the stroke of eleven on a cool April night, a woman
> named Joey Perrone went overboard from a luxury deck
> of the cruise liner M.V. *Sun Duchess*. Plunging toward the
> dark Atlantic, Joey was too dumbfounded to panic.
>
> I married an asshole, she thought, knifing headfirst
> into the waves.
>
> The impact tore off her silk skirt, blouse, panties,
> wristwatch and sandals, but Joey remained conscious
> and alert. Of course she did. She had been co-captain
> of her college swim team, a biographical nugget that
> her husband obviously had forgotten.
>
> Bobbing in its fizzy wake, Joey watched the gaily lit
> *Sun Duchess* continue steaming away at twenty nautical
> miles per hour. Evidently only one of the other 2,049
> passengers was aware of what had happened, and he
> wasn't telling anybody.
>
> Bastard, Joey thought.

How does Hiaasen send us a signal not of distress but of mirth? With his choice of words. What would be your feeling if you were plunging toward the sea from a deck railing many stories high? Joey feels "dumbfounded." Her first thought on hitting the water is "I married an asshole." What's funny here is the contrast of Joey's dire situation with her dry, understated attitude. The technique is simple.

Try it yourself. Invent any disaster, oh, say an airliner plummeting toward a remote mountainside, both its engines trailing smoke. Now play against the expected tone employing your point-of-view character:

> Figures, he thought, wouldn't you know the drinks cart
> hadn't yet reached his row? He really needed a Jack-and-
> Coke. Condemned to die, and he wasn't even getting
> a last request.

In other words, you don't have to make the events of your story funny in themselves. You don't need the zany voice of a first-person comedian. You don't need a big target like Washington, D.C. You don't need a dictionary of words that are automatically funnier than your everyday vocabulary. All you have to do is construct an unexpected contrast to what is happening.

Try it out: Dire circumstances/dry response or dry circumstances/dire response. Coffee spill? Pull the fire alarm. Dating problems? Compose a list of ten reasons why spending a year knitting pashmina shawls in a Himalayan monastery is a great idea. Get it? Or make up your own comic style. Or steal the techniques. Oscar Wilde and Dorothy Parker won't sue and couldn't anyway. They're dead.

Besides, this stuff is free.

If nothing else, try a little hyperbole. Every writer wants humor in her novel. Few have it. For me, I would settle for once in a while having my eyebrows raised or the corners of my mouth twisted into a smirk. Whether over the top or mildly heightened, witty jabs or roundhouse humor, it would be great if reading manuscripts got to be a little more fun.

Even a serious novel needs to occasionally exaggerate for effect. Try it out. Who knows? Maybe you will discover that you have the sensibility of a satirist. If so, you can make shish kebab out of everything in life that bugs you.

Then we'll all be having a nice time.

PRACTICAL TOOLS

Hyperbole

Step 1: Choose anything that a character says or thinks.

Step 2: Hyperbolize it. Exaggerate. Wildly. Go over the top, out of bounds. Make it crazy-wild.

Step 3: Substitute the hyperbole. Watch your readers smile. Okay, you're right, you usually can't see them. Just imagine it.

Step 4: Do a hyperbole draft. In your manuscript, find twenty places to hyperbolize.

Discussion: Using hyperbole is not always about getting a laugh. It is a method of useful heightening in any work of fiction. Whether it's a character or it's you, exaggeration both makes a point and scores a point.

Social Ironies and Literary Parody

Step 1: Ask your protagonist or another character to take a look around at the world. Go on. They don't have anything else to do right now.

Step 2: What seems to this character ironic, weird, stupid, or crazy? Note it.

Step 3: Somewhere in your manuscript, let your character riff on this subject. Counsel her not to hold back. It's okay. No one's listening yet. For now it's just you and her.

Step 4: Is there a literary form that can be parodied in your manuscript? Come to that, is there a business form that can be sent up? A tax form? The key is to play it straight and deadpan. Let just one element provide ridiculous contrast.

Discussion: Your novel may not be comic in intent, but a sideways glance at what is ironic or ridiculous rarely goes amiss. Parody is a little more difficult to insert in an otherwise serious novel. First try creating the parodied element without humor. For instance, realistically lay out an IRS tax form. Make it dry and tedious. Only later need you title it "1040K-9, Individual Canine Return," a form for reporting doggie income and deductions.

Funny Voices, Funny Events

Step 1: Whether using first-person or third-person narration, select a page.

Step 2: Make the narration here wry, dry, snarky, acid, off-hand, loopy, easily distracted, befuddled, paranoid, panic-stricken or whack-o in any other way that comes naturally to you.

Step 3: In your story, pick a small- or medium-sized event.

Step 4: If it's an ordinary event, make the response to it disproportionately huge. If the event is a little unusual or colorful, underplay the response.

Step 5: If the above steps add something positive to your novel, find nine more places to do something similar. If you are going for outright satire, find 150 places to do things similar.

Discussion: Finding a comic narrative tone is easier when you put yourself in the right frame of mind. Get crazy. Become obsessed. Freak out. Oh, you're paying a therapist to help you stop that? Sorry. At any rate, even a novel as serious as a thriller can at times use a little levity. Think of James Bond. Every novel should, somewhere, at least make us crack a smile.

CHAPTER EIGHT

TENSION ALL THE TIME

Unfortunately, there is no test that measures whether any given fiction writer has what it takes to be a career novelist. If it did exist, though, for me that test would put heavy emphasis on one particular trait: an instinct for tension.

Conflict *is* story. We hardly need discuss that any further. Every novelist who's gotten beyond the beginner stage knows it. What many do not grasp, though, including many published novelists, is that what keeps us turning hundreds of pages is not a central conflict, main problem, or primary goal.

Think about it. If that was all it took to keep readers involved to the end, then all you would have to do is set a principal plot problem at the outset. Then you could indulge yourself however you like for hundreds of pages.

Imagine.

Of course, it is not like that. Conflict must be present in smaller ways throughout. Most novelists understand that too, or say they do. Despite that, I am able to skim vast swaths of virtually all manuscripts and portions of many published novels.

Have you ever skimmed a novel you were reading? How much of it? A little generally is not a problem. Skim a lot, though, and you probably will give up on that book, am I right?

What is it, then, that keeps us reading all the way? Is it conflict within each scene? Is it a character in every chapter who has a clearly stated goal? Is it avoiding low-tension traps such as backstory, aftermath, landscape, and weather openings, empty exposition, and unneeded dialogue? Is it keeping the action moving? Is it throwing in sex and violence for occasional jolts of adrenalin and allure? Is it luck?

What keeps us reading every word on every page of a novel is none of that. Consider the page-turners on your shelves that *do* open with weather or scenery, or quickly dump in backstory, or linger in aftermath and indulge in exposition. How do those authors get away with it? Are they so successful that we overlook their flaws? Do they have a free pass?

Doubtful.

Conversely, think about those highly plotted, action-packed novels that didn't hold your attention. Think about the violence that moved you not at all and the sex scenes that you skipped. Weren't those novelists doing it right, writing by the rules? Then, how come you set those novels aside?

Holding readers' attention every word of the way is not a function of the type of novel, or a good premise, tight writing, quick pace, showing not telling, or any of the other frequently taught principles of storytelling. Keeping readers constantly in your grip comes from the steady application of something else altogether.

Micro-tension.

Micro-tension is the moment-by-moment tension that keeps the reader in a constant state of suspense over what will happen, not in the story but in the next few seconds. It is not a function of plot. This type of tension does not come from high stakes or the circumstances of a scene. Action does not generate it. Dialogue does not produce it automatically. Exposition—the interior monologue of the point-of-view character—does not necessarily raise its level.

When you don't have micro-tension, you are slowly losing your reader. When you do have micro-tension, you can do anything. You can open with weather, linger over the landscape, leave in backstory, describe at length, write about pure emotion, build anticipation from a wisp of atmosphere, and even make a riveting passage out of nothing at all.

Micro-tension is easily understood but hard to do. I know this because when teaching it in workshops I watch participants nod in understanding when I explain it, but see them stare helplessly at their pages when they try to do it themselves.

So, let's start with this concept: micro-tension has its basis not in story circumstances or in words: it comes from *emotions* and not just any old emotions but *conflicting emotions*.

Let's see how it works.

TENSION IN DIALOGUE

In real life most of what people say to each other is drivel. Transcripts of genuine dialogue, as in police wire taps, is a chronicle of halting, disjointed, nonlinear incoherence. Really, it's a wonder that we understand each other.

Dialogue in novels is, thank goodness, unnatural. The author has time to think it through. Characters express exactly what they mean. They speak in complete sentences. They do not get interrupted. Even so, much dialogue in manuscripts feels unimportant even when there is a lot to say.

That can be especially true when information is being exchanged. Info dump is nevertheless info dump even when it's batted back and forth in dialogue. But some authors can make an exchange of facts riveting. How do they do it? I can tell you one thing: What makes such dialogue gripping is not the inherent fascination of the topics of viral engineering, corporate case law, or somebody else's crazy family.

Early on in her novel *White Lies* (2008), Jayne Ann Krentz faces the problem of explaining to the readers the defining quality of her heroine, Clare Lancaster: She is a human lie detector. Now, this is not so unusual in the world of Krentz's Arcane Society, subject of a number of her stories. Still, being hip to every white lie you're told must be highly annoying, even paralyzing. How does Clare live with that talent?

In the following passage, Clare explains to hero and romantic interest Jake Salter (himself a parasensitive) how she copes:

"Let me get this straight," he said. "You're a human lie detector and you don't mind that most people lie?"

She smiled slightly. "Let me put it this way. When you wake up one morning at the age of thirteen and discover that because of your newly developed parsenses you can tell that everyone around you, even the people you love, lie occasionally and that you are going to be driven crazy if you don't get some perspective, you learn to get some perspective."

He was reluctantly fascinated. "Just what kind of perspective do you have on the subject?"

"I take the Darwinian view. Lying is a universal talent. Everyone I've ever known can do it rather well. Most little kids start practicing the skill as soon as they master language."

"So you figure there must be some evolutionary explanation, is that it?"

"I think so, yes," she said, calmly serious and certain. "When you look at it objectively it seems obvious that the ability to lie is part of everyone's kit of survival tools, a side effect of possessing language skills. There are a lot of situations in which the ability to lie is extremely useful. There are times when you might have to lie to protect yourself or someone else, for example."

"Okay, I get that kind of lying," he said.

"You might lie to an enemy in order to win a battle or a war. Or you might have to lie just to defend your personal privacy. People lie all the time to defuse a tense social situation or to avoid hurting someone's feelings or to calm someone who is frightened."

"True."

"The way I see it, if people couldn't lie, they probably wouldn't be able to live together in groups, at least not for very long or with any degree of sociability. And there you have the bottom line."

"What bottom line?"

She spread her hands. "If humans could not lie, civilization as we know it would cease to exist."

What is it that holds our attention in that exchange? Is it Clare's highly reasoned discourse on the importance of lying to human survival? Probably not. The tension instead comes from Jake's reluctance to accept what Clare is saying. His opening salvo sets his resistance: "Let me get this straight ..." From there onward he prompts Clare to justify her position.

In other words, it is not information itself that nails us to the page; rather, it is doubt about the facts and skepticism of the deliverer. Tension in dialogue is emotional, not intellectual. It comes from people, not topics. What we want to know is not whether a debate will settle a point of contention but whether the debaters will reconcile.

This testing and defending of the facts is, by the way, the secret behind best-selling stories that depend on large doses of explanation. Does your thriller require that the readers understand a lot about security systems? Are there complex interwoven relationships in your family drama? Do your romantic leads have many reasons to hate each other, especially arising from their past history? If so, it will be necessary to dump a lot of information on your readers.

That usually is dull. Info dump is deadly. Backstory bogs things down. Zipping up information to make it more frightening or relevant doesn't help. Information is still just information. It's dead weight. Many authors attempt to get around that by disguising info dump as dialogue, but unfortunately that does not automatically work. Dialogue drags unless it is infused with tension; but, as we've seen, even that will only be effective when it is a tug-of-war between talkers.

Dialogue between antagonists might seem an easy job, yet even there building tension depends on an artful teasing out of the hostility. The protagonist of Sara Gruen's smash bestseller *Water for Elephants* (2006) is ninety-year-old Jacob Jankowski, who is in an old-age home and not pleased to be there. In the dinner hall one evening, a new resident claims to have worked in the circus carrying water for elephants. This offends Jankowski, who calls the newcomer a liar.

"Are you calling me a liar?" he says slowly.

"If you say you carried water for elephants, I am."

The girls stare at me with open mouths. My heart's pounding. I know I shouldn't do this, but somehow I can't help myself.

"How dare you!" McGuinty braces his knobby hands on the edge of the table. Stringy tendons appear in his forearms.

"Listen pal," I say. "For decades I've heard old coots like you talk about carrying water for elephants and I'm telling you now, it never happened."

"Old coot? *Old coot?*" McGuinty pushes himself upright, sending his wheelchair flying backward. He points a gnarled finger at me and then drops as though felled by dynamite. He vanishes beneath the edge of the table, his eyes perplexed, his mouth still open.

"Nurse! Oh, Nurse!" cry the old ladies.

There's a familiar patter of crepe-soled shoes and moments later two nurses haul McGuinty up by the arms. He grumbles, making feeble attempts to shake them off.

A third nurse, a pneumatic black girl in pale pink, stands at the end of the table with her hands on her hips. "What on earth is going on?" she asks.

"That old S-O-B called me a liar, that's what," says McGuinty, safely restored to his chair. He straightens his shirt, lifts his grizzled chin, and crosses his arms in front of him. "*And* an old coot."

"Oh, I'm sure that's not what Mr. Jankowski meant," the girl in pink says.

"It most certainly is," I say. "And he is too. Pffffft. Carried water for the elephants indeed. Do you have any idea how much an elephant drinks?"

The exchange of insults between these senior citizens is hilarious enough to hold our attention; however, is it the only source of tension in this passage? Have another look. Right away, Gruen gives Jankowski inner conflict. "I know I shouldn't do this, but somehow I can't help myself." Admittedly, Jankowski doesn't try very hard to restrain his impulse, but this mild self-reproach does make us wonder if he will back off. The alarmed and disapproving reactions of the old ladies and the all-powerful nurses only emphasize that Jankowski should shut up. He doesn't, of course, and the deeper he digs himself in the more we wish he would keep quiet.

Or is it the opposite: that we are cheering him on as he defies propriety? Whatever our hope, there is delicious *inner* conflict underneath Jankowski's actions. What keeps us reading is partly a desire to learn the truth of water and elephants, but more powerfully the deeper mystery of what makes Jankowski so prickly on the subject? Gruen clearly is going to answer that question, so we eagerly read on.

What about dialogue between friends? If there is no animosity to exploit, how do you generate tension? In such dialogue the operating principle is friendly disagreement. For example, in Naomi Novik's Napoleonic-era fantasy novel *His Majesty's Dragon* (2006), the relationship between Captain Will Laurence and his battle dragon Temeraire is one of cordiality and respect. Late in the novel Temeraire saves Laurence during an aerial accident, in the process risking the life of a fellow dragon. Laurence must later address Temeraire's misaligned priorities:

> "No, not without cause," Laurence said. "But we are in a hard service, my dear, and we must sometimes be willing to bear a great deal." He hesitated, then added gently, "I have been meaning to speak to you about it, Temeraire: you must promise me in future not to place my life above that of so many others. You must surely see that Victoriatus is far more necessary to the Corps than I could ever be, even if there were not his crew to consider also; you should never have contemplated risking their lives to save mine."

Temeraire curled more closely around him. "No, Laurence, I cannot promise such a thing," he said. "I am sorry, but I will not lie to you: I could not have let you fall. You may value their lives above your own; I cannot do so, for to me you are worth more than all of them. I will not obey you in such a case, and as for duty, I do not care for the notion a great deal, the more I see of it."

Such stalwart loyalty! How noble. And how difficult for Laurence, who now has command of a dragon whom he cannot count upon to adhere to his harsh duty in battle. The strain is understated, but still it is present. The polite tone of their disagreement only underscores its importance.

Where is the tension in your dialogue? Is it present in every line? Why not undertake a dialogue draft? Check every conversation in your story. Are you relying on the circumstances or the topic itself to make it important for us to listen in?

That is dangerous. Instead, find the emotional friction between the speakers. Or externalize your focal characters' inner conflicts. Or pit allies against each other. True tension in dialogue comes not from what is being said, but from inside those who are saying it.

TENSION IN ACTION

Have you ever seen violence up close? One night when I was young my father and I rounded a bend on a Connecticut highway. Ahead of us at an intersection two cars had collided seconds before. One was engulfed in orange flames. Through its windows I could see them roiling in its interior. Sparks shot fifty feet into the air as if the wreck was a Roman candle spewing into the velvet black sky.

"Can we do anything?" I asked my father.

"No," he said slowly. "I don't think so."

Death, I realized, is not a respecter of your plans. It waits around a bend in the highway and you don't get to choose which one. More than thirty years later I can picture those flames.

By contrast, in the last few weeks I have read in novels much more gruesome and violent episodes that I do not remember at all. Perhaps that is understandable. Fiction is fiction, after all, and life is life. Still, shouldn't story violence have an impact? It should, but the truth is that on the page, on TV, and on the movie screen it often affects us very little.

To make matters worse, not all action is violent. Sometimes action merely is meant to be exciting. At other times its purpose is only to create a visual picture of the people in the story in motion. Unless it is violent, though, how is routine action supposed to keep us glued to the page? If we are honest, I think we must admit that frequently it does not. Not even high action necessarily grips us hard.

Writing together, Douglas Preston and Lincoln Child are one of our most reliable crafters of high-voltage thrillers. In their 2006 novel *The Book of the Dead*, they again feature FBI Special Agent Aloysius Pendergast in a story about an Egyptian tomb, which, while under reconstruction at the New York Museum of Natural History, causes all kinds of trouble. (Naturally, it holds a secret that could bring destruction to all of New York.) Pendergast must stop his archenemy, his brother Diogenes, from enacting his evil intentions.

Unfortunately, Pendergast is incarcerated at Herkmoor Correctional Facility, which has never had an escape. Guess what? Pendergast escapes—with considerable help from the tech wizards of his department, it must be said—in a highly planned prison break sequence that is one of the novel's high points. Pendergast first helps a group of convicts stage a diversionary escape of their own, then engineers his own liberation:

> As Glinn had anticipated, the door to guard station 7 had been left unlocked in the hasty departure of the first responders.
>
> Pendergast slipped inside, then threw an arm around the guard's neck and injected him. The guard slumped without a word and Pendergast laid him out on the floor, then half covered the guard's comm mike with his hand

and yelled hoarsely into it, "I see one of them! I'm going after him!"

He quickly undressed the unconscious guard while a burst of shouted countermands came over the speaker, ordering him to remain at his station. In less than a minute, Pendergast was dressed in the guard's uniform, equipped with badge, Mace, Taser, stick, radio, and emergency call unit. He was more slender than the unconscious guard, but a few minor adjustments rendered the disguise quite acceptable.

Next, he reached behind the large rack of servers until he had located the correct port. Then, taking the flash drive from the plastic bag, he inserted it into the port. He then turned his attention back to the guard, taping his mouth shut, his hands behind his back, and his knees together. He dragged the drugged guard back to the nearby men's room, seated him on a toilet, taped his torso to the toilet tank to keep him from falling over, locked the stall, and crawled out beneath the door.

Moving to a mirror, Pendergast pulled the bandages from his face and stuffed them into the waste can. He broke the glass capsule over a sink and massaged the dye into his hair, turning it from white blond to an unremarkable dark brown. Exiting the men's room, he walked down the hall, made a right turn, and—just before coming to the first video camera—he paused to glance at his watch: 660 seconds.

Tick, tick, tick. With clockwork precision, our hero works through every clever step of his plan. Let me ask you, did the passage quoted above have your pulse pounding? No? Does it strike you as a bit mechanical? I'm not surprised.

Granted, we have not experienced the long buildup of Herkmoor's invincible security. We haven't watched as the groundwork of the plan was laid. I've left out some of Pendergast's remarkable feats later in the sequence, too, as when he yanks a line of stitches from his face in order to cover himself in blood. It's a really cunning plan, trust me, and it works. But it's cold. We admire it more than feel it.

Undoubtedly that was the authors' intention, but I believe this passage illustrates that action, when related in strictly visual terms, feels flat. Handled objectively, it does not move us. Emotions are needed to give action force.

Even then, routine emotions are unlikely to get through to us. Fear! Shock! Horror! *Uh-huh. What else have you got?* We are inured to clichés, and that is as true of overused feelings as it is of familiar words and phrases. How to be original in inserting emotions into fast-moving action? Sometimes nothing more is required than honesty, authenticity, and understatement.

Harlan Coben's first stand-alone thriller, *Tell No One* (2001), established Coben's mastery of twisty thrillers. Like Coben's follow-up novels, *Tell No One* is predicated on the possibility that someone who is dead and gone has come back; in this case it's the missing and presumed dead wife of Dr. David Beck, who, it transpires, may still be alive.

David Beck will go to a lot of trouble to find out whether or not mystery e-mails are coming from his wife, but in order for that to be credible Coben knows that we must first believe that Elizabeth was the love of David's life. Coben manages this in a scene that recounts Elizabeth and David's annual ritual of returning to the lakeside camp that was the site of their first teenage kiss. After they have finished making love, David and Elizabeth swim and relax:

> I put my hands behind my head and lay back. A cloud passed in front of the moon, turning the blue night into something pallid and gray. The air was still. I could hear Elizabeth getting out of the water and stepping onto the dock. My eyes tried to adjust. I could barely make out her naked silhouette. She was, quite simply, breathtaking. I watched her bend at the waist and wring the water out of her hair. Then she arched her spine and threw back her head.

My raft drifted farther away from shore. I tried to sift through what had happened to me, but even I didn't understand it all. The raft kept moving. I started losing sight of Elizabeth. As she faded into the dark, I made a decision: I would tell her. I would tell her everything.

I nodded to myself and closed my eyes. There was a lightness in my chest now. I listened to the water gently lap against my raft.

Then I heard a car door open.

I sat up.

"Elizabeth?"

Pure silence, except for my own breathing.

I looked for her silhouette again. It was hard to make out, but for a moment I saw it. Or I thought I saw it. I'm not sure anymore or even if it matters. Either way, Elizabeth was standing perfectly still, and maybe she was facing me.

I might have blinked—I'm really not sure about that either—and when I looked again, Elizabeth was gone.

As action goes, this is pretty tame. A raft drifts. A car door opens. A woman winks from sight. Despite that, wouldn't you agree that this passage is arresting? What makes it so? Is it the nude Elizabeth wringing out her wet hair? That's nice, I'll admit, but I think that what gives this passage its high tension is the contrast between the peace that follows David's decision ("I would tell her everything") and the menacing physical details that quickly follow.

Coben does not need to tell us that David is deeply in love, nor does he need to elaborate that David feels guilty because he is hiding something. That is obvious. (What was it that David planned to confess? Coben makes us wait until the final page to find out.) It is the mix of David's contentment and guilt that snares us in his moment. They are contrasting emotions, almost opposites. They get us because they are difficult to reconcile—and that's the point.

Because we cannot square David's peace and David's torment, we want to. Unconsciously, our brains are seeking to make sense of a contradiction. To work on that we ... well, what do you suppose?

We keep reading.

So, of the above two excerpts, which one has more action? Preston and Child's. Which one has more tension? Coben's. That is weird because less is happening, but it makes perfect sense once you realize that tension in action comes not from the action itself but from inside the point-of-view character experiencing it.

TENSION IN EXPOSITION

Most novels today are written in an intimate third-person point of view. That is to say, we experience the story from inside the head and heart of a point-of-view character. We see what she sees, hear what she hears, think and feel what she thinks and feels. We become the character.

There are many exceptions, of course, but it is a rare novel that does not include healthy doses of what's going on inside its characters' minds. Relating that on the page is an art that is poorly understood. Many novelists merely write out whatever it is that their characters are thinking and feeling; or, more to the point, whatever happens to occur to the author in a given writing session. That is a mistake.

Much exposition stirs faint interest. Pick up any novel off your shelves and read a few pages with a purple highlighter in your hand. Draw a wavy line through the passages that you skim. Your eyes skip lightly over quite a bit, don't they? Much of what you skim is exposition, isn't it? Why doesn't it work?

To write a page-turner means to make it so that your readers read every line on every page. Don't think that because you are writing literary fiction, say, instead of big thrillers that this isn't as important for you. It probably is *more* important, because the subjects of a lot of literary fiction, such as characters' emotional damage, for instance, require that the interior lives of the characters create constant tension.

In other words, exposition always matters. Yet the exposition in many manuscripts and published novels gets the purple highlighter. The most common reason is that such exposition merely restates what is obvious from what we have read: emotions that we felt earlier, thoughts that have already occurred to us. My private term for this is *churning exposition*. It's easy to skim because there's nothing new in it.

Scott Westerfeld's series of futuristic young adult novels—*Uglies* (2005), *Pretties* (2005), *Specials* (2006) and the companion novel *Extras* (2007)—has been a big hit with young readers. The stories are set in a future world where at age sixteen kids are given an operation that makes them perfectly beautiful, thus erasing troublesome differences, jealousy, and conflict. That's the theory. But of course teenage angst doesn't go away just because everyone looks like a supermodel.

The second volume, *Pretties*, finds heroine Tally Youngblood settling into her perfect life as a Pretty, enjoying parties, drinking, and pig-out meals that are easily purged with a pill. Everything is bubbly except that Tally wants to be accepted into one of the New Pretty Town cliques, the Crims. The party at which the Crims are to vote on her is marred by a visit from a masked Ugly from her past, the intrusion of the enforcement Specials, a dive from a balcony, and a cut on her forehead. Despite this, Tally is admitted to the Crims.

Back home at her apartment, Tally listens to a ping (voice message) from friend Peris with the good news, and then digests what it means for her:

> As the message ended, Tally felt the bed spin a little. She closed her eyes and let out a long, slow sign of relief. Finally, she was a full-fledged Crim. Everything she'd ever wanted had come to her at last. She was beautiful, and she lived in New Pretty Town with Peris and Shay and tons of new friends. All the disasters and terrors of the last year—running away to the Smoke, living there in pre-Rusty squalor, traveling back to the city through the wilds—somehow all of it had worked out.
>
> It was so wonderful, and Tally was so exhausted, that belief took a while to settle over her. She replayed Peris's message a few times, then pulled off the smelly Smokey sweater with shaking hands and threw it into the corner. Tomorrow, she would *make* the hole in the wall recycle it.

Tally lay back and stared at the ceiling for a while. A ping from Shay came, but she ignored it, setting her interface ring to sleeptime. With everything so perfect, reality seemed somehow fragile, as if the slightest interruption could imperil her pretty future. The bed beneath her, Komachi Mansion, and even the city around her—all of it felt as tenuous as a soap bubble, shivering and empty.

It was probably just the knock to her head causing the weird missingness that underlay her joy. She only needed a good night's sleep—and hopefully no hangover tomorrow—and everything would feel solid again, as perfect as it really was.

Tally fell asleep a few minutes later, happy to be a Crim at last.

But her dreams were totally bogus.

Needless to say, what's going on in Tally's world is not so nice. Pretties, as well as being made beautiful, also are inflicted with brain lesions that make them lazy, self-centered, and conformist; that is to say, manageable. Although she has temporarily forgotten, Tally is an Ugly who volunteered to become a Pretty in order to test a pill that will reverse the effects of the brain lesions. Tally is in for more trouble.

Take a second look at the passage above. Overtly, all it does is state what we already know Tally will feel upon being made a Crim: happiness. The end of the passage hints that this happiness is "tenuous as a soap bubble, shivering and empty." Even before that, though, Tally is trying too hard to convince herself that her life is now perfect, that "all of it had worked out." Westerfeld overemphasizes her elation to get us to anticipate that it is "bogus," and so we do.

Westerfeld constructs conflicting feelings in this passage. On the one hand Tally is happy, relieved, and content. On the other, she is worried. We unconsciously want her conflict resolved, and so this simple dichotomy causes us to continue reading to see what will happen.

The same effect can be produced when it's not emotions that are involved, but ideas. Thinking can be as conflicted as feeling. Pure intellectual debate is not often found in fiction for the simple reason that it is dry, but even so, wrestling with one's own mind can produce dramatic tension.

In 1980, novelist Marilynne Robinson's *Housekeeping* won a Hemingway Foundation/PEN Award for best first novel, and was also nominated for the Pulitzer Prize. Her second novel, *Gilead* (2004), came twenty-four years later. This time she won both the Pulitzer Prize and the National Book Critics Circle Award for Fiction.

In *Gilead*, the year is 1956. Seventy-six-year-old Rev. John Ames is ailing and writing an account of his life and faith for his six-year-old son by his second, and much younger, wife. Ames meditates upon his grandfather, his father, his sermons, and his struggles, especially his struggle to find Christian forgiveness with respect to John Ames Boughton, the ne'er-do-well son of his best friend and his namesake. Late in the novel Rev. Ames hits a point where forgiveness completely eludes him:

> I have wandered to the limits of my understanding any number of times, out into that desolation, that Horeb, that Kansas, and I've scared myself, too, a good many times, leaving all landmarks behind me, or so it seemed. And it has been among the true pleasures of my life. Night and light, silence and difficulty, it seemed to me always rigorous and good. I believe it was recommended to me by Edward, and also by my reverend grandfather when he made his last flight into the wilderness. I may once have fancied myself such another tough old man, ready to dive into the ground and smolder away the time till Judgment. Well, I am distracted from that project now. My present bewilderments are a new territory that make me doubt I have ever really been lost before.

Admittedly, Robinson's dense prose isn't easy to gloss. Give yourself some time—can I offer you a cup of coppery Ceylon tea?—and reread the passage at your leisure. It's quite beautiful. Have you ever described frustration as a "Kansas"? Have you ever felt that your own sense of inadequacy is "rigorous and good"? Ames stretches to find the beauty in being unable to find forgiveness in his heart.

Is he successful? I'll leave that decision to you. What interests me is that Robinson plagues Ames's mind with contradictory concepts: judgment vs. forgiveness. He tries to find beauty in his dilemma. He is searching for grace and not finding it. Despite that, his attempt to feel good about his desolation is simultaneously a deep expression of his faith. Ames is fighting a battle between conflicting ideas and thus we have a strong reason to keep reading. How will it come out for Ames? Fifty-five pages later in *Gilead* you will find out.

How do you handle exposition? Are there passages of interior monologue in your manuscript that are just taking up space? If there are, you can cut them, or possibly you can dig deeper into your character at this moment in the story and find inside of him contradictions, dilemmas, opposing impulses, and clashing ideas that keep us in suspense.

To put it another way, exposition is an opportunity not to enhance the dangers of the plot (exposition doesn't do that) but to put your characters' hearts and minds in peril. Remember, though, that true tension in exposition comes not from circular worry or repetitive turmoil; it springs from emotions in conflict and ideas at war.

TRANSFORMING LOW-TENSION TRAPS

Weather openings are common—and dull. At my office, we toss them aside with grunts of impatience. "Weather opening" somebody mutters, and we all nod. Most writers are trying to use the weather as foreshadowing, a hint of storms to come. That's fine, but most of the time tension wafts away.

The Uses of Enchantment (2006) was Heidi Julavits's third novel, following *The Mineral Palace* (2000) and *The Effect of Living Backwards* (2003). It begins one afternoon in 1985 when a sixteen-year-old girl, Mary Veal, disappears from the grounds of her prep school in the Boston suburb of West Salem, Massachusetts. Julavits begins her opening this way:

> The following might have happened on a late-fall afternoon in the Boston suburb of West Salem. The afternoon in question was biting enough to suggest the early possibility of snow. The cloud cover made it seem later than the actual time of 3:35 P.M.
>
> The girl was one of many girls in field hockey skirts, sweatpants, and ski shells, huddled together in the green lean-to emblazoned with Semmering Academy's scripted *S*. It had rained all morning and all afternoon; though the rain had temporarily ceased, the playing field remained a patchwork of brown grass and mud bordered by a rain-swept chalk line. Last month a Semmering wing had torn an ankle tendon in similarly poor conditions, but the referee refused to call the game until 4 p.m. because the preparatory school extracurricular activities rules and regulations handbook stipulated that "sporting events shall not be canceled due to weather until one hour past the official start time."
>
> At 3:37, the rain recommenced. The girls whined and shivered while Coach Betsy glowered beneath the brim of her UMASS CREW baseball cap. These girls were not tough girls and they had little incentive, given their eight-game losing streak, to endure a rainy November afternoon.
>
> At 3:42, the girl asked Coach Betsy if she could be excused to the field house. The girl did not say, but she implied that she had her period. Coach Betsy nodded her reluctant permission. The girl departed from the lean-to, unnoticed by her teammates.

The Uses of Enchantment got many starred and glowing reviews, and yet it opens with the weather. What gives? Are rainy November afternoons inherently more interesting in Massachusetts, or because the author's previous two novels were notable? Is it actually the girls in their field hockey skirts that hook our attention? I don't think so.

Julavits uses the drizzle not to invoke atmosphere but as a concrete factor in the story's kickoff, or rather, as an element in the doubt she is planting. Check again her opening line: "The following *might* have happened on a late-fall afternoon ..." (emphasis mine). You may not notice it, it passes so quickly, but that tricky little phrase triggers subconscious suspicions. Is the author telling us the truth?

Julavits deepens the mystery as Mary Veal goes not to the locker room but across the street to clamber into a lurking Mercedes—or does she? The remainder of the novel, inspired in part by Freud's "Dora" case history, teases us with the truth. The weather, here, is not the point. The point is that everybody, including the author, spins their stories in ways that serve their unconscious desires and needs.

To put it differently, the weather has an effect on us not because it is an outward portent but because it is tied to an inward storm. A lightning flash in the sky is just a cliché until it is fused to a bolt of interior tension. Describe the plain old weather and who cares? Provoke anxiety in the readers first and then—*brrr*—the icy November drizzle gives us a chill.

Surveying-the-landscape openings are just as common as weather starts, and equally ineffective. Most of the time. Reed Farrel Coleman's mystery novel *Soul Patch* (2007), discussed previously in chapter four, was a nominee for the Edgar Award for Best Novel. Coleman's gritty series is set in Brooklyn, in this case on Coney Island. Coleman opens *Soul Patch* with the following take on his setting:

> Nothing is so sad as an empty amusement park. And no amusement park is so sad as Coney Island. Once the world's playground, it is no longer the world's anything; not even important enough to be forgotten. Coney Island is the metal basket at the bottom of Brooklyn's sink. So it is that when the County of Kings is stood on end, Coney Island will trap all the detritus, human and otherwise, before it pours into the Atlantic.

Coney Island's demise would be easy to blame on the urban planners, especially Robert Moses, who thought it best to warehouse the niggers, spics and white trash far away from the crown jewel of Manhattan in distant outposts like Rockaway and Coney Island. If they could have built their ugly shoe box housing projects on the moon, they would have. It is no accident that the subway rides from Coney Island and Rockaway to Manhattan are two of the longest in the system. But Coney Island's decay is as much a product of its birth as anything else.

Coney Island, the rusted remnants of its antiquated rides rising out of the ocean like the fossils of beached dinosaurs, clings to a comatose existence. Like the senile genius, Coney Island has lived just long enough to mock itself. And nothing epitomizes its ironic folly better than the parachute jump. A ploughman's Eiffel Tower, its skeleton soars two hundred and fifty feet straight up off the grounds of what had once been Steeplechase Park. But the parachutes are long gone and now only the looming superstructure remains, the sea air feasting on its impotent bones.

So what is it about Coney Island that gives it extra interest? Is it the details of its decline? Is it the thumbnail history? I'd say neither. In fact, as presented there is nothing inherently interesting about Coney Island at all. That's the point. It's the ragged end of nowhere. There's nothing left of it.

Nothing, that is, except the evident sadness—or is it anger?—that the narrator feels about the state of this one-time seaside playground. Read the passage again. Is this narrator dispassionate? Hardly. Is Coney Island itself to blame for its misery? That explanation doesn't satisfy me, but that's not important. What keeps me reading is that the narrator demands an answer to an impossible question. He needs to understand something that cannot be understood. Tension exists not in the place itself but inside the one observing it.

Backstory is the bane of virtually all manuscripts. Authors imagine that readers need, even want, a certain amount of filling in. I can see why they believe that. It starts with critique groups in which writers hear comments such as, "I love this character! You need to tell me more about her!" Yes, the author does. But not right away. As they say in the theater, make 'em wait. Later in the novel backstory can become a revelation; in the first chapter it always bogs things down.

But there are exceptions. Robin Hobb's The Farseer Trilogy revolves around power struggles in the kingdom of the Six Duchies. The second volume, *Royal Assassin* (1996), places young FitzChivalry Farseer into the middle of this mess, charged with protecting the heir apparent while an invasion looms, a usurper schemes, and the king is dying. As the novel opens, Fitz quietly occupies himself with writing a treatise on magic:

> Why is it forbidden to write down specific knowl-
> edge of the magics? Perhaps because we all fear that
> such knowledge would fall into the hands of one not
> worthy to use it.

Right away, Hobb creates below-the-radar apprehension in the readers. Will Fitz get into trouble for setting down his knowledge? Will his discourse on magic fall into the wrong hands? Is he himself unworthy in some way to handle magic entrusted to him? Fitz even pauses in his writing to question his own understanding:

> But when I sit down to the task, I hesitate. Who am
> I to set my will against the wisdom of those who have
> gone before me?

Hobb does not rely on any hypothetical inherent interest in how magic works in her world to carry the readers along. Wisely, she knows that it is Fitz's own inner conflict that makes his musings matter. A little later in the opening, Hobb takes Fitz on a deeper exploration of his motives and, therefore, his fitness (or not) to employ magic:

Power. I do not think I ever wanted it for its own sake. I thirsted for it, sometimes, when I was ground down, or when those close to me suffered beneath ones who abused their powers. Wealth. I never really considered it. From the moment that I, his bastard grandson, pledged myself to King Shrewd, he always saw to it that all my needs were fulfilled. I had plenty to eat, more education than I sometimes cared for, clothes both simple and annoyingly fashionable, and often enough a coin or two of my own to spend. Growing up in Buckkeep, that was wealth enough and more than most boys in Buckkeep Town could claim. Love? Well. My horse Sooty was fond enough of me, in her own placid way. I had the true-hearted loyalty of a hound named Nosy, and that took him to his grave. I was given the fiercest of loves by a terrier pup, and it was likewise the death of him. I wince to think of the price willingly paid for loving me.

Always I have possessed the loneliness of one raised amid intrigues and clustering secrets, the isolation of a boy who cannot trust the completeness of his heart to anyone. I could not go to Fedwren, the court scribe, who praised me for my neat lettering and well-inked illustrations, and confide that I was already apprenticed to the royal assassin, and thus could not follow his writing trade. Nor could I divulge to Chade, my master in the Diplomacy of the Knife, the frustrating brutality I endured trying to learn the ways of the Skill from Galen the Skill Master. And to no one did I dare speak openly of my emerging proclivity for the Wit, the ancient beast magic, said to be a perversion and a taint to any who used it.

Not even to Molly.

Notice how much backstory Hobb slips into the above. We learn a lot about what happened to Fitz in the trilogy's first volume. But is that the point of the passage? No; it is, rather, to develop Fitz's sense of duty toward King Shrewd and set it against his feelings of isolation.

He can confide his problems to no one yet he longs to open his heart. You see? Inner tension. That in turn stirs our own curiosity to learn what will happen to Fitz. Nothing in the backstory itself does that; only Fitz's torn emotions cause us to care.

To put it more simply, Hobbs uses the past to create present conflict. That is the secret of making backstory work.

There was a time when aftermath passages were considered essential to a novel. Even today, some fiction instructors preach the pattern of scene-sequel-scene. The theory goes that after a significant story development, the protagonist (and the readers) needs a pause to digest the significance of this new situation, to make decisions and gather resolve to go forward.

I do not believe in aftermath. The human brain moves faster than any author's fingers can type. The importance of any plot turn is, for most readers, immediately apparent. Mulling it over on the page doesn't add anything fresh. The readers' minds are already racing ahead. In any event, I find that most aftermath is the easiest material in any manuscript to skim. It lacks tension.

Usually.

Kim Edwards wrote a major bestseller in *The Memory Keeper's Daughter* (2005), the story of a doctor, David Henry, who on a snowy night in 1964 finds that he must handle his pregnant wife's delivery, aided only by nurse Caroline Gill. Two babies are born, one a healthy son and the other a daughter with all the indicators of Down's syndrome. Dr. Henry tells his wife that the daughter died, but secretly instructs the nurse to bring the baby to an institution.

Caroline Gill instead contemplates raising the handicapped girl herself. Dr. Henry learns of this and washes his hands of the matter. He wants to know nothing about it and wants his family to remain ignorant, a decision that will haunt everyone involved for years. Following this scene with Dr. Henry, Caroline considers the choice she must make:

> He left, then, and everything was the same as it had
> been: the clock on the mantel, the square of light on
> the floor, the sharp shadows of bare branches. In a few

THE FIRE IN FICTION

weeks the new leaves would come, feathering out on the trees and changing the shapes on the floors. She had seen all this so many times, and yet the room seemed strangely impersonal now, as if she had never lived here at all. Over the years she had bought very few things for herself, being naturally frugal and imagining, always, that her real life would happen elsewhere. The plaid sofa, the matching chair—she liked this furniture well enough, she had chosen it herself, but she saw now that she could easily leave it. Leave all of it, she supposed, looking around at the framed prints of landscapes, the wicker magazine rack by the sofa, the low coffee table. Her own apartment seemed suddenly no more personal than a waiting room in any clinic in any town. And what else, after all, had she been doing here all these years but waiting?

She tried to silence her thoughts. Surely there was another, less dramatic way. That's what her mother would have said, shaking her head, telling her not to play Sarah Bernhardt. Caroline hadn't known for years who Sarah Bernhardt was, but she knew well enough her mother's meaning: any excess of emotion was a bad thing, disruptive to the calm order of their days. So Caroline had checked all her emotions, as one would check a coat. She had put them aside and imagined that she'd retrieve them later, but of course she never had, not until she had taken the baby from Dr. Henry's arms. So something had begun, and now she could not stop it. Twin threads ran through her: fear and excitement. She would leave this place today. She could start a new life somewhere else. She would have to do that, anyway, no matter what she decided to do about the baby. This was a small town; she couldn't go to the grocery store without running into an acquaintance. She imagined Lucy Martin's eyes growing wide, the secret pleasure as she relayed Caroline's lies, her affection for this discarded baby. *Poor old spinster,* people would say of her, *longing so desperately for a baby of her own.*

I'll leave it in your hands, Caroline. His face aged, clenched like a walnut.

"Everything was the same," Edwards writes, but of course it isn't. What has changed? Not the room or the light or the coming spring. What's different is Caroline's perception. Still, Edwards does not leave it at that. From this foundation she erects the tower of Caroline's looming decision. Caroline is not a Sarah Bernhardt, a person given to dramatic and emotionally driven actions. On the other hand, if she keeps the baby she cannot stay in her gossipy small town. "Twin threads ran through her: fear and excitement."

And there you have it: emotional conflict. Competing desires, be safe or be happy. What keeps us reading here is not Caroline's mulling of the pros and cons. We know those. It's her indecision itself. What will she do? You can pretty much guess but even so Edwards keeps a modicum of mystery going by detailing Caroline's inner struggle. Onward we read.

Tension in aftermath comes not from contemplation but from inner conflict.

Also easy to skim in many manuscripts is travel. What does it take to bring us along for the ride? Swiss novelist Pascal Mercier's *Night Train to Lisbon* (2004) spent 140 weeks on the best-seller list in Germany. It's the story of a knowledgeable but unadventurous classics instructor, Raimund Gregorius, whose chance encounter with a Portuguese woman on a rain-slicked bridge awakens him to life. Intrigued soon thereafter by a Portuguese doctor and essayist named Amadeu de Prado, Gregorius impulsively embarks on the night train to Lisbon, there to seek more knowledge of that author. The journey takes him through Paris:

> An hour to Paris. Gregorius sat down in the dining car and looked out into a bright, early spring day. And there, all of a sudden, he realized that he was in fact making this

trip—that it wasn't only a possibility, something he had thought up on a sleepless night and that could have been, but something that really and truly was taking place. And the more space he gave this feeling, the more it seemed to him that the relation of possibility and reailty were beginning to change. Kägi, his school and all the students in his notebook had existed, but only as possibilities that had been accidentally realized. But what he was experiencing in this moment—the sliding and muted thunder of the train, the slight clink of the glasses moving on the next table, the odor of rancid oil coming from the kitchen, the smoke of the cigarette the cook now and then puffed—possessed a reality that had nothing to do with mere possibility or with realized possibility, which was instead pure and simple reality, filled with the density and overwhelming inevitability making something utterly real.

Gregorius sat before the empty plate and the steaming cup of coffee and had the feeling of never having been so awake in his whole life. And it seemed to him that it wasn't a matter of degree, as when you slowly shook off sleep and became more awake until you were fully there. It was different. It was a different, new *kind* of wakefulness, a new kind of being in the world he had never known before. When the Gare de Lyon came in sight, he went back to his seat and afterward, when he set foot on the platform, it seemed to him as if, for the first time, he was fully aware of getting off a train.

Do you often contemplate the relationship of *possibility* and *reality*? I don't, I have to admit, but the vividness of Gregorius's interior life on his trip makes the journey unusually absorbing. Mercier uses the details of the dining car not to set the scene but in service of a moment of awareness: For the first time Gregorius is fully present on a train, his travel not theoretical or planned, and therefore more real. As great as the distance he has traveled to Paris is, the distance between his old and new self is even greater.

It is not the road that keeps us reading but the inner life of the traveler. Note, though, that in the passage above Mercier does not simply relate how his protagonist feels. It is more dynamic than that. Change is delineated, and that in turn raises anticipation in us. What is going to happen to Gregorius? For now it doesn't matter. The change in him is enough to keep us engaged for a while longer.

Violence ought to be a sure-fire attention grabber, but in the majority of manuscripts it is easy to skip through. That is especially true of stalker-killer scenes, easily the most common scene in unpublished fiction. You know how it goes: a ruthless, cold-blooded killer stakes out a victim, creeps up and ... *Noooo!* ... kills him. Such scenes always fall flat.

Vince Flynn is a top writer of political thrillers. In *Consent to Kill* (2005), Flynn has a Saudi billionaire put a $20 million bounty on the head of Flynn's series hero, CIA assassin Mitch Rapp, and naturally the finest killers in the business are eager to fulfill the contract. To heighten the danger, Flynn needs to show these killers in action, and so one of them assassinates a Turkish banker with icy sangfroid:

> He glanced over the top of the paper and made brief eye contact with the man he was about to kill. Casually, he pretended to return his attention to the paper. He glanced across the lake and then to the left. There were a few people about. None of them were close and he doubted they were paying attention. He was now only steps away, and he could see from his peripheral vision that the target was turning away from him. Humans, the only animals in all of nature who willingly turned their back to a potential predator. Harry was almost disgusted with how easy this was going to be.
>
> Stepping toward the target, he followed him quietly for a few steps as the man walked toward the weeping willow. This was turning into a joke. The tree with its drooping wispy branches was the closest thing the park

had to a dark alley, and the Turk was headed right for it. He stopped just short of the outer ring of branches and started to look toward the lake, undoubtedly expecting to see the pedestrian who had interrupted his privacy continuing on his way.

The assassin did not extend the newspaper-encased weapon. He was too practiced for anything so obvious. He merely tiled the paper forward until the angle matched the trajectory that he wanted the bullet to travel. He squeezed the trigger once, and stepped quickly forward. The hollow-tipped bullet struck the Turk directly in the back of the head, flattening on impact, doubling in circumference, and tearing through vital brain matter until it stopped, lodged between the shredded left front lobe and the inner wall of the skull. The impact propelled the financier forward. The assassin had his right hand around the man's chest a split second later. He glanced down at the small coin-size entry wound as he went with the momentum of the Turk's dying body. The newspaper-laded hand cut a swath through the dense branches of the weeping willow, and two steps later he laid the dead man to rest at the foot of the tree. Harry quickly checked himself for blood even though he was almost positive there would be none. The bullet was designed to stay in the body and cause only a small entry wound.

With everything in order, he left the dead body and the shelter of the tree and began retracing his steps. A hundred meters back down the footpath he asked his partner, "Are you free for an early lunch?"

What makes this killer scary? Is it his precision? His bloodless hollow-tipped bullets? His appetite for an early lunch? I would say it is none of those things but rather the line: "Harry was almost disgusted with how easy this was going to be." There isn't enough challenge. This killer craves the thrill of the hunt and is contemptuous when he doesn't get it. I don't know about you, but those mixed feelings make me wonder how Mitch Rapp is going to fare against this whacko.

And so I keep reading.

There is plenty of writing advice on the Web, but no subject inspires so much discussion as sex. Opinions on the best approach to sex scenes are diverse but on one point pretty much everyone agrees: Everyone else writes them badly. That is not surprising. Arousal is a highly individual matter. Your turn on is my turn off. Bulging muscles? Bubble baths? You'd think writers were debating free trade.

There is a second point of agreement, which is that mechanical tab-A-into-slot-B descriptions of the physical act are not arousing. After that it's pretty much a matter of atmosphere, suggestion, and metaphor. How to get it right? It may feel as frustrating as getting that first big score but there's a move that may help: inner conflict.

Jennifer Stevenson's *The Brass Bed* (2008) is the first of a funny urban fantasy trilogy revolving around, guess what, a brass bed. This one is a little different, though. This brass bed is an antique. And haunted. Two centuries ago an English lord offended a witch by being haughtily careless of whether she was satisfied. She magically bound him to the brass bed. Her spell cannot be broken until he satisfies one hundred women. Flash forward. In present day Chicago the brass bed is a prop in a fraudulent sex therapy practice.

Fraud inspector Jewel Heiss goes undercover, as it were, to show that miracle-cure claims for the brass bed are false, unaware that she is woman No. 100 to climb aboard. She dozes and in a dream finds herself in a conference room at the Department of Consumer Services, where a hunk appears:

> *I must be dreaming.* No buff guys ever came within a thousand miles of the Department of Consumer Services. She looked across the conference table at the hunk's unbelievably beefy shoulders and the set of his noble head, like the head of a particularly elegant horse, all dark masculine strength and grace.
>
> He looked right at her. *I'm definitely dreaming.* With all the perky size-five investigators in the room, he

was looking at a six-foot, size-eighteen, dairy-farmer's daughter? He'd be wasted on the size fives. Here was a man big enough for her.

He stood up and beckoned to her. Man, oh, man, was he big. The size fives disappeared, along with the Supervisors in Charge of Talking Slowly at Meetings and the doughnuts and coffee. Good thing, because he was reaching across the table and dragging her by the shoulders into his arms. She was startled at how warm and real his hands felt on her shoulders. In a dream you expect something vague.

Nothing vague about his kiss. Masterful and hot, and yet his lips were cushiony.

She reveled in the dream kiss, letting her back melt against him, letting herself droop across the conference table as if her bodice were being ripped away by a medieval knight, a hunk, half-naked medieval knight who kneaded her bare breasts with strong, hot hands, oh, man, oh *man*!

"Where did you come from?" she murmured when his mouth lifted from hers.

"1811," he said ...

Is "big" your thing? Medieval knights? It doesn't matter. This isn't your idea of perfect seduction, nor mine (although the conference room table is appealing). Since it isn't the particular details with which Stevenson is working that are working on you, what is? Read the passage again. What creates tension is Jewel's simple disbelief at what is happening: "With all the perky size-five investigators in the room, he was looking at a six-foot, size-eighteen, dairy-farmer's daughter?" She wants him yet can't believe that he wants her. *Voilà.* Conflict. Will she get him?

Duh. Of course. Yet it's the uncertainty underlying Jewel's experience that keeps us reading to see how things will turn out. In sex scenes as much as any other part of fiction, true tension flows not from the outer actions but from the inner conflict.

TENSION WHERE THERE IS NONE

Certain passages in manuscripts are antithetical to tension. Among these are passages of description. Ask readers and most will agree: It is the thing that they almost always skim.

How can you remedy that? For the setting of *The Reserve* (2008), esteemed novelist Russell Banks, known especially for *Cloudsplitter* (1998), turns to the rich men's getaway region of the Adirondack Mountains in the 1930s. There he spins the tragic story of left-leaning, married artist Jordan Groves, who becomes romantically entangled with femme fatale Vanessa Cole (discussed in chapter two), a twice-divorced beauty with hidden mental problems. Early in the novel, Banks describes Jordan's Adirondack home:

> The house was an attractive, sprawling, physically comfortable, but essentially masculine structure. Jordan had designed it, in consultation with Alicia, naturally, and had done most of the construction himself, in the process teaching himself basic plumbing, wiring, and masonry. Carpentry had been his father's trade, and Jordan, an only child, had learned it working alongside him as an adolescent and, briefly, after he came home from the war. The unconventional layout of the house and the strict use of local materials and even the fine details of the interior—banister rails made from interwoven deer antlers, yellow birch cabinets with birch bark glued to the facing, hidden dressers built into the walls, and elaborately contrived storage units, with no clutter anywhere and minimal furniture—reflected almost entirely Jordan's taste and requirements, not Alicia's. None of the windows had curtains or drapes or even shades to block the light, and during the daytime the house seemed almost to be part of the forest that surrounded it. And at night the darkness outside rushed in. ...

What strikes you most about Jordan Groves's house? Is it the banisters made from interwoven deer antlers? Is it the portentous hidden drawers or unadorned windows that let the outer darkness in? The house is indeed a model of rustic Adirondack style, but by themselves those are just empty details.

It is the truth behind them that makes them matter: The house is entirely an expression of the masculine needs and ego of Jordan Groves. Banks's passage is littered with foreshadowing, but that too would have little effect if he did not first clue us in to Groves's own selfishness, which will be his undoing.

Banks understands what I wish more novelists would grasp: Description itself does nothing to create tension; tension comes only from within the people in the landscape. A house is just a house until it is occupied by people with problems. When the problems are presented first, then the house builds a metaphor.

Similarly, description of anything can create tension by working backwards to make plain the conflicts of the observer. How would you describe a yak? Let's take a look at how satirist Christopher Moore does it. Moore's novel *Lamb* (2002) is subtitled *The Gospel According to Biff, Christ's Childhood Pal*, which tells you pretty much what you need to know. Biff and Josh, as Christ is called, take a road trip across Asia and the Middle East during Josh's formative years. At one point, while killing time at a monastery in China, Biff is put in charge of the monks' yaks:

> A yak is an extremely large, extremely hairy, buffalo-like animal with dangerous-looking black horns. If you've ever seen a water buffalo, imagine it wearing a full-body wig that drags the ground. Now sprinkle it with musk, manure, and sour milk: you've got yourself a yak. In a cavelike stable, the monks kept one female yak, which they let out during the day to wander the mountain paths to graze. On what, I don't know. There didn't seem to be enough living plant life to support an animal of that size (the yak's shoulder was higher than my head), but there didn't seem to be enough plant life in all of Judea for a herd of goats, either, and herding was one of the main occupations. What did I know?

The yak provided just enough milk and cheese to remind the monks that they didn't get enough milk and cheese from one yak for twenty-two monks. The animal also provided a long, coarse wool which needed to be harvested twice a year. This venerated duty, along with combing the crap and grass and burrs out of the wool, fell to me. There's not much to know about yaks beyond that, except for one important fact that Gaspar felt I needed to learn through practice: yaks hate to be shaved.

Oh, that Biff. What a cut up. What would you say is his attitude toward yaks? Conflicted? I'd agree. More to the point, what does Biff's wry outlook tell you about the journey he is taking with Josh? Ah. Christopher Moore has a big problem in writing the story of Jesus: We know how it turns out. Creating narrative tension is therefore a bit of a challenge. There's really no way to do it except by finding tension elsewhere, and that is primarily within Biff. Moore teases out Biff's conflicted feelings about being the Messiah's buddy for hundreds of pages, keeping us wondering whether he will hang in there all the way to the Resurrection.

Given that emotional conflict is a nuclear generator of tension in all dimensions of a novel, you would think that writing about pure emotions by themselves would be a sure bet to keep readers involved. Not so. Plain emotion can be as dull as description. Just because a character is feeling something doesn't mean we will feel anything other than indifferent.

Susan Minot's highly-praised, and later filmed, novel *Evening* (1998) tells the story of Ann Grant, who in 1994 is dying, and whose memory of the one passionate love of her life is rekindled by the smell of a balsam pillow. In 1954 she travels to a wedding in Maine and there falls in love with fellow guest Harris Arden. Their affair is intense and brief. Then Arden's girlfriend arrives from Chicago for the wedding with the news that she is pregnant. Arden decides to do the right thing. After making his choice, Arden examines his feelings:

> Harris Arden came up around the side of the house. He was not used to so much emotion. It wore him out. This had all caught him off guard. He'd come upon a new road and taken a few steps down that road and now he saw it wasn't the road he was going to take after all. He was going back to the road he knew and would continue walking where he'd been walking for a long time. He'd been walking on that road for a long time for a reason. It suited him, didn't it? Well there wasn't any use in asking whether it suited him or not, it was where his duty took him and where his life had put him and where he would go.
>
> He smelled his sleeve, that was her. She was like a flash of light, surprising him. It had been too sudden. But hadn't it been sudden with Maria also? Why, it could go on being sudden with girls if you let it, one had to put a stop to it somewhere along the line. Having a baby would put a stop to it. Maria was the one he would stop with. And Maria loved him, that was certain. He could not be certain about this new woman. After the brightness faded who knew what would happen, he hardly knew her.

Minot's handling of Arden's feelings is deft. Note how in the first paragraph his reasoning is plodding and detached. Then he thinks of Ann: "He smelled his sleeve, that was her. She was like a flash of light, surprising him." For a second his mind is alive, but then he shuts it down again, rationalizing his choice. Is he worn out by emotion, as he supposes? No, he is pushing it down. He is suppressing his anguish. Had Minot merely portrayed Arden's sadness it would have been fine but it would also have been ordinary.

Because Arden is struggling, we are drawn in. Without being aware of it we are wondering whether he will think away his passion or whether his heart will win. It is a small tension, perhaps, but enough to keep us reading a few pages farther.

Foreshadowing foretells peril—not for the characters but for the novelist. Why? Have you ever groaned over a thudding and clunky piece of portentousness? Then you know. Foreshadowing can have the opposite of its intended effect. Is there a way to cast a shadow without being ridiculously obvious?

E.L. Doctorow's *The March* (2005) was awarded the National Book Critics' Circle and the PEN/Faulkner awards, as well as nominations for the National Book Award and the Pulitzer Prize. It is the story of General Sherman's march through Georgia and the Carolinas late in the Civil War. The burning of Atlanta was just the beginning. A sixty-mile-wide swath of destruction followed behind Sherman. Doctorow uses five points of view to dramatize this calamity.

Toward the beginning of the novel, a plantation family, knowing what is coming, packs their valuables in wagons and departs. They leave behind their slaves who, wearing their Sunday clothes, wait for the emancipation that they believe will arrive with the Union Army. Elder slave Jake Early is the first to sense its approach:

> Jake Early did not have to counsel patience. The fear they had all seen in the eyes of the fleeing Massah and Mistress told them that deliverance had come. But the sky was cloudless, and as the sun rose everyone settled down and some even nodded off, which Jake Early regretted, feeling that when the Union soldiers came they should find black folk not at their ease but smartly arrayed as a welcoming company of free men and women.
>
> He himself stood in the middle of the road with his staff and did not move. He listened. For the longest while there was nothing but the mild stirring of the air, like a whispering in his ear or the rustle of woodland. But then he did hear something. Or did he? It wasn't exactly a sound, it was more like a sense of something transformed in his own expectation. And then, almost as if what he held was a divining rod, the staff in his hand

> pointed to the sky westerly. At this, all the others stood up and came away from the trees: what they saw in the distance was smoke spouting from different points in the landscape, first here, then there. But in the middle of all this was a change in the sky color itself that gradually clarified as an upward-streaming brown cloud risen from the earth, as if the world was turned upside down.

The world of the South and these slaves is indeed about to be turned upside down. What best foreshadows the destruction to come? The columns of smoke on the horizon and the sickly brown hue of the sky are ominous outward signs, to be sure. I wonder, though, if they would bear the same dread had not Doctorow prepared us first with the slaves' hopeful anticipation, wearing their Sunday best, Jake Early wishing they would appear "a welcoming company of free men and women."

Foreshadowing, I believe, is most effective not when it thunders at us but when it stirs within the story's characters a shift of emotion. The signs in the sky are only smoke, really, unless they mark a subtle contrast with characters' feelings.

Every story has static moments; that is, times when nothing in particular is happening. Can those be put on the page? Many writers inadvertently do so. That may seem a failure of self-editing, but I believe that many writers pen such passages because they sense something important in them. What is it they are hoping to capture? And what is the point in trying when there is nothing at all with which to work?

Scottish mystery writer Josephine Tey (1896–1952) did not publish many novels, but one of them featuring her detective, Alan Grant, made her famous: In *The Daughter of Time* (1951), Grant solves a long-standing historical mystery without ever leaving his hospital bed. Laid up with a broken leg, using only history books and pure reason, Grant uncovers the truth of whether Richard III murdered his nephews.

As the novel opens, though, Grant has nothing to do but stare at the ceiling:

Grant lay on his high white cot and stared at the ceiling. Stared at it with loathing. He knew by heart every last minute crack on its nice clean surface. He had made maps of the ceiling and gone exploring on them; rivers, islands, and continents. He had made guessing games of it and discovered hidden objects; faces, birds, and fishes. He had made mathematical calculations of it and rediscovered his childhood; theorems, angles, and triangles. There was practically nothing else he could do but look at it. He hated the sight of it.

He had suggested to The Midget that she might turn his bed around a little so that he could have a new patch of ceiling to explore. But it seemed that that would spoil the symmetry of the room, and in hospitals symmetry ranked just a short head behind cleanliness and a whole length in front of Godliness. Anything out of the parallel was hospital profanity. Why didn't he read? she asked. Why didn't he go on reading some of those expensive brand-new novels that his friends kept on bringing him?

"There are far too many people born into the world, and far too many words written. Millions and millions of them pouring from the presses every minute. It's a horrible thought."

"You sound constipated," said The Midget.

Constipated? Alan Grant is bored. Like Sherlock Holmes needing a fix, he craves a mystery to engage his mind. Until then it is the ceiling. He is able to find in it animals; it recalls geometric formulae. But how does he feel about it? He loathes it.

I ask you, what is it in this classic opening paragraph that actually captures our interest and keeps us reading? The ceiling? No. It's just a ceiling. What keeps us in suspense is whether Alan Grant's boredom will be relieved.

In other words, tension can be made out of nothing at all; or at least, that's how it can appear. In reality it is feelings, specifically feelings in conflict with each other, that fill up an otherwise dead span of story and bring it alive.

Do you feel that your manuscript is brimming with tension? Do agents, editors and reviewers, and vast legions of readers agree? Not yet? Then there is work to do; specifically the work of finding the torn emotions in your characters and using them as the foundation for true tension in dialogue, action, exposition, and anywhere that tension is needed to keep us unsure of what will happen next.

Where is that tension needed? Everywhere.

PRACTICAL TOOLS

Tension in Dialogue

Step 1: Find any passage of dialogue in your manuscript.

Step 2: Create antipathy between the speakers. Set them against each other. Use simple disagreement, a clash of personalities, a struggle over status, competing egos, plain loathing, or any other conflict.

Step 3: Without looking at your original draft, rewrite the dialogue so the conflict between the speakers themselves is impossible to miss.

Discussion: Conflict in dialogue can be as polite as poison, or as messy as hatchets. The approach is up to you. The important thing is to get away from ambling chit-chat and get right to the desire of two speakers to defeat each other. If it's strong on the page, it hardly will matter what they're talking about. Even innocuous chatter can become deadly. For instance, "Would you like sugar for your tea?" is sweet and bland. Try stirring in some acid: "I suppose you'd like sugar for your tea? Never mind. Of course you do. Your type always does."

Tension in Action

Step 1: Find any action in your manuscript. It can be incidental, small, or high action.

Step 2: From whose point of view do we experience this action? What is he feeling at this moment? Find a conflicting emotion.

Step 3: Note visual details of this action which are *oblique;* that is, details that would be noticed only on second look.

Step 4: Without referring to your original draft, and using the results from the steps above, rewrite the action.

Discussion: High action immediately benefits from having torn emotions folded in. What about small and incidental action? Is it too much to add feelings to crossing a room? Maybe. But consider the difference. *He crossed the room.* Not bad. But how about … *He drifted across the room. Was he dreaming? Was he dead?* A bit different, isn't it? Small actions can be overloaded, certainly, but on the other hand there is little tension in plain, everyday action. True tension lies inside.

Tension in Exposition

Step 1: Find any passage of exposition in your manuscript. Sometimes called *interior monologue*, this is any passage in which we experience a character's inner thoughts and feelings.

Step 2: Identify the primary emotion in this passage, then write down its opposite.

Step 3: Look at what this character is thinking. Summarize the main idea in her mind. Now find a conflicting idea.

Step 4: If the passage involves mulling over something that has happened earlier, identify something about the prior occurrence that your character failed to realize or notice. Raise a hitherto unasked question. What *new* reasons does your character have to feel uneasy, anxious, or in danger?

Step 5: Without looking at your original draft, rewrite the exposition incorporating the conflicting emotions or warring ideas. Make the contrast strong. Add fresh questions and worries.

Discussion: Many authors feel it is important to portray what is going on in their characters' heads, but they forget that much of that material has already been felt and thought by the readers. Rehashing what is already obvious does not heighten it. It merely saps tension. Exposition is a time for what is new: extra questions, fresh anxiety, unforeseen angles. Think of exposition as plot turns. It's just plot that plays out in the mind.

Avoiding Low-Tension Traps

Step 1: Find any passage in your manuscript that is a weather or landscape opening, backstory, aftermath, travel, description, or foreshadowing.

Step 2: Determine what your point-of-view character feels most strongly here. Write down the opposite of that.

Step 3: Without looking at your original draft, rewrite this passage and fold in the conflicting emotions you've identified.

Step 4: Find twenty places in your manuscript to repeat the above steps.

Discussion: Tension traps occur in every manuscript. I know because I skim those passages. You don't want that. Generally speaking, it is best to start with action, cut backstory, avoid aftermath, limit description, and use foreshadowing rarely. But why not learn how to transform this material with tension? The range of tools in your story kit will be greater.

Writing Violence

Step 1: Find a violent action in your novel.

Step 2: Deconstruct this violent action into its three, four, or five most distinct visual pictures, the stills that freeze-frame the sequence.

Step 3: Look closely at each still picture. For each, write down something in the image that we would not immediately notice.

Step 4: For each picture, put your point-of-view character in a psychiatrist's chair. Ask, *what do you feel at this precise moment?*

Note: Discard the obvious emotions: shock, horror, fear. For each step of the action, write down a secondary emotion.

Step 5: Without looking at your original draft, rewrite this passage of violence using the results of the steps above. Pick and choose, of course, but draw heavily if not exclusively from your lists.

Discussion: Film directors take a lot of time to storyboard violent action. Each shot is carefully planned, then the shots are edited together to make the sequence. Novelists rarely spend as much time planning their violence. Violence in many manuscripts is rushed. Essential visual action is dry and objective, or sometimes buried and hard to follow. Focusing on less obvious visual details and unexpected emotions can make violence visceral and fresh.

Breaking it down into steps, meanwhile, makes the action easy to follow.

Writing Sex

Step 1: Find a sex scene (or potential sex scene) in your novel.

Step 2: Deconstruct this sex sequence into its four, five, or six most interesting visual pictures, the stills that freeze-frame the sequence.

Step 3: Look around each still picture. For each, write down a visual detail that is oblique, that is not obvious.

Step 4: For each picture, put your point-of-view character in a psychiatrist's chair. Ask, *what do you feel at this precise moment?*
   Note: Discard obvious feelings of desire, longing, lust. Capture secondary emotions.

Step 5: Without looking at your original draft, rewrite this sex scene using the material created in the steps above. Pick and choose, of course, but draw heavily if not exclusively from your lists.

Discussion: Sex scenes in many manuscripts throw off little heat. Some authors feel it is better to draw the curtain. In some stories that may be true. Still, why not practice ways to make the act itself fresh and surprising? Oblique details and secondary emotions can create a sequence that is sensual, exciting, and explicit without being pornographic.

Tension From Nothing

Step 1: Find in your story a moment when nothing at all is happening.

Step 2: Identify the point-of-view character. Write down whatever emotion he is feeling at this moment. Also write down its opposite.

Step 3: Note three or more details of the time and place of this dead moment. What objects are around? What exact kind of light, or darkness? At what pace is time moving? What mood is in the air? What is different now than a day ago?

Step 4: How would your character describe the state of his being at this moment?

Step 5: Create a passage in which this moment of action is filled with everything you created in the steps above, especially the contrasting emotions.

Discussion: Some experience is intangible, yet that which is not outwardly active can still be dynamic. Every minute has a mood. Every moment has meaning. Mood is built from environmental details, and meaning proceeds from emotions. Tension springs from the weaving of these elements into a passage that precisely captures small visual details and surgically dissects the enormous feelings that fill a silence.

CHAPTER NINE

THE FIRE
IN FICTION

Is there such a thing as a bad premise for a story? Without a doubt some story ideas feel familiar. Bandwagon syndrome pretty much guarantees that something successful will soon have imitators. If the imitators are successful you can count on a trend. If a trend lasts, then you can put money on it: that kind of story within a few years will be done to death.

Then again, can we say that whodunits have been done to death? Love conquers all? Save the world? No, these story patterns are durable. They are durable because they are flexible. There are thousands of ways to figure out whodunit. True love has infinite obstacles. The world always needs saving, too, and in different ways in every new decade.

In evaluating manuscripts I look for original stories, but is there anything new under the sun? Not really. Every novel has antecedents. Every author has influences. It is impossible to be wholly original; even so, some novels feel fresh and shake us with their insight. How is that effect achieved, especially when the novel in question is a mystery, romance or thriller of a type we've read a hundred times before?

Mainstream and literary fiction too can feel thin, derivative, or lackluster. If you have you ever read a tastily written debut literary novel that left you feeling hungry, or if you have trudged through four hundred pages of well-reviewed women's fiction only to feel like you've made this journey to self-discovery before, then you know what I mean. What gives a novel not only freshness but the force of the new?

Originality comes not from your genre, setting, plot, characters, voice, or any other element on which you can work. It cannot. It isn't possible. Originality can come only from what you bring of yourself to your story. In other words, originality is not a function of your novel; it is a quality in you.

Are you writing, let's say, a mystery novel? Bad news: you are not the first person to think of starting your story with a murder. Sorry. You are not even close to the front of the line of authors who have created quirky and appealing detectives, either. Too bad. But you do have one advantage over thousands of other mystery writers: You can make your murder and your detective utterly and uniquely your own.

If you are writing mainstream or literary fiction you're covered, right? No worries that your story will feel overly familiar, yeah? How could it possibly? No one's written this story before. Sorry to say, but plenty of mainstream and literary novels do not show us the world in a different way, let alone rock us to the core. What gives any novel the impact of the new is something that does not come from plot or milieu but from a perspective: yours.

Where so many manuscripts go wrong is that, if they do not outright imitate, they at least do not go far enough in mining the author's experience for what is distinctive and personal. So many manuscripts feel safe. They do not force me to see the world through a different lens. They enact the author's concept of what their novel *should* feel like to read rather than what their inner storyteller urgently needs to say. Novelists by and large do not trust themselves. They do not believe that their perspective is important.

Everyone's angry about something. Everyone has been through different things than you or I. Others notice stuff that you and I miss, get passionate about matters that the rest of us haven't considered, or at least not in that way. People are fascinating, don't you find? That means so are you. Your take on the world is not only valid, it is necessary. Your story is not any old story, it is a story that only you can tell and only your own way.

That, at any rate, is how it can be but so often is not. Finding the power buried in your novel is not about finding its theme. I would say, rather, that it is about finding you: your eyes, experience, understanding, and compassion. Ignore yourself and your story will be weak. Embrace the importance of what you have to share with the rest of us and you have the beginning of what makes novels great.

Insuring that your story is powerfully yours is the subject of this final chapter. The fire in fiction is many things, but above and beyond all others it is the fire in you. Let's see how it is sparked and how it can spread in your story.

OUR COMMON EXPERIENCE

Do you hate your job? Many do. Many write manuscripts about it, too. Why should we read them? Mostly we don't have to. I mean, who needs a novel to discover out how horrible life can be from nine to five? Read a blog, or perhaps *Dilbert*, or maybe just punch the clock yourself.

When novels of workplace complaints do become worthwhile it is because they offer us extra levels of humor and insight. We get something more than someone else's war stories over a latte: We get an experience that doesn't feel like work at all. We get, in short, relief and understanding.

In recent years nightmare bosses have become fodder for the bestseller lists. Lauren Weisberger's *The Devil Wears Prada* (2003) and Emma McLaughlin and Nicola Kraus's *The Nanny Diaries* (2002) are two outstanding examples of this genre. But there are many more reasons why work can be a bitch.

We all have heard how much money young associates at law firms and investment banks can earn; we've also heard that they work like slaves and sell their souls. David Bledin, in his novel *Bank* (2007), affirms these truths. So beaten down is everyone in the Mergers & Acquisitions department in his fictional firm that they do not even have real names. The narrator is called Mumbles and his fellow spreadsheet jockeys are The Star, The Defeated One, Postal Boy, and

Clyde, who, perhaps because he has a real name, is doomed. These young associates pull off impossible feats of document prep for bosses like the heartless Sycophant, and consequently have no lives.

So vile is the existence of these young associates that even a coffee run to Starbucks becomes a maneuver fraught with the paranoid fear of being seen by a boss. After just a few chapters of Bledin's detailing of this corporate hell, one begins to wonder why Mumbles doesn't just quit. Indeed, that is the conflict that drives the story: What keeps Mumbles going when any sane person would walk away?

Mumbles's justification for sticking it out at first finds its basis in psychology:

> So this is how it works. By the time you're nearing the end of your second year in the banking world, your compensation has been juiced up to one hundred and forty thousand all-in. Analogously, you're also getting accustomed to the mind-numbing tedium of your position. You can crunch comps in your sleep, tame the two-hundred Excel behemoths, whip out perfectly formatted PowerPoint pie charts like nobody's business. Whether you like it or not, you're turning into the Star.
>
> And let's not ignore the psychological aspect to it, the advent of Stockholm syndrome. The term originates from a bunch of Swedish hostages locked up in a bank vault for six days sometime in the seventies. The hostages gradually grew sympathetic toward their captors, resisted rescue attempts, and later refused to testify at the trial. The psychologists had a field day with this one. The prevailing theory is this: The human psyche is weak. In situations of duress, when we're surrounded by other humans who wield this awesome power over our ephemeral fates, we grow dependent on them. Dependency leads to affection; affection to love.

So in short, I love the Sycophant. Well, not yet, but
I will.

This insight does not keep Mumbles propped up forever. Later in
the story Clyde becomes unhinged after the death of his father and
shows dangerous signs of not caring, such as smoking something outside that is not tobacco. When one afternoon his boss heaps an impossible job on Clyde, The Defeated One calls the other associates to the
rescue but they do not see why they should help out self-destructive
Clyde. The Defeated One blasts them with a kind of pep talk:

> The Defeated One scowls. "It's like this, jackass. We
> slave away at the Bank, these missiles of excrement hail-
> ing down on us from all of the senior guys, and there's
> not a single moment of reprieve: no time for our families,
> our friends, not even five fucking minutes when we get
> home to satisfy that basic human craving for sex. And
> so, let me ask you this: What do we have left if we turn
> on one another? I'll tell you—*zip*. Nada."
> He takes a deep breath, turning to Postal Boy.
> "Look, I'm not trying to be Clyde's protector, and I'm
> not going to force you to stay away from the Toad. If you
> really feel the need to lie down on his couch and unbur-
> den your woes, then I won't stop you. But think about
> what's helping us survive here—not the Toad, not the
> Sycophant. It's the ability to rely on one another."

The young associates are, like soldiers under fire, a band of brothers. It is their camaraderie that keeps them alive. Bledin continues their torment for one hundred more excruciating and hilarious
pages, holding out meager carrots, moments of petty revenge, and
for Mumbles, the promise of a relationship with the skittish The
Woman With The Scarf.

In the end, Mumbles quits. Some of the taskmasters get their
comeuppance, but tying up plot threads is not Bledin's main concern.
His intent is to show us why and how human beings persist. Working

at a bank is, for Bledin, not just a springboard for comedy but a teller's window onto the human condition.

Ed Park's *Personal Days* (2008) has as its driving narrative force a tension that is the opposite of that in Bledin's novel: instead of angst over quitting, the people in Park's nameless firm are fearful of getting fired. And with good reason. The firm's new owners, referred to as the Californians, begin to fire people with a randomness that breeds paranoia.

Like Bledin, Park lovingly details office absurdities. As the firings take their toll, though, worker morale declines so far that Park's text assumes the format of a legal brief, each paragraph a numbered and lettered subclause. The novel's final section is in the form of a long e-mail rant at the end of which the writer, a survivor named Jonah, reveals to a fired friend a reason for the firings (the inability of management to identify a criminal at the firm) and also Park's statement of why their torment matters:

> I'm sorry, Pru, sorry I couldn't say all that I wanted to, tonight, but in truth it was as much about imagining I was saying something to you as it was about actually saying anything: You said yourself, once, waiting for stuff by the asthmatic printer, that the office generates at least one book, no, one *novel* every day, in the form of correspondence and memos and reports, all the reams of numbers, hundreds of sentences, thousands of words, *but no one has a mind to understand it,* no one has the eyes to take it all in, all these potential epics, *War and Peace* lying in between the lines; so maybe just think of this letter as one such novel, one such book, cobbled from the data all around me, and I'm trusting that at worst you'll ignore the NEW E-MAIL flashing in your in-box, bothering your screen, but at least you'll be conscious of it, as you sit at your desk or your worktable with the sewing machine, over there at Sharmila Maternity Wear, and slowly the unread message will invade your thoughts, and curiosity will get the

better of you, as you wonder what I could possibly have
to say to you after all this time, and why I remain,—Your
friend,—JONAH

In the existential wilderness of corporate America, then, there is
this scrap of hope: Working at least gives you friends. It would have
been a cinch for Park simply to trash the office, but that is too easy.
There is meaning buried in every experience, and here Park cares
enough to bring it out.

What is routine in your story? What happens that in real life
would pass by unnoticed and unexamined? A kiss on the cheek? A
wait at a red light? A Big Mac? You can edit out low-tension stuff
like that or, alternately, you can find in it the drama and significance
that it can have if we will but see it.

Meaning lies not in the experiences that you select to portray—I
mean, how much cosmic significance is there to a Big Mac?—but
rather in what that experience means to your characters; and, before
that, what it means to you. If there is importance, great, use it. If
there isn't, cut it and move on.

OUR UNCOMMON EXPERIENCES

Where were you on 9/11? That is one question that everyone can answer: We were all in close proximity to the World Trade Center on
that day, or feel as if we were. The impulse to write about it has stuck
many authors, among them Ken Kalfus, Jonathan Safran Foer, Martin Amis, Jay McInerny, and John Updike. But what, really, is there
to add to what the news has shown us and history has played out?

That, in a way, was a point made even before 9/11 by novelist Don
DeLillo, who has long been concerned that terrorism is the narrative
that in our times overwhelms any possible fiction (see his novel *Mao
II*, 1991). In an essay in *Harper's* a few months after 9/11, DeLillo
wrote, "The narrative ends in the rubble and it is left to us to create
the counternarrative." Adding to the 9/11 story, then, for DeLillo
means building *from* the ruins, looking at what came after.

It is perhaps for that reason DeLillo's novel *Falling Man* (2007) does not portray, until its end, the actual 9/11 events. It begins with a fortyish lawyer, Keith Neudecker, who has escaped just before the south tower's fall, turning up at the door of Lianne, the wife from whom he has been separated for several years. In his hand is someone else's briefcase.

Falling Man has no real plot. Keith finds the owner of the briefcase. His son Justin watches the sky for more planes. His wife notices Muslims everywhere, and all of New York is unsettled by the appearance of a suit-wearing performance artist known as Falling Man, who dangles himself from bridges and buildings. DeLillo captures the emotional numbness of the months following the attack with upsetting accuracy. His characters' paralysis is profound. Setting us adrift, one wonders whether DeLillo intends for *Falling Man* to be a novel or instead a re-immersion in the experience of that day.

Falling Man would be almost unbearable reading except that DeLillo excavates from the rubble a scrap of insight about the survivors, which he comes to in this passage about Keith's wife Lianne:

> It's interesting, isn't it? To sleep with your husband, a thirty-eight-year-old woman and a thirty-nine-year-old man, and never a breathy sound of sex. He's your ex-husband who was never technically ex, the stranger you married in another lifetime. She dressed and undressed, he watched and did not. It was strange but interesting. A tension did not build. This was extremely strange. She wanted him here, nearby, but felt no edge of self-contradiction or self-denial. Just waiting, that was all, a broad pause in recognition of a thousand sour days and nights, not so easily set aside. The matter needed time. It could not happen the way things did in normal course. And it's interesting, isn't it, the way you move about the bedroom, routinely near-naked, and the respect you show the past, the deference to its fervors of the wrong kind, its passions of cut and burn.
>
> She wanted contact and so did he.

Human connection, therefore, is the need that unites DeLillo's survivors. The hope that they'll find it is the tension that underlies *Falling Man*. The novel is bleak reading, no question, but DeLillo's purpose is to illuminate what is dark in our memories. In *Falling Man*'s final pages we return with Keith Neudecker to his office on the morning the plane strikes just a few floors above his own. Keith tries, and fails, to save an office mate, then makes his way down the hellish fire stairs to the outside just as the first tower collapses. The intensity of these events is, in DeLillo's hands, horrifying, but when it is over we have connected with the victims and we, like them, rise and go on.

Andre Dubus III, who wowed the literary world with *House of Sand and Fog* (1999), also turned his attention to 9/11 in *The Garden of Last Days* (2008). Dubus focuses not on the immediate aftermath but on the week preceding the attack. Before they departed for their deaths, several of the terrorists taking flight training in Florida spent their last night at a strip club. In *The Garden of Last Days*, Dubus imagines that night in a place he calls the Puma Club for Men. There a terrorist named Bassam, torn by his attraction and repulsion to the exposed flesh of Western women, pays for two hours of solo time in the club's Champagne Room with a young stripper who calls herself Spring.

The encounter between Spring (real name April) and Bassam (who calls himself Mike) is a power struggle over identity, boundaries, and understanding. Bassam wishes to know why Spring dances and whether her flesh can be bought. Spring is stripping to support her three-year-old daughter Franny whom, lacking a babysitter, Spring unfortunately has brought to the club that evening. The contest between Bassam and Spring focuses on money and Spring's cesarean scar:

> "Do you believe in nothing?"
> "I believe in some things."
> "What please?"
> "Like keeping your word, Mike. I believe in that."

"What does this mean?" He was squinting at her, though the smoke in the room had cleared.

"You asked me why I danced." She nodded at the wad still in his hand. "You put eight of those down and asked me."

"But I know why it is for you doing this, April."

"Spring."

"April." He stood and sat back down on the love seat, the cash in his hand. So much of it. "Stand, please."

She didn't feel like standing. He pulled a hundred from the fold and dropped it in front of her.

Such easy, easy money.

...

He smiled, letting his bad teeth show. For the first time all night he looked genuinely pleased about something. He kept his eyes on hers and separated three more hundreds from the fold. Two drifted down onto the black cushion, the other bent over itself and fell to the floor.

"What's that for, Mike?"

"For that." He nodded at her crotch.

"What?"

"Where they cut you."

"It's just a scar. You don't want to touch a scar."

Two more hundreds floated and spun like playing cards onto the other two. Six hundred. He was crazy in some way, and unless he came back and did this again, she would never have another night like this ever.

...

"You do it for skin—what is the way you say?—for flesh."

"Flesh?"

"Yes, for your love of it. Even if you had no children you would sell your flesh."

"I don't sell my flesh. I dance."

...

He sat up, took the bottle of Rémy, poured some into his snifter. "You do it because you think it is allowed." He picked up his glass and swirled the cognac.

He stared into it like there was something in there only he could see. "But it is not. Not for you. Not for any of you."

What is it that Dubus wants us to conclude? Who is right? Who is wrong? In postmodern fashion, he doesn't say. He simply offers us different experiences, or rather struggles. Bassam is torn: purity vs. flesh. Spring is also torn: her body vs. money. It is their conflicted yearning that interests Dubus, and which causes him to bring together these two representatives of irreconcilable human desires in a scene as old as myth and as raw as yesterday.

In the course of *The Garden of Last Days* we learn of the death of Bassam's brother in their beloved American muscle car. We also find out how deeply Spring cares about her daughter. Other characters are portrayed in detail too: a club bouncer, a disgruntled patron, the ailing babysitter. Dubus does not indulge in stereotypes. He brings these people individually to life. His research was thorough. His detailing is minute. He cares, but then so do all authors. Or so they say. The difference is that Dubus digs deeper, imagines more completely, and does not allow himself to see his characters dishonestly or through filters.

Both DeLillo and Dubus approach 9/11 in ways that may strike some as timid, as if the enormity of 9/11 robbed or humbled them to the point that only the fringes of the event could be examined. I would say, rather, than these authors have written respectfully. They do not try to top history or outdo the news. They do not cook up thriller heroes who ridiculously defeat terrorism and set right all that is wrong.

DeLillo and Dubus acknowledge the impossibility of encompassing so vast a tragedy, but they also do not surrender to it. From the rubble each pulls something for us to hold onto. Their stories may be microcosmic, but then aren't all stories? Through the small, the particular, and the personal we can understand what is common to us all. Even when the characters are strange and the territory unfamiliar, what makes a story universal is what the author causes us to feel.

What does it mean to write for the ages? Must one have a moral or reveal a universal truth? Or is it enough to merely plumb the depths of human experience so that we all can relate? It doesn't matter. Power in fiction comes from touching readers. Touching readers comes from your own compassion.

Whether you are burning to say something or immersed in curiosity about your characters and what happens to them, what's important is to get it all down in detail and with conviction. Merely writing well is not enough. Fine prose is empty unless it is charged with your own deep feeling.

THE MORAL OF THE STORY

What if your intent is precisely to make a point? Suppose you *want* to stack the deck, run the game, play God, or in some other way manipulate your story for a purpose? How is that done without being hokey and undermining your own message?

Deeanne Gist, one of the most entertaining writers in the Christian romance market, is known especially for her spirited heroines. *Courting Trouble* (2007) introduces the unconventional Essie Spreckelmeyer, who scandalizes her 1894 hometown of Corsicana, Texas, with her outlandish hats and bicycle bloomers. Unmarried at thirty, Essie is practically an old maid. To remedy her situation she draws up a list of Corsicana's eligible bachelors and writes down their good and bad qualities. The most appealing of the bunch is the unfortunately named Hamilton Crook, owner of a general store.

Essie sets about to get hired. She is an excellent saleswoman, it turns out, and in time it looks as if Hamilton will propose. But it is not to be. Bitterly disappointed, Essie quits to assist her father in running Corsicana's first oil field. Among the help is a handsome drifter named Adam Currington, with whom she falls in love. Eventually he seduces her and runs off. Essie is ruined. Gist does not indulge in modern morality but stays true to the times: Essie is indeed spoiled, her marriage prospects forever lost.

But then a ray of possible salvation arrives in the form of Ewing Wortham, a seminary student seven years her junior who returns to town and discovers that his boyhood crush on Essie has not diminished. Despite her fallen state, he wishes to marry her. It is almost too good to be true—and so it proves. Set to become the town minister, Ewing requires that Essie comport herself in a manner more becoming a preacher's wife. This means, among other things, that she must tone down her hats and, worse, give up riding her bicycle. In the end, Essie is unable to conform. She calls off the engagement, knowing her last hope is gone.

This is a romance? Actually, no. Gist has a different intent. Essie's devastation is profound. How can she go on? The answer comes from her father in a talk toward the novel's end:

> Sorrow etched the lines in Papa's face. "You do not need a man to be a whole person."
>
> "Then why would God send me Ewing if not for the purpose of marrying him?"
>
> "Perhaps because the Lord wants to see if you will trust Him. If you will choose Him over being married."
>
> "But marriage was His idea. He sanctified it."
>
> "Marriage is a good thing, but it may not be the highest and best for you. Are you willing to give it up for Him, if that is what He wishes?"
>
> Moisture once again rushed to her eyes. "But I don't want Him to wish that for me. Why would He?"
>
> "I don't know. All I'm saying is, if you truly trust God, and if He is the most important thing in your entire life, then you will accept and believe that He knows what is best for you. And you will accept it joyfully. Willingly."
>
> She pulled her hands away, propping an elbow on the table and resting her head against his palm. "Who will hug me in my old age? Who will eat at my table when you and Mother are gone?"

"Christ will meet your needs, Essie. If you let Him."

Does Essie's fate seem to you harsh? Gist does not mean it to be. Later Essie considers her future, writes out a list of God's good and bad points, and prays:

> She took a trembling breath. *I will embrace the life you have laid out for me, Lord, and I will live it joyfully so that I may be a witness to how great you are.*
>
> Her tears slowed to a trickle, leaving her cheeks slick and salty. She wondered if she really could live the life of a spinster with joy.
>
> Images of herself old and gray, of this house empty and quiet, rattled her resolve. How could she embrace such a thing?
>
> Help me be joyful, Lord. I'm afraid. Afraid of being alone.
>
> *I will never leave you.*

As God speaks to Essie, Gist's purpose is revealed. *Courting Trouble* was never intended to be a romance. Is it instead a morality tale about abstinence before marriage? The novel certainly portrays premarital sex as dangerous. But Gist's message is larger: Put your trust in God, she is saying. In faith you will find strength and the answer to life's essential loneliness.

Gist encourages our expectation of a happy romantic outcome precisely so she can thwart it. How do you shape the events of your story to your purpose? Are you afraid that if you did so readers would reject what you have to say? You are not alone. It has become unfashionable to make statements in fiction. In our politically correct, post-9/11 world, is it perhaps even unwise to assert our views?

I believe that the danger lies in not doing so. Stories draw their power from their meaning. If you ask me, challenging readers' beliefs is not a weakness but a strength. Did you ever have someone tell you the harsh truth about yourself? It was hard to hear, wasn't it, but today aren't you glad you listened? A similar dynamic is at work in fiction. Truth can be uncomfortable. It can also be comforting. Whatever it is, it is necessary to speak it.

War has been portrayed in countless works of fiction such as Stephen Crane's *The Red Badge of Courage* (1895), Erich Maria Remarque's *All Quiet on the Western Front* (1929), Ernest Hemingway's *A Farewell to Arms* (1929), Norman Mailer's *The Naked and the Dead* (1948), James Jones's *From Here to Eternity* (1951), and Tim O'Brien's *Going After Cacciato* (1978). Science fiction has also speculated about the future of war in novels like Robert A. Heinlein's *Starship Troopers* (1959), Joe Haldman's *The Forever War* (1975), and Orson Scott Card's *Ender's Game* (1985). Considering all that, what is there left to say about it?

In one sense there is nothing new to say. How could there be? There are, however, men and women who have experienced war whose perspectives on it *are* new to us. Even the future of war can be imagined in fresh ways. One recent science-fiction novel that did that was John Scalzi's *Old Man's War* (2005), which posits a future in which old folks don't have to die, they can instead enlist and live again in rejuvenated bodies that are enhanced for fighting with improvements like SmartBlood and BrainPal, an implanted computer.

After the death of his wife, seventy-five-year-old John Perry joins the Colonial Defense Force and bonds with a group of similar recruits who ironically dub themselves the Old Farts. They are separated but stay in touch as they fight alien species on faraway planets. With the superenhanced bodies, Scalzi's characters naturally evoke the classic science-fiction question of what it means to be human.

Old Man's War would be a retread of prior SF novels, but Scalzi is not content merely to raise familiar issues. In a deft turn of the plot, Scalzi has John Perry meet his dead wife Jane, now in a young female soldier's body. John Perry now must struggle not to remain human but to escape his humanity and the emotional agony that entails. It is not war that is inhumane in *Old Man's War*, it is instead being human itself that causes suffering. By the end of the novel John Perry has let his wife go and embraced his identity:

> Eventually I asked to go back into combat. It's not that
> I like combat, although I'm strangely good at it. It's just

that in this life, I am a soldier. It was what I agreed to be and to do. I intended to give it up one day, but until then, I wanted to be on the line. I was given a company and assigned to the *Taos*. It's where I am now. It's a good ship. I command good soldiers. In this life, you can't ask for much more than that.

That would be a fine and challenging enough conclusion to *Old Man's War*, but Scalzi then twists the story again in a mental exchange (a ping) between John and his wife that closes the novel:

> *You once asked me where Special Forces go when we retire, and I told you that I didn't know*—she sent. *But I do know. We have a place where we can go, if we like, and learn how to be human for the first time. When it's time, I think I'm going to go. I think I want you to join me. You don't have to come. But if you want to, you can. You're one of us, you know.*
>
> I paused the message for a minute, and started it up again, when I was ready.
>
> *Part of me was once someone you loved*—she sent. *I think that part of me wants to be loved by you again, and wants me to love you as well. I can't be her. I can just be me. But I think you could love me if you wanted to. I want you to. Come to me when you can. I'll be here.*
>
> That was it.
>
> I think back to the day when I stood before my wife's grave for the final time, and turned away from it without regret, because I knew that what she was was not contained in that hole in the ground. I entered a new life and found her again, in a woman who was entirely her own person. When this life is done, I'll turn away from it without regret as well, because I know she waits for me, in another, different life.
>
> I haven't seen her again, but I know I will. Soon. Soon enough.

Old Man's War, then, is not about what it means to be human; it is about what it means to be a soldier. Being human can be set aside; it can also be taken up again. Scalzi's message differs from *war is hell*. It is also different from the many novels about the silent suffering of veterans after the battle, like Sloan Wilson's *The Man in the Gray Flannel Suit* (1955). Scalzi is saying that it is important to be a soldier but it is equally important to leave soldiering behind. War doesn't erase humanity, in Scalzi's story; it simply is part of it.

How do the events of your story make your point? Do you even have a point? I believe that you do. How do I know? Because I know that you are not a person lacking principles and void of passion. That isn't possible. You are, after all, writing fiction. That is not an activity taken up by those without a heart. If you know love, if you have lived life, then you have stories in you: stories that are completely yours. For those stories to resonate it is important not to tell them in the same old way that others have.

Think about it. Hackneyed plots and stereotypical characters don't work. We brush them off. Stories that stretch our minds and characters who challenge our view of ourselves ... ah, those are the ones we remember. They are the stuff of which classics are made. So start by making sure that you put yourself into your novel: your views, your hurts, your questions, your convictions, your crazy-weird take on it all. Give all that to your characters or simply give it to yourself when you write. You've kept it inside for too long. It is time to let it out and to let it make a noise.

If you are worried that your plot will feel calculated or contrived to your readers, don't. Actually, the more you let your passionate self inform your novel, the more it will strike your readers with a moral force.

THE FIRE IN FICTION

What is the truth that you most wish the rest of us would see? That is the purpose of your novel. That is your message. I wish more manuscripts had them. A great many do not.

Some bemoan the decline of reading and lament the sad state of contemporary fiction. Are they right? Sometimes I wonder.

Many contemporary novels focus on daughters, journeys home, and the aftermath of significant events. Another trend is to make characters of Jane Austen, Edgar Allan Poe, and Arthur Conan Doyle or to borrow their creations. What has happened to us? Have we lost confidence in our own imaginations? Are we afraid of portraying grand characters and big events? Do we identify only with victims? Is the story of our age no more than a tale of survival?

Perhaps. Contemporary fiction reflects who we are. And who are you? How do you see our human condition? Where have you been that the rest of us should go? What have you experienced that your neighbors must understand? What have I missed? What makes you angry? What wisdom have you gleaned? Are there questions we're not asking? Do the answers of the past no longer serve, or are they more apt than ever?

Simply put, what the hell do you want to say to me? If I remember nothing else, what would you have me recall when I close your novel's covers?

Having something to say, or something you wish us to experience, is what gives your novel its power. Identify it. Make it loud. Do not be afraid of what's burning in your heart. When it comes through on the page, you will be a true storyteller.

PRACTICAL TOOLS

The Uncommon in Common Experience

Step 1: Is your story realistic? Are your characters ordinary people?

Step 2: What in the world of your story makes you angry? What are we not seeing? What is the most important question? What puzzle has no answer? What is dangerous in this world? What causes pain?

Step 3: Where in the world of your story is there unexpected grace? What is beautiful? Who is an unrecognized hero? What needs to be saved?

Step 4: Give your feelings to a character. Who can stand for something? Who can turn the main problem into a cause?

Step 5: Create a situation in which this character must defend, explain, or justify his actions. How is the problem larger than it looks? Why does it matter to us all?

Discussion: Passion is expansive. It sweeps us up, carries us away. What is your passion? Get it into your story, especially through your characters. What angers you can anger them. What lifts them up will inspire us in turn. Ordinary people don't need to be bland. They can be poets, prophets, and saints. Their world is a microcosm. Why else are you writing about it?

The Common in Uncommon Experience

Step 1: Is your story about uncommon events? Are your characters out of the ordinary? Is your novel an historical?

Step 2: Find for your hero a failing that is human, a universal frustration, a humbling setback, or any experience that everyone has had. Add this early in the manuscript.

Step 3: What in the world of the story is timelessly true? What cannot be changed? How is basic human nature exhibited? What is the same today as a hundred years ago, and will be the same a hundred years ahead?

Step 4: What does your protagonist do the same way as everyone? What is her lucky charm? Give this character a motto. What did she learn from her mom or dad?

Step 5: Create a situation in which your exceptional protagonist is in over her head, feels unprepared, is simply lost, or in any other way must admit to herself that she's not perfect.

Discussion: While racing to save the world, it's nice to know that your Herculean hero is human after all. Even the most rarefied or ancient milieu is, in some way, just like the world in which you and I toil. Including those details and moments makes your extraordinary story one to which all readers can relate.

The Moral of the Story

Step 1: Is there a moral or a lesson in your story?

Step 2: When does your protagonist realize that he got something wrong?

Step 3: Who in the story can, at the end, see things in a completely different way?

Step 4: At the end, how is your hero better off?

Step 5: At the end, what does your hero regret?

Step 6: Who, in the midst of the story, is certain that there is no solution nor is there any way to fully comprehend the problem?

Step 7: Why is the problem positive, timely, universal, or fated?

Discussion: Providing something for the readers to take away doesn't require lecturing or teaching a lesson. Your story's main problem is itself the lesson. The students are your characters. Make your points through them—simply. The more you hammer your readers with your moral, the less likely they are to acknowledge your point.

The Fire in Fiction—A Master Technique

Step 1: Choose any scene in your manuscript that seems to you weak. Who is the point-of-view character?

Step 2: Identify whatever this character feels most strongly in this scene. Fury? Futility? Betrayal? Hope? Joy? Arousal? Shame? Grief? Pride? Self-loathing? Security?

Step 3: Recall your own life. What was the time when you most strongly felt that emotion which you identified in Step 3?

Step 4: Detail your own experience: When precisely did this happen? Who was there? What was around you? What do you remember best about the moment? What would you most like to forget? What was the quality of the light? What exactly was said? What were the smallest—and largest—things that were done?

Step 5: Did this real life experience twist the knife, or put the icing on the cake? It would have stirred this feeling anyway, but what *really* provoked it was … what?

Step 6: What did you think to yourself as the importance of this experience struck you?

Step 7: Give the details of your experience to your character, right now, in this very scene.

Discussion: Steal from life. That's what it's for, isn't it? How often, when something bad happened to you, did you think to yourself, *at least this will be good material for a story some day!* Well, now's your chance. What has happened to you, its details and specifics, are a tool to make this scene personal and strong. They are what make any story feel real. Use this method whenever you are stuck or if inspiration is low. It is the way to put fire in your fiction every day.

INDEX

ABOUT THE AUTHOR

Donald Maass heads the Donald Maass Literary Agency in New York City, which represents more than 150 novelists and sells more than 150 novels every year to publishers in America and overseas. He is a past president of the Association of Authors Representatives, Inc., and is the author of several books of interest to fiction writers: *The Career Novelist* (now available as a free download from his agency's Web site), *Writing the Breakout Novel*, and *Writing the Breakout Novel Workbook*. His Web site is www.maassagency.com.